HELP,
I'M TRAPPED
IN MY DUVET

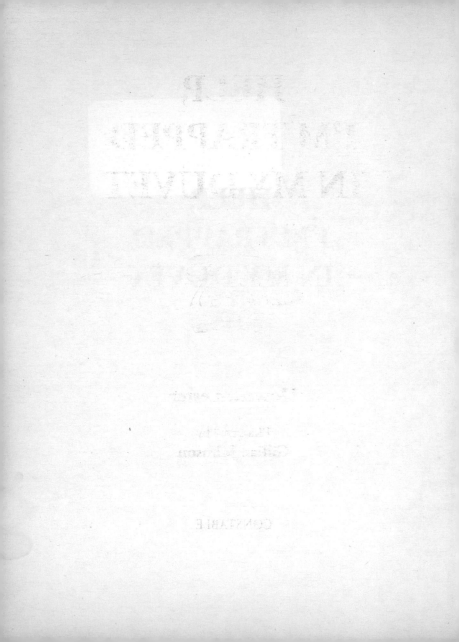

HELP, I'M TRAPPED IN MY DUVET

Howard Lester

Illustrated by
Gillian Johnson

CONSTABLE

Constable & Robinson Ltd
55-56 Russell Square
London WC1B 4HP

This edition published by Constable,
an imprint of Constable & Robinson Ltd 2012

A copy of the British Library Cataloguing in Publication Data
is available from the British Library

ISBN-13: 978-1-47210-255-3

Designed by Design 23
Printed and bound in the European Union

1 3 5 7 9 10 8 6 4 2

MIX
Paper from
responsible sources
FSC
www.fsc.org   FSC® C018072

INTRODUCTION

Ordinary people understand that emergency numbers such as 999 in the UK and 911 in the US are only to be used when absolutely necessary. So it is bewildering to discover the astonishing range of trivial and absurd situations in which callers attempt to persuade the emergency services to intervene.

The callers documented in this book are reacting to everything from an angry goose to a sad seagull, from a non-existent Big Mac to a recalcitrant teenager who won't tidy his room, and from a window that won't open to a borrowed jumper. One caller has used the emergency number to report a cat who won't stop playing with string and it is 'doing her head in'. One can only admire the patience and common sense of the emergency line operators who not only have to deal with this lunacy, but who spend the rest of their time serving their community in the most useful way possible. The emergency services often publicise these kinds of calls in an attempt to persuade people not to misuse the emergency number in future, though it seems they are in a losing battle.

Hearing about these calls is simultaneously hilarious and mindboggling, especially as it sets some of the best elements of the human race in a direct confrontation with some of its most idiotic members.

Operator: What is your emergency?

Caller: I'm in a sandwich shop and I've specifically asked for a little turkey, a little ham, lots of cheese and lots of mayonnaise. They're not doing it properly.

Operator: You're calling emergency services because you're not happy with the way they're making your sandwiches?

Caller: Yes, I don't think they're ever going to make the sandwiches how I like them. They're playing games with me. Can you send somebody down here?

Operator: …?

Caller: I need to find out when the chemist is open.

Operator: Is this an emergency?

Caller: Yes, I have a terrible headache and need to buy some painkillers immediately.

Operator: The details should be on your local chemist's door.

Caller: No, I don't want to go out in this rain if it's not open. Can't you send somebody round there so you can tell me when it's open?

Operator: ...?

In the depths of winter, a woman dialled 999 and asked for paramedics to come round and bring in her washing. She told the operator that the path was too icy to walk down and the washing needed to be brought in.

A Liverpool man phoned 999 to complain that a local takeaway pizza company had put mushrooms on his pizza, even though he hated them. He wanted the police to demand that the pizza restaurant remove the offending vegetable and give the owners a caution.

Operator: What emergency service do you require?

Caller: Hello, I want to report a goose that's staring at me.

Operator: A goose is staring at you?

Caller: Yes, I'm in the park and there's a mean looking goose sitting under the bench opposite me. It's staring and it has a plastic thing around its leg. I think it's recording me. It might be a spy device.

Operator: OK, so there's a goose staring at you

with a plastic tag on its leg and you think it's spying on you?

Caller: Yes, what can you do?

Operator: Please stay where you are sir. I'm sending some paramedics to help you.

Caller: I need you to send a police car right away.

Operator: You want the police? What is your emergency?

Caller: I've missed the last bus home and I have no money for a taxi. I'm stranded.

Operator: Sorry, I can't help you.

Caller: But I need to get home.

Operator: Sorry sir, emergency services cannot take you home.

A man in Newcastle telephoned 999 because his local takeaway was closed. He told them that according to their sign they should be open so it was suspicious that nobody was there and asked for police to be dispatched to find the staff.

A caller telephoned 999 after finding a dead pigeon in her garden. She asked if paramedics could come round to resuscitate the bird.

A drunken dad requested the police to go and get his children from the pub. He had taken them there so he could spend the afternoon drinking but got so drunk that he left them there when he went home. He claimed he was now too drunk to go back and fetch them.

A young man asked for an ambulance to be sent because he had severe facial bleeding. When paramedics got there, the 'facial haemorrhage' turned out to be a spot that he had picked at and that was bleeding.

On Christmas Eve, a man called the emergency number to ask what the temperature was. He also wanted to know the weather forecast over Christmas. He was told to watch television or listen to the radio.

Caller: I want the police
Operator: What is your emergency sir?
Caller: A car just drove past and splashed me when it went through a puddle.

Operator: That's not the sort of emergency that we deal with.

Caller: Well, I've got his registration number and I want to report him for dangerous driving. I'm soaked.

Operator: This number is for real emergencies. I'm hanging up now.

A man demanded that the fire brigade come to his house because he had dropped his TV remote down the back of the sofa and couldn't reach it. He wanted them to bring cutting equipment to get the remote out.

A woman dialled 999 because her local takeaway had put too many onions in her curry.

A woman dialled 999 and asked for an ambulance because she was having difficulties with her vision. It turned out that she had simply got shampoo in her eyes.

Caller: I want to report a burglary. Someone has broken into my house and taken a bite out of my homemade apple crumble.
Operator: Are the intruders still there? Was anything else taken?
Caller: No, they've left but all they did was have a bite of my apple crumble. It's happened before and I'm getting tired of it.

A man in Romford dialled 999 and asked for advice on what to do because his wife had got on the wrong bus after going out shopping.

Caller: I want the police

Operator: You want police assistance?

Caller: Well, I don't know who else to call. Can you tell me how to cook a shoulder of lamb?

Operator: …?

A man demanded an ambulance because he couldn't breathe. When the paramedics arrived, he was discovered to have a bad cold and a blocked nose. He told them that he had called because his cold was worse than it had been two days previously.

Caller: Hi, I'm having a lot of difficulty breathing. My chest feels really tight and I feel very faint. I might be about to pass out.

Operator: Can you tell me where you are?

Caller: I'm at the pay phone on Steward Street.

Operator: OK sir, I'm sending an ambulance to you now. Do you have emphysema or asthma?

Caller: No

Operator: So did the shortness of breath come on suddenly? Have you any idea what caused it?

Caller: Yes, I'm being chased by the police.

A young man asked for police assistance because the credit on his mobile phone had run out and the only number he could call was the emergency services.

A young woman was walking home alone one night and wanted someone to talk to so she dialled 999 for 'a chat'.

One caller asked the emergency services to telephone a taxi for her because she had no credit left on her phone.

Caller: I want the fire brigade

Operator: Are you reporting a fire?

Caller: Yes, in a way. There's a big firework display going on in the park and I think some of the larger ones might land on my house. Could you send a fire engine round just in case?

Operator: It is a registered firework display sir and precautions will have been taken. I can't send a fire engine 'in case' there's a fire.

Caller: Well then, you're useless, I won't call you even if there *is* a fire!

Caller: I feel as if I have something swimming inside my arms and legs.

Operator: Do you need an ambulance?

Caller: Yes, I think so. My arms and legs have gone all weird.

Operator: OK. I'll get an ambulance to you.

Caller: Will you need a fish tank too?

Operator: A fish tank?
Caller: Yes, for the fish inside my arms and legs.
Caller: I need help right now.
Operator: What is your emergency?

A grandmother telephoned the emergency number to ask what the weather would be like the next day. She wanted to take her grandchildren on a picnic.

Caller: There's a hamster behind my wardrobe.
Operator: What did you say?
Caller: There's a hamster stuck behind my wardrobe and I need someone to come round and move the wardrobe so I can get it. It's too heavy for me.
Operator: Can't you just ask a neighbour?

Caller: No! I don't want to leave it alone in case it thinks I've abandoned it.

Operator: …?

A mum at the end of her tether called the police because her son wouldn't get out of bed. She thought it would make him get up and get ready for school. Unfortunately, she was charged with wasting police time.

Caller: I want to report my wife to the police.

Operator: Why what has she done?

Caller: She's gone out without making me any lunch.

Operator: I'm afraid that doesn't count as an emergency sir.

Caller: Of course it does, I'm starving. She's my

wife, she makes all the meals. She always has until today. Something must be very wrong. I need the police!

Operator: …?

A man in Manchester dialled 999 to complain about the lack of buses in his area. He wanted the police to investigate the matter.

A woman in Coventry wanted the fire brigade to come round and get a rat out of her kitchen.

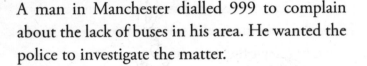

A woman bought a rabbit from an advertisement a local breeder had put in the newsagent's window. When she collected the rabbit its ears were not floppy enough so she asked for the police to go and arrest him for fraud.

Caller: I'm in Ashton-under Lyne, looking for B&Q and I can't find it.

Operator: B&Q? This isn't an emergency life or death situation, is it madam?

Caller: No, but I am very, very distressed. I have been driving around looking for it all morning, and I can't find it. I am in tears now. I might be about to have some sort of breakdown.

Operator: Madam, this isn't the kind of thing you should be calling 999 for. This is for emergency calls only

Caller: I suppose so. I'm so sorry. Could you just tell me how to find it since you're on the line?

Operator: Try asking someone on the street.

Caller: Oh… Goodbye then.

A woman in Dover asked for the fire brigade to be sent round because she had a tap that she couldn't turn off. She was advised to get a plumber.

An elderly woman in Blackpool dialled 999 to get a stain out of her carpet. She asked for the fire brigade to come round with their 'specialist' equipment.

A woman dialled the emergency number to ask for Tony Blair's telephone number. She said that she needed the number because he was her 'sort of chap'. After a two minute conversation with the operator she hung up telling them they were useless.

A woman asked the emergency services operator to ask how to top up the credit on her mobile phone.

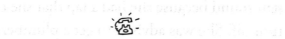

Caller: Hello?

Operator: What emergency service do you require?

Caller: I really need to know what todays's date is.

Operator: Is this a matter of life and death?

Caller: No, but could you tell me anyway?

A woman telephoned the police after hearing a lot of yelling and shouting in the flat below her. When the police arrived they knocked on the door of the basement flat and it was answered by the man who lived there. They told him why they were there and he looked a bit embarrassed. He had been on the toilet doing his business and the shouts were the sounds he made as he did it.

Caller: Has time stopped?

Operator: Excuse me; I don't think I heard you right. Could you repeat that?

Caller: Yes, has time stopped? It's been two o'clock for about two hours.

Operator: You probably need to get a new battery for your watch sir. It's half past four.

A male caller demanded an ambulance after calling the emergency number because he had toothache.

Operator: Emergency services.

Caller: Hi! I was just checking to see if my new mobile phone worked.

A man asked for an ambulance because he had had itchy eyes for three weeks. It transpired that he was merely suffering from hay fever.

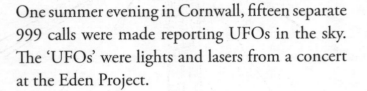

One summer evening in Cornwall, fifteen separate 999 calls were made reporting UFOs in the sky. The 'UFOs' were lights and lasers from a concert at the Eden Project.

Someone dialled 999 to report a large owl sitting on top of a telegraph pole. They wanted the fire brigade to turn up with ladders to get it down. The operator reminded him that owls are birds and that they could fly if necessary.

Caller: I need an ambulance.

Operator: Is it for you sir.

Caller: No, there's a dog stuck in the river, it's in distress and I need paramedics to treat it.

Operator: I'm sorry sir, ambulances are for human casualties. You need to call the RSPCA.

Caller: That's very cruel of you. You should look after all creatures.

Caller: The Chinese takeaway I ordered is 45 minutes late. I want you to prosecute the takeaway for ripping me off.

Operator: I'm afraid we can't do that sir. This line is for emergencies.

Caller: I need the police.

Operator: Can I ask you what the problem is?

Caller: Can one of your officers come around to my house to tell my sons to stop fighting?

A man called the police because his drug dealer had short-changed him. He claimed that he'd paid £60 for some cocaine but the amount of the drug he was given was worth only £20.

In Liverpool at the weekends the 999 service becomes clogged up with club-going youths who don't have enough money for a taxi home. They usually phone about a very 'drunk friend' before attempting to climb inside the ambulance themselves.

Caller: 'I have lost my shoplifting ticket I was given when I was arrested last week.
Operator: …?

Caller: 'There's been a pigeon in my back garden for the past three days – it's got a tag on its leg. Who does it belong to?
Operator: I don't know.

Caller: I'd like to report a theft.

Operator: What was taken?

Caller: Someone has taken my snowman from outside my house. It was there last night and now it's gone.

Operator: Do you think it might have melted madam?

Caller: No, it was very cold before I went to bed last night. I went outside to check. It was out there and cold. This morning it has gone. It's definitely been stolen.

Operator: …?

Caller: Can you put me in touch with whoever deals with noise pollution?

Operator: What service do you require?

Caller: Well, there is a builder using an angle grinder outside.

Operator: I'm sorry madam. It's not illegal to be a builder.

Caller: Well it should be!

Caller: (whispering) I can't see anything, I think I've been kidnapped, I'm wearing a blindfold…

Operator: Are you moving?

Caller: No I'm lying still. Wait, I'm trapped

Operator: Are you OK? Can you sit up?

Caller: Oh, yes, hold on a minute. It's just my duvet. I woke up with it covering my head and

thought someone had done something to me.
Operator…?

Caller: I bought a pair of boots at a shop last
week and took them back but the shop won't
give me a refund. I only wore them once.
Operator: There's nothing I can do about that.

A boy in Brighton called 999 to report that he
had got his fingers trapped in his DVD player.

A student was doing some ironing and somehow
the board collapsed, trapping him underneath
it. He had to wriggle across the room still

my power has gone off. Will my Black forest gateau defrost in the freezer if I keep the door shut and how long would it take?

trapped in the ironing board to his phone to call the emergency services.

Caller: I'm watching *The X Factor* and I can't get through to make a vote.
Operator: I don't think I can help you with that.
Caller: But…then would you please telephone them yourself and put a vote on for me?

A mother telephoned the emergency number to ask how she could do CPR on her daughter's pet squirrel. She said that she'd found him comatose on the patio. It turned out that the squirrel had gone into hibernation.

Operator: Hello, 999 emergency services.
Caller: Is that 999?
Operator: How can I help you?
Caller: I've left my coat on the bus.

Operator: Hello, emergency services.
Caller: My Playstation pictures have gone all fuzzy and I can't play Grand Theft Auto.
Can you send somebody round to fix it?
Operator: No.

A woman called 999 because she had just got in from work and her boyfriend refused to warm up her feet.

Caller: My car will not start and I'm locked inside it. Nothing works, I can't open the door because it's electronically locked and I'm getting so hot that I feel really unwell.

Operator: Have you tried pulling up the lock on the door?

Caller: Oh, yes I can get out now thank you. That's better.

Operator: …

A woman dialled 999 after not receiving as many prawns in her fried rice as usual. She demanded that the police turn up to investigate. She had ordered extra prawns and she told the operator that, they were over charging her because she couldn't see any extra prawns amongst the rice.

A woman called 999 to complain that her local McDonalds had run out of Chicken McNuggets. She had already placed her order and was waiting for her food when she was told that they had run out of McNuggets. Since they had processed the transaction through the till they asked her to choose something else off the menu but she was furious and called the police telling them that it was an emergency and demanding that a police officer came to help her. Unsurprisingly, it wasn't enough of an 'emergency' for no police support to be dispatched. Her biggest issue was that she only wanted the McNuggets and refused offers of any other food. This particular emergency call made news around the world.

Operator: Emergency services.
Caller: Hello, I'm five years old. Can you help me
with my science homework?

A man called the police after being refused entry to a Leeds nightclub. He was being denied entry because he was too drunk, but the man ranted on until police turned up, at which point he was arrested for being drunk and disorderly.

Caller: I need help.
Operator: What is wrong?
Caller: Where is Tesco's???

A school pupil used his mobile phone to call the

police after he was disciplined by a teacher. The boy was sent outside the classroom for disruptive behaviour where he pulled his phone out of his pocket and dialled 999. Unfortunately, since he gave his full name and his school, the police were able to turn up and tell the head teacher about his calls.

A drunken woman called the emergency number to try and find a boyfriend. She called four times insisting that the emergency services find her a partner. She told the operator what she looked like and gave her height and weight as if she was joining a dating agency. Each time a different operator told her that they couldn't help her.

A woman telephoned 999 to get a spider removed from her bathroom. She requested the London

Metropolitan Police come round and take the spider away. However, the operator told her that the police couldn't help her on this occasion and advised her to seek help from a neighbour.

A man in Kingston-Upon-Thames climbed into his little boys' toy car and became stuck. His wife had to call the fire brigade to get him cut out of it.

Caller: I'm just calling to enquire about the penalties for growing marijuana. Could you tell me er... how much trouble you can get into for growing just one plant?

Operator: Are you in the process of committing a crime?

Caller: Err...possibly.

Caller: I understand that it's not really an emergency but I just want to ask you about a bright round stationary object across the valley from me.

Operator: OK.

Caller: I wondered if perhaps you could tell me what it is. It's been there at least an hour and it's still there.

Operator: It's been there for an hour. Right. Is it actually on land or in the sky?

Caller: It's in the sky.

Operator: I will try to find out for you what it is.
Caller: Good. [Short pause]
Operator: Sir, I'm being told that it's the moon.

Caller: Hi, I'm on my way home from Asda and I want to report the buses.
Operator: What about the buses?
Caller: There are none.
Operator: Excuse me?
Caller: There are no buses and my feet hurt.
Operator: Is that all?
Caller: No! There weren't any taxis either. My feet hurt. I just want a lift home.

A woman in Devon dialled 999 because her boyfriend had put her hamster out in the rain. She asked for police to come and arrest him with handcuffs and put him in the cells overnight. The operator politely declined to comply with her request.

A man in Bolton called 999 because he was stuck in the middle of an icy road. He told the operator that he was scared of going backwards or forwards and asked them to send someone to help him across the road.

A man called 999 because his iPhone was not working properly. He demanded to be put through to Apple headquarters so that he could make his complaint directly to the bosses. When the operator told him that they couldn't redirect him he hung up and called 999 again with the same request.

Caller: My fingernail is broken. Can you get help for me?

Operator: No this number is for emergencies only.

Caller: This *is* an emergency. Besides, you're public servants so you should serve me.

Operator: …?

Caller: My gerbil's having babies and I don't know what to do.

Operator: Madam, you need a vet, not an ambulance

Caller: Don't you have vets? My gerbil might die. Couldn't you just send some paramedics round to help me?

Operator: No, I'm sorry madam. You need to look in the phone book for an emergency vet if you're worried about your pets.

A woman dialled 999 to tell police that she'd lost her slippers. She told them that they might have been stolen and asked if they would come round and investigate.

An elderly woman telephoned for assistance from a paramedic, telling the operator that she'd fallen. When the paramedics arrived she was fine and just asked them if they'd get a packet of cigarettes for her.

Caller: I'm trying to put a light bulb in my living room lamp but none of them seem to fit. Can you send someone round to help me?

A family in Kent got lost in a hay maze and had to call 999 because they couldn't find their way out. Police turned up and found them within ten minutes. A police spokesperson pointed out that since the field didn't actually have any wire or stone fencing around it all they had to do was listen out for traffic and then head in that direction.

Caller: I need someone to come to my house.

Operator: Could you tell me what's happened?

Caller: My glass coffee table has been smashed.

Operator: Are you calling to report an assault? Is anyone hurt?

Caller: No, no one's hurt but there's glass all over the carpet.

Operator: I don't understand. What service do you require?

Caller: I want someone to come round and clear it up before my dog cuts his paws on it.

A woman called 999 after the superglue that she'd been using splashed onto her jeans causing them to stick to her.

A woman dialled 999 because she had forgotten the pass code for her mobile phone and it had become locked. She wanted to know if an expert at the police station could unlock it for her.

Caller: Hello, I need help.

Operator: What's the problem you have?

Caller: I have burnt my face badly.

Operator: OK, can you tell me how you did that?

Caller: I think I was in the sun for too long yesterday

Operator: So it's sunburn?

Caller: Yes.

Operator: …!

Caller: I need to go to hospital

Operator: Can you tell me what's happened?

Caller: A cat attacked me.

Operator: Was it your pet or a stray?

Caller: No, it belongs to next door.

Operator: Can you tell me how bad your injuries are?

Caller: Yes, I have a scratch on my right hand.

Operator: How deep is it? Are you bleeding heavily?

Caller: No, I'm not bleeding. It's a scratch about three inches long but it's not bleeding.

Operator: So it's just a scratch?

Caller: Yes, it's just a scratch, but I'm worried that it might become infected without immediate medical treatment.

Operator: How can I help?

Caller: Hi, this is an emergency. It's been going on for two hours now and it's 'doing my head in'.

Operator: What's happening there?

Caller: My cat's been playing with string.

Operator: …

Caller: I think I have a moth in my ear.

Operator: Can you tell me how that happened?

Caller: Yes, I came into the kitchen and the moth

flew near me and now I can't find it.

Operator: Can you feel it in your ear?

Caller: No, but I can't see it so I think that's where it is.

Operator: Are you sure it's not somewhere where you just can't see it?

Caller: No…oh hold on. Yes, now I can see it. It's flying round the lamp in the hall.

Caller: I think a poltergeist has deleted files from my computer.

Operator: A poltergeist?

Caller: Yes, they were there this morning but they've vanished. It must be a poltergeist because I live alone and this sort of thing happens often.

Operator: What did you think we could do about it?

Caller: Well, can't the police do something about

it? This isn't the first time. It chases me through the house sometimes.

Operator: A poltergeist?

Caller: Yes.

Operator: No.

Caller: I'd really like my phone reconnected. Can you put me through to Orange please?

Operator: Unfortunately there is no way I can do that, this is an emergency line.

Caller: But this IS an emergency – I've got no contact with the outside world

Caller: Hi. I've just been asked to show my ID in a shop. I'm actually 20 and I have a criminal record. Could you get the police to look me up on their system and then confirm with the

shop keeper that I'm 20 because I've lost my ID?

Operator: Sorry no, there is no way I can do that for you, this is an emergency line.

Caller: It'll only take a minute; I'm not even trying to buy alcohol, just cigarettes.

Operator: I'm sorry but I cannot tell the man in the shop you are 20 so that you can buy alcohol or cigarettes. Please clear the line

Caller: Help! Help! Send the police and an ambulance. I've been stabbed.

Operator: You said you've been stabbed?

Caller: Yes, I've been stabbed

Dispatcher: How many times were you stabbed?

Caller: This is the first time.

Caller: I have no electricity.

Operator: Yes, we're aware of that. Is there an emergency?

Caller: No, there's no emergency. I just want to make sure I'm not being charged when there's no electricity. Will I have to pay?

Operator: No sir, you won't be charged for the electricity you didn't use because the service is unavailable.

Caller: That's great news!

A woman dialled 999 to tell the police that there was a roll of carpet in her front garden. It turned out that her husband had put it there after clearing out the garage.

Caller: Someone is building late at night and it's keeping me awake.

Operator: A noise complaint is not an emergency call. You'll have to call your local authority in the morning.

Caller: Well if I went over there to stab them, would it be an emergency then?

Operator: Yes, it would.

Caller: Alright.

Caller: I need an ambulance. Can you send one or do I need to call someone else?

Operator: I can do that for you sir. Please calm down. What's the problem?"

Caller: I saw a medical documentary on TV last night about a rare disease, and I think I have all the symptoms. My neighbour thinks I do, too.

Operator: You need to see your own doctor sir. This is for emergency medical situations.

Operator: Emergency services.
Caller: There's a leopard sunbathing on the wall.
    Operator: Are you sure it's a leopard?
Caller: Yes, it's a small one but it's covered in spots.
    I'm sure it's a leopard.

During a very bad winter, a woman called 999 to complain that the overnight gritting trucks were making too much noise for her to sleep.

A man called 999 because he thought he saw someone driving his car and assumed it had been stolen. The police took down his registration number and set out to look for the car. They couldn't find it anywhere. When he got home he saw that his car was still on the driveway and realised that he'd made a mistake. He then tried to pretend to the police that the thief must have brought the car back again. The police were not impressed.

Caller: I want to talk to the police.

Operator: What is the problem?

Caller: I'm sixteen and I want to know if I can disown my mum.

Operator: That's not an emergency.

Caller: Yes it is. She won't give me any money and I want to go to a party on Saturday. I really need the money today so I can buy a new pair of jeans.

Operator: This is emergency calls only; needing new jeans is not an emergency.

Caller: You haven't seen my old jeans.

A woman called 999 because she could hear screams coming from her neighbour's house. When police went to investigate, a couple inside the house were arguing about which Nintendo game they were going to put on their console. They were throwing the remote controls at each other.

Operator: Which emergency service do you require please?

Caller: I want the police to come round.

Operator: What is the problem?

Caller: I want to remove a man from my sofa.

Operator: Is he an intruder or being violent?

Caller: No, it's just that he's sleeping on my end of the sofa.

Operator: He's *asleep*?

Caller: Yes, but he's sleeping at *my* end
of the sofa and I can't move him.
Operator: Can you sleep on the other side of the
sofa?
Caller: No, I like it at my end.
Operator: This isn't really an emergency is it?
Caller Yes it is. I'm very tired and I need someone
to move him.
Operator: …?

Operator: 999 emergency services
Caller: My friend needs an ambulance.
Operator: What is the problem?
[Voice in the background]: Get rid of the dope,
quickly.
Caller: He's unconscious.
[Another voice in the background]: I'm getting
rid of it right now, I'm doing it now!
Operator: Has he taken any drugs?

[Voice in the background]: It's gone; I put it in John's car.
Caller: No!

Caller: I need to get another burger
Operator: Is this an emergency?
Caller: Yes, I brought home a hamburger and whilst I was in the bathroom my cats ate it.
Operator: Your cats ate your burger?
Caller: Yes, I've been working all day and I'm starving hungry, I'm so hungry that I don't have the strength to go out to get another. I want you to call the burger place and have them send me another one.
Operator: I'm sorry madam, we can't do that.
Caller: If you don't I'll be in need of an ambulance later when I pass out from hunger. So you might as well get started now.
Operator:…?

Caller: There's a black cat the size of a hog just gone past my house.
Operator: What…?

Caller: I want to report my boyfriend.
Operator: What has he done?
Caller: Well, for my birthday he gave me perfume.

Operator: Is that a problem, this is an emergency number?

Caller: Yes, I wanted drugs. I know he has drugs; he just won't give them to me. I can use drugs more than I can use perfume.

Operator: Are you saying that your boyfriend is in possession of drugs?

Caller: Yes, of course he is and I want some.

Operator: Can you give me his name and address please?

Caller: Yes, his name is [...] and he lives at [...] When you get over there can you get some drugs off him for me?

Operator: Thank you for your information.

Caller: Uhh?

A woman in London dialled 999 because her boyfriend wouldn't let her switch over to *Eastenders* during a football match.

Caller: I'm trapped inside my house.

Operator: Trapped? Is someone holding you there against your will?

Caller: Someone? No, I'm alone but there's a very large rat on my front doorstep.

Operator: A rat?

Caller: Yes, a huge, aggressive looking rat.

Operator: Well yes, but why can't you leave the house?

Caller: I have already told you. There is a rat on my front doorstep and I am terrified of rats.

Operator: Is there any other door in the house that you could use instead?

Caller: No. I have only one door and I can't get out of it with the rat sitting there.

Operator: You could take a brush or newspaper and move the rat off the doorstep couldn't you?

Caller: No, I can't do that. I keep telling you, I am terrified of rats. It might attack me, and go for my throat.

Caller: I want to report an intruder in my home

Operator: Are they violent? Are they still there?

Caller: Yes, they're still here. They're probably not what you'd call violent, no. I just want rid of them.

Operator: Do you know the intruder sir?

Caller: Yes, it's my mother-in-law

Operator: Your *mother-in-law*?

Caller: Yes, she's been here nearly three weeks and I want her to go home. Can she be arrested for intruding?

Operator: Is this an emergency?

Caller: Of course it's an emergency. I'm beginning to want to kill her.

A woman called 999 from outside Tesco's because she couldn't find a £1 coin for the shopping trolley.

A young man called 911 sounding frantic and told them that his cousin had stolen his Playstation video game console. He ranted to the operator that he was going over to his cousin's house to get it back and gave her his address. The operator told him that that was unwise and he should wait for the police to handle it. The young man then rang off telling the operator that he was off to his cousin's house to kill him. When police arrived, the man told them that his cousin had a gun and that they ought to shoot him. He then told the police that he had a gun and if they didn't shoot his cousin, he would shoot them. He was later arrested. The Playstation was subsequently found at his house. It hadn't been stolen – it was broken and he was hoping to claim for a new one on his home insurance.

Operator: 911, Can you tell me what your emergency is?

Caller: Yes, my wife's being attacked by a huge dog and I need an ambulance."

Operator: Ok, we're sending an ambulance to you right now. Can you give me your address?

Caller: 48766 Sycamore Drive.

Operator: Can you spell that please?

Caller: (long silence) Er…no. Look I'll drag her over to Langton Street and you can come and get her there.

Operator: Emergency, how can I help you?

Caller: I'm outside Burger King

Operator: What is your emergency?

Caller: It's a drive through.

Operator: Yes?

Caller: I have asked them five times to get me a flame grilled burger and they keep giving me the wrong burger, I get hamburger, lettuce, tomato, cheese and onion but no bacon and no barbeque sauce. They're just clearing up and ignoring me now.

Operator: Yes?

Caller: …she just gave me another one, it's still wrong. How hard is it to get a flame grilled burger?

Operator: What exactly do you want us to do?

Caller: Well, you should come down here and tell them to make it properly.

Operator: Sorry ma'am we are unable to intervene – this is an emergency line.

Caller: What am I supposed to do?

Operator: You need to speak with the manager.

Caller: She just told me that she wouldn't deal with it.

Operator: I suggest you get your money back and go elsewhere for your burger.

Caller: …You're supposed to protect me. Help me out.

Operator: Consider that we're protecting you from the 'wrong' burger ma'am. This is not a criminal issue. Please clear the line.

A woman called 999 from a beauty salon to complain that her nails had been cut too short. She was refusing to pay the nail technician the full price and wanted her arrested for incompetence. The police told her that they couldn't do anything about nails being too short and that she had to discuss her issues with the manager.

Caller: Well… this isn't exactly an emergency but…could you please tell me if there are any barber's shops around here that are open?

Operator: No, I can't do that from a 999 number. It's for emergencies only.

Caller: 999, oh I thought I dialled 998.

Operator: No, you dialled 999.

Caller: Oh, sorry. Bye bye then.

Operator: Bye.

Caller: I want to speak to the police.

Operator Yes, what is your emergency?

Caller: Well…it's a bit hard to explain.

Operator: Go on.

Caller: Well, I'm psychic and I'm sure that my friend is going to be involved in a car crash tomorrow or the day after.

Operator: I'm sorry. This number is for emergency calls only. I can't deal with things that might happen in the future.

Caller: But I'm trying to prevent an accident. It will save you time and resources. Can you not just follow her in her car tomorrow if I give you the registration number and keep her out of harm?

Operator: No.

Caller: Oh, OK bye then.

Operator: Bye.

A man in Florida once called 911 sixteen times over a news article that was on ABC. On one call he was recorded shouting into the phone that the TV news needed to be arrested. When he was told that that didn't count as an emergency he agreed that it wasn't an emergency but reiterated that he wanted the news to be arrested.

Caller: Hello, I'm on the M1, just past junction 24.

Operator: Yes, what emergency service do you require? Has there been an accident?

Caller: No, but I've just seen a slow moving tortoise crawling along in the slow lane.

Operator: A tortoise?

Caller: Yes, I mean I'm concerned about the tortoise but cars are swerving round it and it might cause an accident.

Operator: I'm sending the transport police round
  to investigate now sir.
[It turned out to be a squashed football]

Operator: How can I help you?
Caller: Hello, er…I'm in a hotel room and I'm
  stuck in the hot tub.
Operator: You can't get out of the hot tub?

Caller: No, that's right.

Operator: Do you want me to send help?

Caller: Yes please, I'm naked. Could you bring some marshmallows and a towel as well?

Operator: What?

Caller: I really want to eat some marshmallows in here and I also need a towel because I can't get out until I have a towel.

Operator: You're stuck in a hot tub and you want me to bring marshmallows and a towel? In what way are you stuck sir?

Caller: Well, like I said I'm naked…and there are no towels.

A Californian man in his early thirties telephoned 911 because he wanted his mother to be arrested. He told the emergency services operator that she had taken away his beer and he wanted them to come and get her. His words on the phone were so slurred that it was obvious to police why she'd decided to take his beer away in the first place.

Operator: 911 Emergency, how can I help you?

Caller: Hello…?

Operator: What is your emergency sir?

Caller: I think me and my wife have poisoned ourselves. We are both very sick and time is running very slowly.

Operator: I can call an ambulance for you. Can you tell me how you have been poisoned?

Caller: Yes, we ate some chocolate brownies with a special ingredient and now we're dying. We might already be dead. I'm having an 'out of body' experience.

Operator: Could you tell me what the special ingredient was?

Caller: Didn't I already tell you? I've now been on the phone for over an hour to you. Why aren't you doing anything?

Operator: You have been on the phone for three minutes sir.

Caller: No! I think someone is trying to break down my door. I think it's the CIA. They know about our secrets.

Operator: That is the paramedics sir. If you can, please let them in so they can assist you.

Caller: Why are the paramedics here? I think they're just pretending to be paramedics.

Operator: What ingredient did you put in the brownies sir?

Caller: Marijuana. I feel very weird. My wife can't stop laughing and she says she feels dizzy. Are we OK? Have we overdosed? Will we die?

Operator: Please let the paramedics in so they can assist you.

Caller: OK. Bye then.

A woman from New Jersey was caught speeding on the local highway and was given a ticket. Later that evening, she called 911 to find out the name of the traffic cop who booked her, telling the operator that he was 'cute'. The emergency operator told her that she was unable to give her the policeman's name and number.

An American man once called 911 because he could see the shadow of a 'huge angry looking creature' standing in his yard. He described the intruding creature as being about 6ft 9in tall. It turned out to be his own shadow, cast by the porch security light.

A woman in Florida was charged with misusing 911 after she called them to report that her local burger chain had run out of lemonade. She told the operator that she had ordered a complete meal that included lemonade but had been told that they had run out of lemonade and could she please order something else instead. The woman refused and called 911 to force the burger shop to go and find her some lemonade. She also refused to accept that it was not an emergency and remained arguing on the line for about twenty minutes. She was eventually arrested by two policemen, who turned up whilst she was still on the phone.

Caller: I'm in Subway getting some sandwiches for lunch and it's all going wrong.

Operator: What is your problem sir?

Caller: The meatballs are dry.

Operator: The meatballs are dry?

Caller: Yes, you know...they might poison me or something. I think they've been here all night

Operator: This is not an emergency is it sir?

Caller: Well it would be if I was poisoned. You ought to send someone round here to arrest them.

Operator: Maybe you should go somewhere else for your lunch?

Caller: No, someone else might get poisoned if nobody does anything.

Operator: This line is for emergency calls only. Nobody has been poisoned. Please clear the line sir.

Caller: Oh…OK then.

Caller: There's a chicken running around my front garden. It's scratching my trees and trampling the flower beds.

Operator: A chicken?

Caller: Yes, a big chicken. I have a knife – can I kill it if I catch it?

Operator: Do you know who it belongs to?

Caller: No, no one has any chickens round here. I can't think where it has come from. It's probably escaped. If I kill it will I be arrested for animal cruelty?

Operator: I'm not sure. You should contact the RSPCA. They will be able to advise you. This number is an emergency line. It's not for chickens.

Caller: OK.

Operator: 911 Emergency, how can I help you?

Caller: Sorry to bother you but could you get me the phone number for my friend in Boston?

Operator: What is your emergency?

Caller: I've just seen her boyfriend out with someone else and I want to warn her as quickly as possible.

Operator: Ma'am that is not an emergency.

Caller: Of course it is – they're getting married

next spring. She needs to know what he's like immediately.

Operator: Sorry ma'am we can't help you with that.

Operator: Emergency, how can I help you?

Caller: I'm at a drive through KFC. I've ordered a kids' meal for my daughters and I told them that I don't want any cheese because they don't like cheese. I asked for corn on the cob instead but they went ahead and gave me cheese.

Operator: This is not an emergency is it sir?

Caller: Yes it is. They should be arrested for incompetence.

Operator: Please clear the line sir or you'll be arrested.

Caller: I need to talk to the police right now.

Operator: OK how can I help you?

Caller: It's my refrigerator, it's broken.

Operator: Ma'am, you need to call appliance repair.

Caller: Can't you call them for me?

Operator: No, this line is for emergency calls only.

Caller: This is an emergency. There's left over take-out food in there and I want it for my lunch. It will go off.

Operator: Sorry, we can't help with things like that.

A woman once rang 999 for the fire brigade because her bedroom window wouldn't open. She asked if they could come round and get it open from the outside by using the ladders attached to the fire engines. Unsurprisingly they declined to turn up and suggested that she call a builder to prise them open.

Caller: I want to report a cricket outside my door.

Operator: A cricket?

Caller: Yes, it's a big one. It jumps around.

Operator: Just the one?

Caller: Yes, but the noise is driving me mad.

Operator: What would you like us to do?

Caller: Can't you send someone round to take it away?

Operator: No I'm afraid we can't do that madam.

Caller: I'm worried about what might happen if I kill it. Will I be in trouble? I'm not going to be able to take this much longer. Will I be arrested if I kill it?

Operator: I don't think so madam.

Caller: Are they a protected species?

Operator: I don't know but I'm sure you'll be OK.

Caller: Well, alright then I'm going to kill it. Are you sure that doesn't make me a bad person?

Operator: Is that all?

Caller: Yes, thank you.

Caller: I'm not working at the moment and I'm desperate to find a job. Can you help me?

Operator; Sorry sir, this is an emergency line. We can't help you. Please clear the line.

Caller: So, are you short staffed?

Operator: Excuse me?

Caller: Since you don't have time to talk to me I'm assuming you're short staffed. Could I get a job with you?

Operator: No sir, I'm just asking you to clear the line for real emergency calls.

Caller: But if I worked there you would have

another line wouldn't you? I'd really love to work there.

Operator: No sir, I'm sorry we are fully staffed.

Caller: Well, it doesn't sound like it to me. I'll say good bye then. Thanks for being so helpful.

Operator: Good bye sir.

Operator: What emergency service do you require?

Caller: Mneh mneeh hne Ntonge

Operator: Speak as calmly and clearly as you can. What is your location, I can send an ambulance to you immediately?

Caller: Yeeees… have… nbit… mhery… tunge.

Operator: Did you say you've bit your tongue?

Caller: Nyeees.

Operator: Does it need stitches?

Caller: Mnoh… mnoh…s'ok

Operator: Is this an emergency sir?

Caller: n'it hurts.

Operator: Do you require an ambulance?

Caller: Mnoh.

Operator: What do you want me to do?

Caller: Mnothing…really.

Operator: Ok then is that all?

Caller: Mnn. Bye.

Caller: Yes, I want to tell you about my central heating. It's not hot enough.

Operator: It's not hot enough? This is an emergency number. What do you want us to do?

Caller: Well, it broke and a chap came to fix it. Now it's working again but it's not as hot as it used to be. I think he must've stolen some heat from me. I want to tell the police. I've got his card with his number on it.

Operator: Are you saying that your boiler engineer stole some heat from you?

Caller: Well, he must have done or else why is it not as hot as it was before?

Operator: Have you tried your thermostat sir?

Caller: What's a thermostat?

Operator: It's a little dial usually on your wall. It regulates the temperature. You may just need to turn it up.

Caller: Well, OK thank you I'll try that. Can I call you back if it becomes clear that he's still stolen some heat?

Operator: I'd rather you didn't sir.

A new mother phoned an ambulance because she had run out of calpol. She said her infant was upset and she needed the medicine immediately because it was the middle of the night and she couldn't get to sleep.

In the UK, Northumbria Police was once called by a woman who claimed two spiders were attacking her in her cellar.

A man telephoned 999 wanting to report a dangerous driver, who was riding a moped. He demanded that the police come and identify the rider and arrest him because he claimed that the moped had nearly run him down. When he was told that if he was unhurt there was no emergency, he told the operator that he was off to find the moped and its rider and try to get him to run him down again – just to prove hat he was telling the truth.

Caller: I want to report a seagull.

Operator: Can you tell me why? What is the seagull doing?

Caller: It's sitting in my garden looking sad. It's raining heavily outside.

Operator: Looking sad? What emergency service do you need?

Caller: Can't you send someone to look after it?

Operator: I'm afraid not. You could try a local bird sanctuary.

A woman dialled 999 from a high street because she had walked past a doorway that was being painted and had got paint on her clothes. She wanted the painters arrested for negligence.

A teenager telephoned for an ambulance from a party because she had been hit on the head by a party popper. She had also been drinking heavily which accounted more for her dizziness and loss of balance than the tiny plastic bottle striking her on the ear.

Caller: Hello, I haven't been able to sleep you
see.

Operator: What is your emergency?

Caller: I'm trying to explain...I couldn't sleep...
so I didn't want to take sleeping tablets, you
see?

Operator: Yes, how can we help you?

Caller: Yes, so I went to get a beer.

Operator: You got a *beer*? So, what is your
problem?

Caller: Well...I can't open it.

Operator: You need to ask your neighbours to
help you. Is that all?

Caller: Oh, Ok, Thank you. Goodbye

Operator: Goodbye.

An elderly man in Manchester once telephoned the emergency services to try to get the police to come round to his house to shoot a blackbird that kept waking him up in the morning. When they explained that they couldn't comply with his request he threatened to buy a gun illegally and shoot every bird he could find.

Caller: I want to report my postman.

Operator: Why, what has he done?

Caller: He hasn't been today.

Operator: I'm sorry this is an emergency line; you should contact your local postal sorting office.

Caller: But you see there were days last week when he didn't come either. What if he's stealing peoples post on the days when he doesn't turn up? I might be reporting a theft.

Operator: This is not an emergency. Please contact your postal office.

Caller: But it could be theft couldn't it? Identity theft, stealing parcels, that kind of thing?

Operator: Sorry, I can't help you. Please contact your post office.

A woman made an emergency call because she was upset that her son was so distressed after failing his driving test. Apparently she was worried about his actions. She had seen him look very upset and go upstairs to his room. When she knocked on his door a little while later, there was no answer. She opened the door and couldn't find him but the window was open. Concerned that he must have done something stupid she called 999. Police and paramedics came to look for him but he turned up walking down the street. He had apparently gone over to his friend's house without telling his mum and she hadn't heard him go.

Caller: Help, I've got a real problem.

Operator: What is your emergency madam?

Caller: I can't get my cat to stop meowing. What can I do?

Operator: This is not an emergency is it?

Caller: Well it is to me...I don't know what to do.

Operator: You either need to contact a vet or feed it.

Caller: Feed it? Oh...OK

Operator: Yes, feed it. Is that all?

Caller: Yes, thank you. Good bye.

Operator: Is this an emergency? What do you want us to do about it?

Caller: Well I telephoned them and they refuse to come and empty them before Wednesday morning.

Operator: What day do they normally come on?

Caller: Wednesday but it's only Monday today and it's driving me mad. They won't come out right now when I need them.

Operator: I think you need to talk with your local council.

Caller: I just did. That's why I'm calling you. They won't help me.

Operator: This is not a matter for the emergency services. Please clear the line.

The mother of a teenage girl who had just had her ears pierced telephoned 999 demanding an ambulance because she thought her daughter's ear had become infected.

The younger of two sisters called emergency services because her older sister wouldn't let her borrow her clothes. She wanted a member of the police to explain to her sister how to 'be a kind sister'.

Caller: I want to report the dustbin men. My bins are overflowing and it's making me very ill with stress.

A man called the police to say he'd locked his keys inside his car. When the operator told him to call a locksmith, he told them that his children were locked inside the car. When the police turned up there were no kids. There was just a man locked out of his car.

Caller: I saw a chair in the window of the RSPCA charity shop.

Operator: Yes?

Caller: I wonder … could you contact them and reserve it for me?

Operator: No I'm sorry we can't do that. This is an emergency number.

Caller: But it is urgent. What if it sells before I get there?

Operator: I'm sorry we can't help you with something like that.

Caller: Why is there so much traffic on this highway?

Operator: Is this an emergency sir?

Caller: Yes, I want to know why there is so much traffic on this road. It is an emergency.

Operator: Sir, it doesn't sound like an emergency; it sounds as if you're stuck in traffic. Is that the only reason for your call?

Caller: Yes, so you can't tell me?

Operator: I'm afraid not sir.

A man in Louisiana called 911 after he was pulled over by a police car because of speeding and also given a caution because his car stereo could be heard over 25 feet away. The man wanted the operator to tell the policeman that the noise level law was only for 'young kids playing their awful music'. He was 65 and had been listening to an easy listening radio station.

Caller: My smoke alarm keeps beeping. Does that mean that something is on fire?

Operator: Can you see or smell any fire?

Caller: No. There is no fire.

Operator: If you can't see any fire, then you can switch it off.

Caller: But doesn't it mean that there is a fire somewhere even if I can't see or smell it?

Operator: Not necessarily. It probably needs new batteries.

Caller: Oh, I didn't realise that. Thank you. Bye

Late one evening, during a bad downpour of rain, a man attempted to clear leaves from his gutter because the water was overflowing. However, when he put the ladders up against the house they wouldn't reach to the gutter. He then dialled the emergency services to ask them to come out with a longer ladder. He was told that his case didn't qualify as an emergency and that he should contact a roofing specialist the next day.

Caller: Yes, my friend was wondering... If she takes in a homeless man to live with her... Is it against the law?

Operator: No I don't believe it is.

Caller: What even if they get married or have sex? They won't be in trouble?

Operator: No as long as they're both in agreement.

Caller: Oh that's great!! Bye now!

Caller: My girlfriend went and sold my TV whilst I was out getting more tacos.

Operator: She *sold* your TV?

Caller: Yes, it's gone and she said she's sold it.

Operator: Do you know who she sold it to?

Caller: Yes, some guy down the street.

Operator: You need to all talk to each other. Talk and then call back and I'll contact the police if it can't be sorted out.

Caller: [mumbling noises in background] Oh, it's

OK. It was just a joke. They're bringing it back.

A youth on drugs called 999 to try to get someone from the emergency services to come to his home and get him a drink from the fridge. He told them he was too 'spaced out' to get it from himself.

Caller: Help! I'm desperate. My dog won't stop barking.

Operator: Do you know what's causing the barking?

Caller: No, I don't know what it is.

Operator: Are you alone in your house?

Caller: Yes, but the dog is barking at the cupboards.

Operator: Try opening the cupboard.

Caller: Ahg! There's a mouse in here. That's why. Can you send someone out to get rid of a mouse?

Operator: I'm sorry sir, that's not the sort of thing that we deal with. This is an emergency line.

People have often made emergency calls regarding televisions. One woman called to tell someone that she thought her TV needed tuning, whilst an elderly man phoned to complain that his TV wouldn't turn on. Both needed someone familiar with the appliance, not emergency services.

Caller: Hello, I'm a retired detective and I want to report someone trapped inside a bag.
Operator: Are they moving? Is it like a sleeping bag or a rubbish bag?
Caller: Yes, they're running around by the field. I don't know how to describe the bag. It's sort of big and red.

Operator: We'll send someone out to you sir.

Caller: Oh wait a minute. No…it's OK I think it's a dog stuck in a picnic blanket. Yes, it is. It's OK. Sorry to have bothered you. Bye.

A man called 911 to make a complaint about McDonalds. They had forgotten to put his orange juice in the bag with his order. Instead of returning to the restaurant, the man demanded that police go back there and get it for him. He refused to go and speak to them himself. Eventually he was fined for wasting police time.

A woman once telephoned for an ambulance because she had a paper cut on her finger. She told the operator that she knew it wasn't life threatening but wanted medical attention because it hurt so much.

In the north west of England, emergency services were called to rescue a hedgehog that had got its head stuck in a yoghurt pot. It was suggested to them that they really ought to have contacted a vet.

Caller: I want my ex-girlfriend arrested.

Operator: What has she done?

Caller: She won't give me my favourite jumper back.

Operator: Your jumper?

Caller: Yes, it's clearly theft. She's stolen it.

Operator: Have you tried asking for it back?

Caller: Yes, but she's ignoring me. That's why I want her arrested.

Operator: I'm sorry, that's not an emergency. You need to contact your local police station if you can't sort it out between yourselves. Please clear the line.

Caller: I'm trying to report a THEFT!

Operator: Emergency services cannot help you in this case.

Caller: Useless people.

Operator: OK?

Caller: S'ppose I'll have to be if you won't help me. Bye.

Operator: Bye.

Someone phoned for an ambulance because they had a bad headache. They told the operator that they had taken some paracetemol ten minutes earlier but it still hadn't worked. As the caller was on the phone answering the operator's questions, the pain killer kicked in and the headache disappeared.

A drunken man demanded the police and fire brigade attend to him after getting his key stuck in the front door. He claimed that a burglar was inside his house and had deliberately locked him outside.

Caller: Hello, I think I ate something dodgy and now I feel sick.
Operator: Can you remember what you ate?
Caller: Yes, I ate some pizza that was sitting in a bin

last night. It looked alright and I was hungry and
I'd been drinking.

Operator: A bin?

Caller: Yes, it looked alright…

A mother called an ambulance for her son who
was sleeping and 'making a funny noise' when he
breathed. It turned out that he was just snoring.

Operator: 999 emergency services.

Caller: [Raspy voice] Hello, I've been diagnosed
with tonsillitis and my throat hurts.

Operator: Has it got worse since your diagnosis?

Caller: No, I just want someone to come and stop
it hurting!

A woman once spent 20 minutes on an emergency call because she was scared but she didn't know what she was scared of and wanted the operator to help her work out why she was so frightened. When they had been through the list of possibilities the woman realised that she had nothing to be scared of. She thanked the operator and hung up.

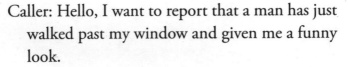

Caller: Hello, I want to report that a man has just walked past my window and given me a funny look.

Operator: He gave you a funny look? Did you know him?

Caller: No, he just sort of glared at me and then walked on. I've looked outside and I can't see him.

Operator: OK sir, if he comes back you can call us again. OK?

Caller: Oh, yes of course. Thank you. Bye now.

A woman telephoned the police because she believed that someone had put a black magic curse on her husband. The woman demanded that police go round to the house of the woman who she believed had cursed her husband. The police told her that they couldn't make an arrest or conduct an investigation based on supernatural claims. The woman phoned back five minutes later and told them that they should go round to the same woman's house because she wanted to charge her with stealing her washing from the line. It turned out that her husband was having an affair with the woman.

Caller: Yes, I called you earlier regarding a burglary?

Operator: Can you give me your details madam?

Caller: Yes it's [...]

Operator: I thought that call was responded to by

the police department.

Caller: Yes, they came and took notes and secured my house and everything. It's just that now they've gone I feel really, really stressed. Could you send someone back to sit with me?

Caller: Hi, I need medical help.

Operator: What is the nature of your emergency?

Caller: I have real bad stomach pain and I am finding it difficult to stand up.

Operator: I can call you an ambulance. How long have you had your symptoms?

Caller: Since I ate.

Operator: What did you eat?

Caller: A family tub of KFC, two Whopper Burgers, large coke, fries and ice-cream.

Operator: That's just you? By yourself?

Caller: Yeah, I'm on my own. I think I ate too much. Can you die from eating too much in

one sitting? How much would you have to eat? Do I need to go to hospital?

Operator: You've eaten too much? Were you fine before you ate?

Caller: Yes, I think maybe I've eaten too much.

Operator: You probably don't need medical attention at this stage.

Caller: OK. Goodbye then.

A priest called emergency services at an airport because the shop he was in wouldn't let him use their staff toilet. There were public toilets at the airport but he didn't want to use them because he was a priest.

A woman called 999 for help saying that she had a serious hand wound and was bleeding badly. When an ambulance arrived at her home, they found she had scratched her hand on a nail but she was 'worried it might get infected'.

Caller: Hi, yes, a black cat has just walked into my house and I can't get rid of it.

Operator: What help do you require ma'am?

Caller: Can you send somebody round to get it out for me?

Operator: I'm sorry we don't deal with things like that

this is an emergency number.

Caller: Well, it's an emergency to me. What can I do?

Operator: Try chasing it out with a broom.

A man called the emergency number whilst he was being arrested for driving without a license and complained to the emergency services that two police officers were harassing him and he didn't know why. He didn't realise that he was being put through to the same people that were in the process of arresting him.

A youth dialled 999 after he drank a can of cola that was out of date. He said he was worried it might have poisoned him and wanted immediate medical help.

Caller: I want someone to help me with my dog.
Operator: What is wrong with your dog sir?
Caller: I can't stop it snoring.
Operator: It's snoring?
Caller: Yes, very loudly.
Operator: You need to call your vet.

A woman demanded an ambulance to take her to the doctors. The previous day she had been slapped across the face by another family member and had reported it to the police as an assault. Because the slap left a red mark on her face, the police suggested that she see a doctor to get it documented. She lived in an area not served by buses and had no money for a taxi. She was furious when the operator refused to send an ambulance for her.

A woman rang 999 for an ambulance after being bitten by her daughter's hamster.

A man called 999 because he couldn't get rid of a noise in his ear. He said he had gone deaf in the affected ear and it was buzzing inside his head. When paramedics came round they found a small honey bee had become lodged in his ear.

A man phoned emergency services from a public toilet because there was no toilet paper. He wanted them to get him some more. Because it was a public toilet he decided that it was a community issue. Operators refused so the man threatened to 'call the authorities on them'. Perhaps he didn't realise that he was already talking to 'the authorities'.

Caller: There are ladybirds climbing up my wall.

Operator: There are *ladybirds* climbing up your wall? What emergency service do you need sir?

Caller: I need someone to come round and remove them.

Operator: I'm sorry sir we don't deal with ladybirds.

Caller: Well, what do I do with them?

Operator: You could try collecting them yourself or phone your local council pest control and see if they can help you.

Caller: OK I'll do that. Thank you!

A young woman requested an ambulance because her very high heeled new shoes had left her with blisters on her feet.

A man dialled 999 because he thought he had a bat hanging upside down in the corner of his bedroom ceiling. He knew that bats were a protected species so thought an emergency line could help. When the police went round to investigate they found that the 'bat' was in fact a patch of damp on the ceiling.

Caller: Is it safe to eat an out-of-date yoghurt?
Operator: I'm sorry we can't help you with that.
Caller: But might I need medical assistance?
Operator: That is not a matter for the emergency services.
Caller: I've been followed home by a cat.

Operator: What do you want emergency services to do about it?

Caller: Well, it might be lost, can't someone come and get it and take it home?

Caller: Oh hello, our son was taken into custody this morning.

Operator: Yes, what emergency service do you need?

Caller: Well, his dad and me are back at home now and we can't find where he put the remote control for the TV.

Two young shoplifters in the USA were caught when a mobile phone in one of their pockets accidentally dialled 911 whilst they were in the process of stealing from a shop. The operator heard them discussing what they were stealing and when they came out of the store police were waiting to arrest them.

A drunken man called 999 demanding to speak to the police so that he could complain that a local take-away had ruined his kebab by putting too much chilli sauce in it. As he ranted he also demanded that they come and get him and take him to a better take-away where they wouldn't put chilli sauce on it without asking him. He claimed that he was merely 'calling for assistance' in order to procure the meal that he wanted.

A young man was keen to build up his muscles and bought some weight lifting equipment to use at home. After the first attempt at exercising with them he suffered pain in his arms. He called for an ambulance without initially explaining that he had been lifting weights. When paramedics arrived they looked at the weights and realised that the weights he had been trying to lift were the equivalent of the weight of a small horse.

Caller: Hello, I had a dream my friend has been shot. I tried to ring him, but no one answered. Can you go round and make sure he is OK?

Caller: Hi yes, I'm calling to find out if there's a pizza place still open around here.

Operator: This is an emergency line only and that is not a life or death emergency.

Caller: Yes, it is…my wife is pregnant see, and she has a desperate craving for pizza, so it's kind of a medical emergency with her being pregnant isn't it?

Operator: I'm sorry sir, we can't help you with that, can you clear the line please.

Operator: 999 emergency services.

Caller: Hello, my boyfriend has a boil on his

bum and he can't sit down. I think we need an ambulance.

Operator: That isn't really a medical emergency. He should visit his GP.

Caller: But he can't do that until tomorrow morning and he's in pain now!

Operator: I'm sorry I can't send an ambulance for a boil. Please contact your GP in the morning.

Operator: How can I help you?

Caller: I need help ... I've been stung by a bee!

Operator: OK, are you allergic to bee stings? Do you have an adrenaline shot with you?

Caller: I don't know. I've never been stung before.

Operator: How is your breathing? Is there any tightness in your throat?

Caller: No! I've been stung on the arm. Why are you talking about my throat? There's nothing wrong with my throat.

Operator: So you don't suffer from anaphylactic shock then?

Caller: What the hell is that? I'm calling you because I've been stung by a bee and I have a red lump on my arm.

Operator: I don't think you need emergency treatment.

A man dialled 999 because he was having an argument with his wife and he wanted to throw his wedding ring at her. When he realised that he couldn't get it off his finger, he made a request to the emergency services to send a fireman round to cut it off his finger so that he could throw it at her.

A Texan woman called 911 to complain that her husband wouldn't eat the dinner she had cooked for him. On previous occasions she had called the emergency services because she couldn't find certain items of clothing and also because her dogs had got loose in the yard. She was eventually charged with abuse of the emergency number.

Caller: I want to report a theft.

Operator: OK, can you tell me what has been stolen sir?

Caller: Yes, there's a bag of rice missing from my cupboard.

Operator: Is there anything else missing?

Caller: No, just a bag of rice.

Operator: I don't think you need emergency services for that.

Operator: Hello, emergency services…

Caller: How much will my car license cost this year?

Caller: How many ounces in a pound?

Caller: What's the capitol of Romania?

Caller: Can you call someone, my cars broken down?

Caller: What year did the internet start?

Caller: There's a grey squirrel in my garden but there are no hazelnut trees around here. Will it die?

Caller: I can't find the cinema and the film starts in 5 minutes.

And finally…

Caller: I was just calling to thank you for all the amazing work you do. The emergency services are so brave and help so many people…

Operator: That is very kind of you madam. But you shouldn't be calling this line to say that. There may be real emergencies trying to get through.

Caller: But I wanted to thank someone in person…

Operator: Thank you for your call. But now I am going to hang up.

Caller: But, wait…

Operator: …

LITTLE LORD
FAUNTLEROY

Frances Hodgson Burnett

Harper Press
An imprint of HarperCollins*Publishers*
77–85 Fulham Palace Road
Hammersmith
London W6 8JB

This Harper Press paperback edition published 2012

Frances Hodgson Burnett asserts the moral right to be identified as the author of
this work

A catalogue record for this book is available from the British Library

ISBN: 978-0-00-744992-7

Printed and bound in Great Britain by Clays Ltd, St Ives plc

FSC™ is a non-profit international organisation established to promote the
responsible management of the world's forests. Products carrying the FSC
label are independently certified to assure consumers that they come
from forests that are managed to meet the social, economic and
ecological needs of present and future generations.

Find out more about HarperCollins and the environment at
www.harpercollins.co.uk/green

Life & Times section © Gerard Cheshire
Classic Literature: Words and Phrases adapted from
Collins English Dictionary
Typesetting in Kalix by Palimpsest Book Production Limited,
Falkirk, Stirlingshire

10 9 8 7 6 5 4 3 2 1

History of Collins

In 1819, millworker William Collins from Glasgow, Scotland, set up a company for printing and publishing pamphlets, sermons, hymn books and prayer books. That company was Collins and was to mark the birth of HarperCollins Publishers as we know it today. The long tradition of Collins dictionary publishing can be traced back to the first dictionary William published in 1824, *Greek and English Lexicon*. Indeed, from 1840 onwards, he began to produce illustrated dictionaries and even obtained a licence to print and publish the Bible.

Soon after, William published the first Collins novel, *Ready Reckoner*, however it was the time of the Long Depression, where harvests were poor, prices were high, potato crops had failed and violence was erupting in Europe. As a result, many factories across the country were forced to close down and William chose to retire in 1846, partly due to the hardships he was facing.

Aged 30, William's son, William II took over the business. A keen humanitarian with a warm heart and a generous spirit, William II was truly 'Victorian' in his outlook. He introduced new, up-to-date steam presses and published affordable editions of Shakespeare's works and *Pilgrim's Progress*, making them available to the masses for the first time. A new demand for educational books meant that success came with the publication of travel books, scientific books, encyclopaedias and dictionaries. This demand to be educated led to the later publication of atlases and Collins also held the monopoly on scripture writing at the time.

In the 1860s Collins began to expand and diversify

and the idea of 'books for the millions' was developed. Affordable editions of classical literature were published and in 1903 Collins introduced 10 titles in their Collins Handy Illustrated Pocket Novels. These proved so popular that a few years later this had increased to an output of 50 volumes, selling nearly half a million in their year of publication. In the same year, The Everyman's Library was also instituted, with the idea of publishing an affordable library of the most important classical works, biographies, religious and philosophical treatments, plays, poems, travel and adventure. This series eclipsed all competition at the time and the introduction of paperback books in the 1950s helped to open that market and marked a high point in the industry.

HarperCollins is and has always been a champion of the classics and the current Collins Classics series follows in this tradition – publishing classical literature that is affordable and available to all. Beautifully packaged, highly collectible and intended to be reread and enjoyed at every opportunity.

Life & Times

About the Author

Frances Hodgson Burnett was born in 1849 into an impoverished family in the slums of Manchester, England during the Industrial Revolution. Her father died when she was five years old, leaving the family in dire straits. Her mother was struggling to raise Frances and her four siblings when a considerate uncle urged them to emigrate to the USA. When her mother died, Frances was left to care for her siblings at the age of 18.

Frances turned to writing with the very specific idea of making money to feed the family. Within a year she had managed to sell her first story to a monthly magazine and begun to establish herself as a professional author. She published her first novel in 1877 and by 1886 she had written a number of novels. Her best seller, *Little Lord Fauntleroy* sold so well that it quickly made her a lady of independent means.

In the late 1890s Hodgson Burnett returned to England and took up residence in Great Maytham Hall, in the county of Kent. On exploration of the grounds of the property she discovered a walled garden untended for a number of years. She took it upon herself to restore the garden to floral splendour and then used the space as a place to sit and write. It was here that she conjured the idea for her children's novel *The Secret Garden*, which was published in 1911.

The Secret Garden

In *The Secret Garden*, Hodgson Burnett imagined her home of Maytham Hall to be populated by other people. She herself claimed that a robin had shown her where to find the key for the real walled garden, so she used this as a device to allow her protagonist to discover her way into the secret garden in the story. The heroine of the narrative is an orphaned girl named Mary Lennox, who finds herself living at the home of her uncle. The girl is lonely and inquisitive, leading her to find the secret garden. She soon realises that there is another child living in the manor house; her cousin Colin Craven.

Colin is a sickly child, confined to his bedroom, but slowly a friendship forms between them and Mary begins to open up Colin's world by taking him outside to visit the garden she has discovered. It turns out that Colin's father is overly protective and has kept him shut away for the good of his health. He is initially displeased to discover that his son has been venturing outside, but he is soon overcome with joy at seeing his son's subsequent recovery to good health and grateful to Mary for her part.

The theme of the book is essentially about the restorative properties of nature. On her arrival at Maytham Hall Mary was an ill-tempered and neglected child, but the garden soothes her and helps her to piece her life back together again. It has a similar calming affect on Colin, who suffers from psychosomatic illness partly brought about by the obsessive nature of his father. His father remains in mourning for his late wife, but he too eventually finds solace and happiness through the garden.

Little Lord Fauntleroy

The phrase 'Little Lord Fauntleroy' has become a byword for a boy who is spoilt and has a sense of entitlement. This idea is completely at odds however with the true nature of the child described in Hodgson Burnett's *Little Lord Fauntleroy* (1886). It seems that this misapprehension must have come from people who had never read the book or else missed the point entirely.

The boy in the story is, in fact, an American named Cedric Errol, who has lived his life so far with his mother in a downtrodden neighbourhood of New York City. He discovers that he is the next in line to become Lord Fauntleroy in England and reluctantly goes to live with his grandfather, the Earl of Dorincourt, who is an indefensible snob. In fact, the Earl refused to have anything to do with Cedric's mother because she was an American. Cedric has been raised with the idea that his grandfather is a philanthropist and benefactor, when in fact he is a misanthrope and a miser. However, the old man soon falls for the child and has no wish to disappoint him and to the amazement of others, he begins to show generosity and concern for their wellbeing. Ultimately the Earl learns that his idea of aristocratic behaviour was at fault and that the boy has taught him the importance of compassion and empathy. He accepts Cedric and his mother, having realised the value and importance of tolerance and connection. So, Cedric is anything but the conceited character that the phrase 'Little Lord Fauntleroy' is used to imply.

Following the release of the novel there was a curious fashion amongst the aspiring classes for dressing young boys in 'Little Lord Fauntleroy' outfits – velvet jumpsuits with lace collars. It seems that this image persisted in the public consciousness though few ever read the story, and this led to the misconception that the character was pompous and demanding, based simply on appearance. The author was keenly aware of the differences between cultures in England and America, because she had emigrated to the US at the age of 16. The idea that Americans were brash and uncouth was commonplace among the English upper class, because the US was founded on the notion that anyone had the right and opportunity to succeed – The Land of the Free. Hodgson Burnett was evidently keen to express her view that it was the intrinsic qualities of a person that mattered and not perceived etiquette and affectations designed to divide society.

The Edwardian Era

The Secret Garden was written in the Edwardian era, just before the outbreak of World War I. Queen Victoria had died at the turn of the 20th century and the British Empire covered an astonishing quarter of the globe. Hodgson Burnett was a working-class Mancunian, but she also had a worldly view because of her time spent in the States. Consequently, she had cultivated a romanticised and slightly bittersweet view of English aristocracy.

Her heroine Mary had been cruelly neglected by her well-to-do parents living in colonial India and then orphaned by their deaths from cholera. Her uncle was also rather remote from his son Colin, demonstrating Hodgson Burnett's view of the upper-class English as being stiff and lacking in emotional connection. She uses the secret garden as a form of therapy for the children, indicating that she recognises the value in keeping one's feet on the ground, literally as well as metaphorically. The children are also helped in their recuperation by the working-class staff at the manor.

This idea of the importance of socially connecting is paralleled in *Howards End*, written by E. M. Forster and published the year before *The Secret Garden*, in 1910. Forster's book addresses relationships between people of different classes and cultures, as the central characters are Germans living in pre-war England. Following World War I, the world was left a very different place. The British Empire had had its foundations shaken and was about to be razed to the ground. Similarly the class structure in England was eroding with the redistribution of wealth and opportunity.

Hodgson Burnett had already moved back to America by 1909, having secured US citizenship. She lived in New York State for the remainder of her life, where she continued to write. In *The Secret Garden* she had experimented with ideas about curing ailments through mind over matter, and this became something of central interest in her autumn years. This was expressed in her practising theosophy, which was essentially a blend of religion and philosophy. It seems that her mind required a belief system, but she was reluctant to think of herself as religious and invest her entirety in religion alone.

Hodgson Burnett was also a playwright, but she is best known as a children's writer and fantasy novelist. *The Secret Garden* has become a staple of English literature because it is the kind of story that can be enjoyed by both child and adult together. Moreover, many children grow into adults with a fondness for the story and then introduce their own offspring to its charm. For that reason, the book has remained popular for a century.

LITTLE LORD FAUNTLEROY

CONTENTS

Chapter 1	A Great Surprise	1
Chapter 2	Cedric's Friends	11
Chapter 3	Leaving Home	36
Chapter 4	In England	42
Chapter 5	At the Castle	54
Chapter 6	The Earl and His Grandson	74
Chapter 7	At Church	96
Chapter 8	Learning to Ride	104
Chapter 9	The Poor Cottages	114
Chapter 10	The Earl Alarmed	121
Chapter 11	Anxiety in America	140
Chapter 12	The Rival Claimants	152
Chapter 13	Dick to the Rescue	161
Chapter 14	The Exposure	167
Chapter 15	His Eighth Birthday	172

CHAPTER 1

A Great Surprise

Cedric himself knew nothing whatever about it. It had never been even mentioned to him. He knew that his papa had been an Englishman, because his mamma had told him so; but then his papa had died when he was so little a boy that he could not remember very much about him, except that he was big, and had blue eyes and a long moustache, and that it was a splendid thing to be carried around the room on his shoulder. Since his papa's death, Cedric had found out that it was best not to talk to his mamma about him. When his father was ill, Cedric had been sent away, and when he had returned, everything was over; and his mother, who had been very ill too, was only just beginning to sit in her chair by the window. She was pale and thin, and all the dimples had gone from her pretty face and her eyes looked large and mournful, and she was dressed in black.

'Dearest,' said Cedric (his papa had called her that always, and so the little boy had learned to say it), 'dearest, is my papa better?'

He felt her arms tremble, and so he turned his curly head, and looked in her face. There was something in it that made him feel that he was going to cry.

'Dearest,' he said, 'is he well?'

1

Then suddenly his loving little heart told him that he'd better put both his arms around her neck and kiss her again and again, and keep his soft cheek close to hers; and he did so, and she laid her face on his shoulder and cried bitterly, holding him as if she could never let him go again.

'Yes, he is well,' she sobbed; 'he is quite, quite well, but we – we have no one left but each other. No one at all.'

Then, little as he was, he understood that his big, handsome young papa would not come back any more; that he was dead, as he had heard of other people being, although he could not comprehend exactly what strange thing had brought all this sadness about. It was because his mamma always cried when he spoke of his papa that he secretly made up his mind it was better not to speak of him very often to her, and he found out, too, that it was better not to let her sit still and look into the fire or out of the window without moving or talking. He and his mamma knew very few people, and lived what might have been thought very lonely lives, although Cedric did not know it was lonely until he grew older and heard why it was they had no visitors. Then he was told that his mamma was an orphan, and quite alone in the world when his papa had married her. She was very pretty, and had been living as companion to a rich old lady who was not kind to her, and one day Captain Cedric Errol, who was calling at the house, saw her run up the stairs with tears on her eyelashes; and she looked so sweet and innocent and sorrowful that the Captain could not forget her. And after many strange things had happened, they knew each other well and loved each other dearly, and were married, although their marriage brought them the ill-will of several persons. The one who was most angry of all, however, was the Captain's father, who lived in England, and was a very rich and important old nobleman, with a very bad temper, and a very violent dislike to America and Americans. He had two sons older than Captain Cedric; and it was the law that the elder of these sons should inherit the family title and estates, which were very rich and splendid; if the eldest son died the next one would be heir; so though he was a member of such a great family, there was little chance that Captain Cedric would be very rich himself.

But it so happened that Nature had given to the younger son gifts which she had not bestowed upon his elder brothers. He had a beautiful face and a fine, strong, graceful figure; he had a bright smile and a sweet, gay voice; he was brave and generous, and had the kindest heart in the world, and seemed to have the power to make everyone love him. But it was not so with his elder brothers; neither of them was handsome, or very kind or clever. When they were boys at Eton, they were not popular; when they were at college, they cared nothing for study, and wasted both time and money, and made few real friends. The old Earl, their father, was constantly disappointed and humiliated by them; his heir was no honour to his noble name, and did not promise to end in being anything but a selfish, wasteful, insignificant man, with no manly or noble qualities. It was very bitter, the old Earl thought, that the son who was only third, and would have only a very small fortune, should be the one who had all the gifts, and all the charms, and all the strength and beauty. Sometimes he almost hated the handsome young man because he seemed to have the good things which should have gone with the stately title and the magnificent estates; and yet, in the depths of his proud, stubborn old heart, he could not help caring very much for his youngest son. It was in one of his fits of petulance that he sent him off to travel in America; he thought he would send him away for a while, so that he should not be made angry by constantly contrasting him with his brothers, who were at that time giving him a great deal of trouble by their wild ways.

But after about six months, he began to feel lonely, and longed in secret to see his son again, so he wrote to Captain

Cedric and ordered him home. The letter he wrote crossed on its way a letter the Captain had just written to his father telling of his love for the pretty American girl, and of his intended marriage; and when the Earl received that letter, he was furiously angry. Bad as his temper was, he had never given way to it in his life as he gave way to it when he read the Captain's letter. His valet, who was in the room when it came, thought his lordship would have a fit of apoplexy, he was so wild with anger. For an hour he raged like a tiger, and then he sat down and wrote to his son, and ordered him never to come near his old home, nor to write to his father or brothers again. He told him he might live as he pleased, and die where he pleased, that he should be cut off from his family for ever, and that he need never expect help from his father as long as he lived.

The Captain was very sad when he read the letter; he was very fond of England, and he dearly loved the beautiful home where he had been born; he had even loved his ill-tempered old father, and had sympathized with him in his disappointments; but he knew he need expect no kindness from him in the future. At first he scarcely knew what to do; he had not been brought up to work, and had no business experience, but he had courage and plenty of determination. So he sold his commission in the English army, and after some trouble found a situation in New York, and married. The change from his old life in England was very great, but he was young and happy and he hoped that hard work would do great things for him in the future. He had a small house in a quiet street, and his little boy was born there, and everything was so gay and cheerful, in a simple way, that he was never sorry for a moment that he had married the rich old lady's pretty companion just because she was so sweet and he loved her and she loved him. She was very sweet indeed, and her little boy was like both her and his father. Though he was born in so quiet and cheap a little home, it seemed as if there never had been a more fortunate baby. In the first place he was always well, and so he never gave anyone trouble; in the second place he had so sweet a temper and ways so charming that he was a pleasure to everyone; and in the third place he was so beautiful to look at that he was quite a picture. Instead of being a bald-headed baby, he started in life with a quantity of soft, fine, gold-coloured hair, which curled up at the ends, and went into loose rings by the time he was six months old; he had big brown eyes and long eyelashes and a darling little face; he had so strong a back and splendid sturdy legs that at nine months he learned suddenly to walk; his manners were so good, for a baby, that it was delightful to make his acquaintance. He seemed to feel that everyone was his friend, and when anyone spoke to him, when he was in his carriage in the street, he would give the stranger one sweet serious look with the brown eyes, and then follow it with a lovely, friendly smile; and the consequence was, that there was not a person in the neighbourhood of the quiet street where he lived – even to the grocery-man at the corner, who was considered the crossest creature alive – who was not pleased to see him, and speak to him. And every month of his life he grew handsomer and more interesting.

When he was old enough to walk out with his nurse, dragging a small wagon and wearing a short white kilt skirt, and a big white hat set back on his curly yellow hair, he was so handsome and strong and rosy that he attracted everyone's attention, and his nurse would come home and tell his mamma stories of the ladies who had stopped their carriages to look at and speak to him, and of how pleased they were when he talked to them in his cheerful little way, as if he had known them always. His greatest charm was this cheerful, fearless, quaint little way of making friends with people. I think it arose from his having a very confiding nature, and a kind little heart that sympathized with everyone, and wished to make everyone as comfortable as he liked to be himself. It made him very quick to understand the feelings of those about him. Perhaps this had grown on him too, because he had lived so much with his father and mother, who were always loving and considerate and tender and well bred. He had never heard an unkind or uncourteous word spoken at home; he had always been loved and caressed and treated tenderly, and so his childish soul was full of kindness and innocent warm feeling. He had always heard his mamma called by pretty, loving names, and so he used them himself when he spoke to her; he had always seen that his papa watched over her and took great care of her, and so he learned too to be careful of her.

So when he knew his papa would come back no more and saw how very sad his mamma was, there gradually came into his kind little heart the thought that he must do what he could to make her happy. He was not much more than a baby, but that thought was in his mind whenever he climbed upon her knee and kissed her, and put his curly head on her neck, and when he brought his toys and picture books to show her, and when he curled up quietly by her side as she used to lie on the sofa. He was not old enough to know of anything else to do, so he did what he could, and was more of a comfort to her than he could have understood.

'Oh, Mary,' he heard her say once to her old servant, 'I am sure he is trying to help me in his innocent way – I know he is. He looks at me sometimes with a loving, wondering little look, as if he were sorry for me, and then he will come and pet me or show me something. He is such a little man, I really think he knows.'

As he grew older he had a great many quaint little ways which amused and interested people greatly. He was so much of a companion for his mother that she scarcely cared for any other. They used to walk together and talk together and play together. When he was quite a little fellow he learned to read; and after that he used to lie on the hearth-rug, in the evening, and read aloud – sometimes stories, and sometimes big books such as older people read, and sometimes even the newspaper; and often at such times Mary, in the kitchen, would hear Mrs Errol laughing with delight at the quaint things he said.

'And, indade,' said Mary to the grocery-man, 'nobody cud help laughin' at the quare little ways of him – and his ould-fashioned sayin's! Didn't he come into my kitchen the noight the new prisident was nominated and shtand afore the fire, lookin' loike a pictur', wid his hands in his shmall pockets, an' his innocent bit of a face as sayrious as a jedge? An' sez he to me: "Mary," sez he, "I'm very much int'rusted in the 'lection," sez he. "I'm a 'publican, an' so is Dearest. Are you a 'publican, Mary?" "Sorra a bit," sez I; "I'm the bist o' dimmycrats!" An' he looks up at me wid a look that ud go to yer heart, and sez he: "Mary," sez he, "the country will go to ruin." An' nivver a day since thin has he let go by widout argyin' wid me to change me polytics.'

Mary was very fond of him, and very proud of him too. She had been with his mother ever since he was born; and after his father's death, had been cook and housemaid and nurse and everything else. She was proud of his graceful, strong little body and his pretty manners, especially proud of the bright curly hair which waved over his forehead and fell in charming love-locks on his shoulders. She was willing to work early and late to help his mamma to make his small suits and keep them in order.

"Ristycratic, is it?' she would say. 'Faith and I'd loike to see the choild on Fifth Avey-*noo* as he looks loike him an' shteps out as handsome as himself. An' ivvery man, woman and choild lookin' afther him in his bit of a black velvet skirt made out of the misthress's ould gownd; an' his little head up an' his curly hair flyin' an' shinin'. It's like a young lord he looks.'

Cedric did not know that he looked like a young lord; he did not know what a lord was. His greatest friend was the grocery-man at the corner – the cross grocery-man, who was never cross to him. His name was Mr Hobbs, and Cedric admired and respected him very much. He thought him a very rich and powerful person, he had so many things in his store – prunes and figs and oranges and biscuits – and he had a horse and wagon. Cedric was fond of the milkman and the baker and the apple-woman, but he liked Mr Hobbs best of all, and was on terms of such intimacy with him that he went to see him every day, and often sat with him quite a long time discussing the topics of the hour. It was quite surprising how many things they found to talk about – the Fourth of July, for instance. When they began to talk about the Fourth of July there really seemed no end to it. Mr Hobbs had a very bad opinion of 'the British', and he told the whole story of the Revolution, relating very wonderful and patriotic stories about the villainy of the enemy and the bravery of the revolutionary heroes, and he even generously repeated part of the Declaration of Independence. Cedric was so excited that his eyes shone and his cheeks were red and his curls were all rubbed and tumbled into a yellow mop. He could hardly wait to eat his dinner after he went home, he was so anxious to tell his mamma. It was perhaps Mr Hobbs who gave him his first interest in politics. Mr Hobbs was fond of reading the newspapers, and so Cedric heard a great deal about what was going on in Washington; and Mr Hobbs would tell him whether the President was doing his duty or not. And once, when there was an election, he found it all quite grand, and probably but for Mr Hobbs and Cedric the country might have been wrecked. Mr Hobbs took him to see a great torch-light procession, and many of the men who carried torches remembered afterwards a stout man who stood near a lamp-post and held on his shoulder a handsome little shouting boy, who waved his cap in the air.

It was not long after this election, when Cedric was between seven and eight years old, that the very strange thing happened which made so wonderful a change in his life. It was quite curious, too, that the day it happened he had been talking to Mr Hobbs about England and the Queen, and Mr Hobbs had said some very severe things about the aristocracy, being specially indignant against earls and marquises. It had been a hot morning, and after playing soldiers with some friends of his, Cedric had gone into the store to rest, and had found Mr Hobbs looking very fierce over a piece of the *Illustrated London News*, which contained a picture of some Court ceremony.

'Ah,' he said, 'that's the way they go on now; but they'll get enough of it some day, when those they've trod on rise and blow 'em up sky-high – earls and marquises and all! It's coming, and they may look out for it!'

Cedric had perched himself as usual on the high stool and pushed his hat back, and put his hands in his pockets in delicate compliment to Mr Hobbs.

'Did you ever know many marquises, Mr Hobbs?' Cedric inquired; 'or earls?'

'No,' answered Mr Hobbs with indignation; 'I guess not. I'd like to catch one of 'em inside here; that's all! I'll have no grasping tyrants sittin' 'round on my biscuit barrels!'

And he was so proud of the sentiment that he looked around proudly and mopped his forehead.

'Perhaps they wouldn't be earls if they knew any better,' said Cedric, feeling some vague sympathy for their unhappy condition.

'Wouldn't they!' said Mr Hobbs. 'They just glory in it! It's in 'em. They're a bad lot.'

They were in the midst of their conversation when Mary appeared. Cedric thought she had come to buy some sugar, perhaps, but she had not. She looked almost pale as if she were excited about something.

'Come home, darlint,' she said; 'the misthress is wantin' yez.'

Cedric slipped down from his stool. 'Does she want me

to go out with her, Mary?' he asked. 'Good morning, Mr Hobbs. I'll see you again.'

He was surprised to see Mary staring at him in a dumb-founded fashion, and he wondered why she kept shaking her head. 'What's the matter, Mary?' he said. 'Is it the hot weather?'

'No,' said Mary, 'but there's strange things happenin' to us.'

'Has the sun given Dearest a headache?' he inquired anxiously.

But it was not that. When he reached his own house there was a coupé standing before the door, and someone was in the little parlour talking to his mamma. Mary hurried him upstairs and put on his best summer suit of cream-coloured flannel with the red scarf around the waist, and combed out his curly locks.

'Lords, is it?' he heard her say. 'An' the nobility an' gintry. Och! bad cess to them! Lords indade – worse luck.'

It was really very puzzling, but he felt sure his mamma would tell him what all the excitement meant, so he allowed Mary to bemoan herself without asking many questions. When he was dressed, he ran downstairs and went into the parlour. A tall, thin old gentleman with a sharp face was sitting in an armchair. His mother was standing near by with a pale face, and he saw that there were tears in her eyes.

'Oh, Ceddie!' she cried out, and ran to her little boy and caught him in her arms and kissed him in a little frightened, troubled way. 'Oh, Ceddie darling!'

The tall old gentleman rose from his chair and looked at Cedric with his sharp eyes. He rubbed his thin chin with his bony hand as he looked. He seemed not at all displeased.

'And so,' he said at last slowly, 'and so this is little Lord Fauntleroy.'

CHAPTER 2

Cedric's Friends

There was never a more amazed little boy than Cedric during the week that followed; there was never so strange or so unreal a week. In the first place, the story his mamma told him was a very curious one. He was obliged to hear it two or three times before he could understand it. He could not imagine what Mr Hobbs would think of it. It began with earls; his grandpapa, whom he had never seen, was an earl; and his eldest uncle, if he had not been killed by a fall from his horse, would have been an earl too in time; and after his death, his other uncle would have been an earl, if he had not died suddenly, in Rome, of fever. After that, his own papa, if he had lived, would have been an earl; but since they had all died and only Cedric was left, it appeared that he was to be an earl after his grandpapa's death – and for the present he was Lord Fauntleroy.

He turned quite pale when he was first told of it.

'Oh, Dearest,' he said, 'I should rather not be an earl. None of the boys are earls. Can't I *not* be one?'

But it seemed to be unavoidable. And when, that evening, they sat together by the open window looking out into the shabby street, he and his mother had a long talk about it. Cedric sat on his footstool, clasping one knee in his favourite attitude and wearing a bewildered little face rather red from the exertion of thinking. His grandfather had sent for him to come to England and his mamma thought he must go.

'Because,' she said, looking out of the window with sorrowful eyes, 'I know your papa would wish it to be so, Ceddie. He loved his home very much; and there are many things to be thought of that a little boy can't quite understand. I should be a selfish little mother if I did not send you. When you are a man you will see why.'

Ceddie shook his head mournfully. 'I shall be very sorry to leave Mr Hobbs,' he said. 'I'm afraid he'll miss me, and I shall miss him. And I shall miss them all.'

When Mr Havisham – who was the family lawyer of the Earl of Dorincourt, and who had been sent by him to bring Lord Fauntleroy to England – came the next day, Cedric heard many things. But somehow it did not console him to hear that he was to be a very rich man when he grew up, and that he would have castles here and castles there, and great parks and deep mines and grand estates and tenantry. He was troubled about his friend, Mr Hobbs, and he went to see him at the store soon after breakfast in great anxiety of mind.

He found him reading the morning paper, and he approached him with a grave demeanour. He really felt it would be a great shock to Mr Hobbs to hear what had befallen him, and on his way to the store he had been thinking how it would be best to break the news.

'Hallo!' said Mr Hobbs. 'Mornin'!'

'Good morning,' said Cedric.

He did not climb up on the high stool as usual but sat down on a biscuit box and clasped his knee, and was so silent for a few moments that Mr Hobbs finally looked up inquiringly over the top of his newspaper.

'Hallo!' he said again.

Cedric gathered all his strength of mind together.

'Mr Hobbs,' he said, 'do you remember what we were talking about yesterday morning?'

'Well,' replied Mr Hobbs, 'seems to me it was England.'

'Yes,' said Cedric; 'but just when Mary came for me, you know?'

Mr Hobbs rubbed the back of his head.

'We *was* mentioning Queen Victoria and the aristocracy.'

'Yes,' said Cedric rather hesitatingly, 'and – and earls; don't you know?'

'Why, yes,' returned Mr Hobbs; 'we *did* touch 'em up a little; that's so!'

Cedric flushed up to the curly hair on his forehead. Nothing so embarrassing as this had ever happened to him in his life. He was a little afraid that it might be a trifle embarrassing to Mr Hobbs too.

'You said,' he proceeded, 'that you wouldn't have them sitting 'round on your biscuit barrels.'

'So I did!' returned Mr Hobbs stoutly. 'And I meant it. Let 'em try it – that's all!'

'Mr Hobbs,' said Cedric, 'one is sitting on this box now!'

Mr Hobbs almost jumped out of his chair.

'What!' he exclaimed.

'Yes,' Cedric announced with due modesty; '*I* am one – or I am going to be. I shan't deceive you.'

Mr Hobbs looked agitated. He rose up suddenly and went to look at the thermometer.

'The mercury's got into your head!' he exclaimed, turning back to examine his young friend's countenance. 'It *is* a hot day! How do you feel? Got any pain? When did you begin to feel that way?'

He put his big hand on the little boy's hair. This was more embarrassing than ever.

'Thank you,' said Ceddie; 'I'm all right. There is nothing the matter with my head. I'm sorry to say it's true, Mr Hobbs.

That was what Mary came to take me home for. Mr Havisham was telling my mamma, and he is a lawyer.'

Mr Hobbs sank into his chair and mopped his forehead with his handkerchief.

'*One* of us has got a sunstroke!' he exclaimed.

'No,' returned Cedric, 'we have not. We shall have to make the best of it, Mr Hobbs. Mr Havisham came all the way from England to tell us about it. My grandpapa sent him.'

Mr Hobbs stared wildly at the innocent, serious little face before him.

'Who is your grandfather?' he asked.

Cedric put his hand in his pocket and carefully drew out a piece of paper, on which something was written in his own round, irregular hand.

'I couldn't easily remember it, so I wrote it down on this,' he said. And he read aloud slowly: '"John Arthur Molyneux Errol, Earl of Dorincourt". That is his name, and he lives in a castle – in two or three castles, I think. And my papa, who died, was his youngest son; and I shouldn't have been a lord or an earl if my papa hadn't died; and my papa wouldn't have been an earl if his two brothers hadn't died. But they all died, and there is no one but me – no boy – and so I have to be one; and my grandpapa has sent for me to come to England.'

Mr Hobbs seemed to grow hotter and hotter. He mopped his forehead and his bald spot and breathed hard. He began to see that something very remarkable had happened; but when he looked at the little boy sitting on the biscuit box with the innocent, anxious expression in his childish eyes, and saw that he was not changed at all, but was simply as he had been the day before, just a handsome, cheerful, brave little fellow in a black cloth suit and red neck-ribbon, all this information about the nobility bewildered him. He was all the more bewildered because Cedric gave it with such ingenuous simplicity and plainly without realizing himself how stupendous it was.

'Wha – what did you say your name was?' Mr Hobbs inquired.

'It's Cedric Errol, Lord Fauntleroy,' answered Cedric. 'That was what Mr Havisham called me. He said when I went into the room: "And so this is little Lord Fauntleroy!"'

'Well,' said Mr Hobbs, 'I'll be – jiggered!'

This was an exclamation he always used when he was very much astonished or excited. He could think of nothing else to say just at that puzzling moment.

Cedric felt it to be quite a proper and suitable ejaculation. His respect and affection for Mr Hobbs were so great that he admired and approved of all his remarks. He had not seen enough of society as yet to make him realize that sometimes Mr Hobbs was not quite conventional. He knew, of course, that he was different from his mamma, but then his mamma was a lady, and he had an idea that ladies were always different from gentlemen.

He looked at Mr Hobbs wistfully.

'England is a long way off, isn't it?' he asked.

'It's across the Atlantic Ocean,' Mr Hobbs answered.

'That's the worst of it,' said Cedric. 'Perhaps I shall not see you again for a long time. I don't like to think of that, Mr Hobbs.'

'The best of friends must part,' said Mr Hobbs.

'Well,' said Cedric, 'we have been friends for a great many years, haven't we?'

'Ever since you was born,' Mr Hobbs answered. 'You was about six weeks old when you were first walked out on this street.'

'Ah,' remarked Cedric with a sigh, 'I never thought I should have to be an earl then!'

'You think,' said Mr Hobbs, 'there's no getting out of it?'

'I'm afraid not,' answered Cedric. 'My mamma says that my papa would wish me to do it. But if I have to be an earl, there's one thing I can do: I can try to be a good one. I'm not going to be a tyrant. And if there is ever to be another war with America I shall try to stop it.'

His conversation with Mr Hobbs was a long and serious one. Once having got over the first shock, Mr Hobbs was not so rancorous as might have been expected; he endeavoured to resign himself to the situation, and before the interview was at an end he had asked a great many questions. As Cedric could answer but few of them he endeavoured to answer them himself, and being fairly launched on the subject of earls and marquises and lordly estates, explained many things in a way which would probably have astonished Mr Havisham, could that gentleman have heard it.

But then there were many things which astonished Mr Havisham. He had spent all his life in England, and was not accustomed to American people and American habits. He had been connected professionally with the family of the Earl of Dorincourt for nearly forty years, and he knew all about its grand estates and its great wealth and importance; and, in a cold business-like way, he felt an interest in this little boy who, in the future, was to be the master and owner of them all – the future Earl of Dorincourt. He had known all about the old Earl's disappointment in his elder sons and all about his fierce rage at Captain Cedric's American marriage, and he knew how he still hated the gentle little widow and would not speak of her except with bitter and cruel words. He insisted than she was only a common American girl who had entrapped his son into marrying her because she knew he was an earl's son. The old lawyer himself had more than half believed this was all true. He had seen a great many selfish, mercenary people in his life, and he had not a good opinion of Americans. When he had been driven into the cheap street, and his coupé had stopped before the cheap small house, he had felt actually shocked. It seemed really quite dreadful to think that the future owner of Dorincourt Castle and Wyndham Towers and Chorlworth, and all the other stately splendours, should have been born and brought up in an insignificant house in a street with a sort of greengrocery at the corner. He wondered what kind of a child he would be, and what kind of a mother he had. He rather shrank from seeing them both. He had a sort of pride in the noble family whose legal affairs he had conducted so long, and it would have annoyed him very much to have found himself obliged to manage a woman who would seem to him a vulgar, money-loving person, with no respect for her dead husband's country and the dignity of his name. It was a very old name and a very splendid one, and Mr Havisham had a great respect for it himself though he was only a cold, keen business-like old lawyer.

When Mary handed him into the small parlour he looked around it critically. It was plainly furnished, but it had a home-like look; there were no cheap, common ornaments, and no cheap, gaudy pictures; the few adornments on the walls were in good taste, and about the room were many pretty things which a woman's hand might have made.

'Not at all bad so far,' he had said to himself; 'but perhaps the Captain's taste predominated.' But when Mrs Errol came into the room, he began to think she herself might have had something to do with it. If he had not been quite a self-contained and stiff old gentleman, he would probably have started when he saw her. She looked in the simple black dress, fitting closely to her slender figure, more like a young girl than the mother of a boy of seven. She had a pretty, sorrowful young face, and a very tender, innocent look in her large brown eyes – the sorrowful look that had never quite left her face since her husband had died. Cedric was used to seeing it there; the only times he had ever seen it fade out had been when he was playing with her or talking to her, and had said some old-fashioned thing, or used some long word he had picked up out of the newspapers or in his conversations with Mr Hobbs. He was fond of using long words, and he was always pleased when they made her laugh, though he could not understand why they were laughable; they were quite serious matters with him. The lawyer's experience taught him to read people's characters very shrewdly, and as soon as he saw Cedric's mother he knew that the old Earl had made a great mistake in thinking her a vulgar, mercenary woman. Mr Havisham had never been married, he had never even been in love, but he divined that this pretty young creature with the sweet voice and sad eyes had married Captain Errol only because she loved him with all her affectionate heart, and that she had never once thought it an advantage that he was an earl's son. And he saw he should have no trouble with her, and he began to feel that perhaps little Lord Fauntleroy might not be such a trial to his noble family after all. The Captain had been a handsome fellow, and the young mother was very pretty, and perhaps the boy might be well enough to look at.

When he first told Mrs Errol what he had come for, she turned very pale.

'Oh,' she said, 'will he have to be taken away from me? We love each other so much! He is such a happiness to me! He is all I have. I have tried to be a good mother to him.' And her sweet young voice trembled, and the tears rushed into her eyes. 'You do not know what he has been to me!' she said.

The lawyer cleared his throat.

'I am obliged to tell you,' he said, 'that the Earl of Dorincourt is not – is not very friendly towards you. He is an old man, and his prejudices are very strong. He has always especially disliked America and Americans, and was very much enraged by his son's marriage. I am sorry to be the bearer of so unpleasant a communication, but he is very fixed in his determination not to see you. His plan is that Lord Fauntleroy shall be educated under his own supervision; that he shall live with him. The Earl is attached to Dorincourt Castle, and spends a great deal of time there. He is a victim to inflammatory gout, and is not fond of London. Lord

Fauntleroy will, therefore, be likely to live chiefly at Dorincourt. The Earl offers to you as a home Court Lodge, which is situated pleasantly, and is not very far from the Castle. He also offers you a suitable income. Lord Fauntleroy will be permitted to visit you; the only stipulation is, that you shall not visit him or enter the park gates. You see you will not be really separated from your son, and I assure you, madam, the terms are not so harsh as – as they might have been. The advantage of such surroundings and education as Lord Fauntleroy will have, I am sure you must see, will be very great.'

He felt a little uneasy lest she should begin to cry or make a scene, as he knew some women would have done. It embarrassed and annoyed him to see women cry.

But she did not. She went to the window and stood with her face turned away for a few moments, and he saw she was trying to steady herself.

'Captain Errol was very fond of Dorincourt,' she said at last. 'He loved England, and everything English. It was always a grief to him that he was parted from his home. He was proud of his home, and of his name. He would wish – I know he would wish – that his son should know the beautiful old places, and be brought up in such a way as would be suitable to his future position.'

Then she came back to the table and stood looking up at Mr Havisham very gently.

'My husband would wish it,' she said. 'It will be best for my little boy. I know – I am sure the Earl would not be so unkind as to try to teach him not to love me; and I know – even if he tried – that my little boy is too much like his father to be harmed. He has a warm, faithful nature, and a true heart. He would love me even if he did not see me; and so long as we may see each other I ought not to suffer very much.'

'She thinks very little of herself,' the lawyer thought. 'She does not make any terms for herself.'

'Madam,' he said aloud, 'I respect your consideration for your son. He will thank you for it when he is a man. I assure you Lord Fauntleroy will be most carefully guarded, and every effort will be used to ensure his happiness. The Earl of Dorincourt will be as anxious for his comfort and well-being as you yourself could be.'

'I hope,' said the tender little mother, in a rather broken voice, 'that his grandfather will love Ceddie. The little boy has a very affectionate nature; and he has always been loved.'

Mr Havisham cleared his throat again. He could not quite imagine the gouty, fiery-tempered old Earl loving anyone very much; but he knew it would be to his interest to be kind, in his irritable way, to the child who was to be his heir. He knew too that if Ceddie were at all a credit to his name, his grandfather would be proud of him.

'Lord Fauntleroy will be comfortable, I am sure,' he replied. 'It was with a view to his happiness that the Earl desired that you should be near enough to him to see him frequently.'

He did not think it would be discreet to repeat the exact words the Earl had used, which were in fact neither polite nor amiable.

Mr Havisham preferred to express his noble patron's offer in smoother and more courteous language.

He had another slight shock when Mrs Errol asked Mary to find her little boy and bring him to her, and Mary told her where he was.

'Sure I'll foind him aisy enough, ma'am,' she said; 'for it's wid Mr Hobbs he is this minnit, settin' in his high shtool by the counther an' talkin' pollytics, most loikely, or enj'yin' hisself among the soap an' candles an' pertaties, as sinsible an' shwate as ye plase.'

'Mr Hobbs has known him all his life,' Mrs Errol said to the lawyer. 'He is very kind to Ceddie, and there is a great friendship between them.'

Remembering the glimpse he had caught of the store as he passed it, and having a recollection of the barrels of potatoes and apples and the various odds and ends, Mr Havisham felt his doubts arise again. In England gentlemen's sons did not make friends of grocery-men, and it seemed to him a rather singular proceeding. It would be very awkward if the child had bad manners and a disposition to like low company. One of the bitterest humiliations of the old Earl's life had been that his two elder sons had been fond of low company. Could it be, he thought, that this boy shared their bad qualities instead of his father's good qualities.

He was thinking uneasily about this as he talked to Mrs Errol until the child came into the room. When the door opened he actually hesitated a moment before looking at Cedric. It would perhaps have seemed very queer to a great many people who knew him, if they could have known the curious sensations that passed through Mr Havisham when he looked down at the boy, who ran into his mother's arms. He experienced a revulsion of feeling which was quite exciting. He recognized in an instant that here was one of the finest and handsomest little fellows he had ever seen. His beauty was something unusual. He had a strong, lithe, graceful little body and a manly little face; he held his childish head up, and carried himself with quite a brave little air; he was so like his father that it was really startling; he had his father's golden hair and his mother's brown eyes, but there was nothing sorrowful or timid in them. They were innocently fearless eyes; he looked as if he had never feared or doubted anything in his life.

'He is the best-bred-looking and handsomest little fellow I ever saw,' was what Mr Havisham thought. What he said aloud was simply: 'And so this is little Lord Fauntleroy.'

And after this the more he saw of little Lord Fauntleroy the more of a surprise he found him. He knew very little about children, though he had seen plenty of them in England

– fine, handsome, rosy girls and boys, who were strictly taken care of by their tutors and governesses, and who were sometimes shy, and sometimes a trifle boisterous, but never very interesting to a ceremonious, rigid old lawyer. Perhaps his personal interest in little Lord Fauntleroy's fortunes made him notice Ceddie more than he had noticed other children; but, however that was, he certainly found himself noticing him a great deal.

Cedric did not know he was being observed, and he only behaved himself in his ordinary manner. He shook hands with Mr Havisham in his friendly way when they were introduced to each other, and he answered all his questions with the unhesitating readiness with which he answered Mr Hobbs. He was neither shy nor bold, and when Mr Havisham was talking to his mother, the lawyer noticed that he listened to the conversation with as much interest as if he had been quite grown up.

'He seems to be a very mature little fellow,' Mr Havisham said to the mother.

'I think he is, in some things,' she answered. 'He has always been very quick to learn, and he has lived a great deal with grown-up people. He has a funny little habit of using long words and expressions he has read in books, or has heard others use, but he is very fond of childish play. I think he is rather clever, but he is a very boyish little boy sometimes.'

The next time Mr Havisham met him he saw that this last was quite true. As his coupé turned the corner he caught sight of a small group of small boys, who were evidently much excited. Two of them were about to run a race, and one of them was his young lordship, and he was shouting and making as much noise as the noisiest of his companions. He stood side by side with another boy, one little red leg advanced a step.

'One to make ready!' yelled the starter. 'Two to be steady. Three – and away!'

Mr Havisham found himself leaning out of the window of his coupé with a curious feeling of interest. He really never remembered having seen anything quite like the way in which his lordship's lordly little red legs flew up behind his knicker-bockers and tore over the ground as he shot out in the race at the signal word. He shut his small hands and set his face against the wind; his bright hair streamed out behind.

'Hooray, Ced Errol!' all the boys shouted, dancing and shrieking with excitement. 'Hooray, Billy Williams! Hooray, Ceddie! Hooray, Billy! Hooray! 'Ray! 'Ray!'

'I really believe he is going to win,' said Mr Havisham. The way in which the red legs flew and flashed up and down, the shrieks of the boys, the wild efforts of Billy Williams, whose brown legs were not to be despised as they followed closely in the rear of the red legs, made him feel some excitement. 'I really – I really can't help hoping he will win!' he said, with an apologetic sort of cough.

At that moment the wildest yell of all went up from the dancing, hopping boys. With one last frantic leap the future Earl of Dorincourt had reached the lamp-post at the end of the block and touched it, just two seconds before Billy Williams flung himself at it panting.

'Three cheers for Ceddie Errol!' yelled the little boys. 'Hooray for Ceddie Errol!'

Mr Havisham drew his head in at the window of his coupé and leaned back with a dry smile.

'Bravo, Lord Fauntleroy!' he said.

As his carriage stopped before the door of Mrs Errol's house, the victor and the vanquished were coming towards it, attended by the clamouring crew. Cedric walked by Billy Williams and was speaking to him. His elated little face was very red, his curls clung to his hot, moist forehead, his hands were in his pockets.

'You see,' he was saying, evidently with the intention of making defeat easy for his unsuccessful rival, 'I guess I won because my legs are a little longer than yours. I guess that was it. You see, I'm three days older than you, and that gives me a 'vantage. I'm three days older.'

And this view of the case seemed to cheer Billy Williams so much that he began to smile on the world again, and felt able to swagger a little, almost as if he had won the race instead of losing it. Somehow Ceddie Errol had a way of making people feel comfortable. Even in the first flush of his triumphs, he remembered that the person who was beaten might not feel so gay as he did, and might like to think that he *might* have been the winner under different circumstances.

That morning Mr Havisham had quite a long conversation with the winner of the race – a conversation which made him smile his dry smile, and rub his chin with his bony hand several times.

Mrs Errol had been called out of the parlour, and the lawyer and Cedric were left together. At first Mr Havisham wondered what he should say to his small companion. He had an idea that perhaps it would be best to say several things which might prepare Cedric for meeting his grandfather, and perhaps for the great change that was to come to him. He could see that Cedric had not the least idea of the sort of thing he was to see when he reached England, or of the sort of home that waited for him there. He did not even know yet that his mother was not to live in the same house with him. They had thought it best to let him get over the first shock before telling him.

Mr Havisham sat in an armchair on one side of the open window; on the other side was another still larger chair, and Cedric sat in that and looked at Mr Havisham. He sat well back in the depths of his big seat, his curly head against the cushioned back, his legs crossed and his hands thrust deep into his pockets, in a quite Mr Hobbs-like way. He had been watching Mr Havisham very steadily when his mamma had been in the room, and after she was gone he still looked at him in respectful thoughtfulness. There was a short silence after Mrs Errol went out, and Cedric seemed to be studying Mr Havisham, and Mr Havisham was certainly studying Cedric. He could not make up his mind as to what an elderly gentleman should say to a little boy who won races, and wore short knickerbockers and red stockings on legs which were not long enough to hang over a big chair when he sat well back in it.

But Cedric relieved him by suddenly beginning the conversation himself.

'Do you know,' he said, 'I don't know what an earl is?'

'Don't you?' said Mr Havisham.

'No,' replied Ceddie. 'And I think when a boy is going to be one he ought to know. Don't you?'

'Well – yes,' answered Mr Havisham.

'Would you mind,' said Ceddie respectfully, 'would you mind 'splaining it to me?' (Sometimes when he used his long words he did not pronounce them quite correctly.) 'What made him an earl?'

'A king or queen in the first place,' said Mr Havisham. 'Generally he is made an earl because he has done some service to his sovereign, or some great deed.'

'Oh,' said Cedric; 'that's like the President.'

'Is it?' said Mr Havisham. 'Is that why your presidents are elected?'

'Yes,' answered Ceddie cheerfully. 'When a man is very good and knows a great deal, he is elected president. They have torchlight processions and bands, and everybody makes speeches. I used to think I might perhaps be a president, but I never thought of being an earl. I didn't know about earls,' he said rather hastily, lest Mr Havisham might feel it impolite in him not to have wished to be one. 'If I'd known about them, I dare say I should have thought I should like to be one.'

'It is rather different from being a president,' said Mr Havisham.

'Is it?' asked Cedric. 'How? Are there no torchlight processions?'

Mr Havisham crossed his own legs and put the tips of his fingers carefully together. He thought perhaps the time had come to explain matters rather more clearly.

'An earl is – is a very important person,' he began.

'So is a president!' put in Ceddie. 'The torchlight processions are five miles long, and they shoot up rockets, and the band plays! Mr Hobbs took me to see them.'

'An earl,' Mr Havisham went on, feeling rather uncertain of his ground, 'is frequently of very ancient lineage –'

'What's that?' asked Ceddie.

'Of very old family – extremely old.'

'Ah,' said Cedric, thrusting his hands deeper into his pockets. 'I suppose that is the way with the apple-woman near the park. I dare say she is of ancient lin-lenage. She is so old it would surprise you how she can stand up. She's a hundred, I should think, and yet she is out there when it rains even. I'm sorry for her, and so are the other boys. Billy Williams once had nearly a dollar, and I asked him to buy five cents worth of apples from her every day until he had spent it all. That made twenty days, and he grew tired of apples after a week; but then – it was quite fortunate – a gentleman gave me fifty cents and I bought apples from her instead. You feel sorry for anyone that's so poor and has such ancient lin-lenage. She says hers has gone into her bones and the rain makes it worse.'

Mr Havisham felt rather at a loss as he looked at his companion's innocent, serious little face.

'I am afraid you did not quite understand me,' he explained. 'When I said "ancient lineage" I did not mean old age; I meant that the name of such a family has been known in the world a long time; perhaps for hundreds of years persons bearing that name have been known and spoken of in the history of their country.'

'Like George Washington,' said Ceddie. 'I've heard of him ever since I was born, and he was known about long before that. Mr Hobbs says he will never be forgotten. That's because of the Declaration of Independence, you know, and the Fourth of July. You see, he was a very brave man.'

'The first Earl of Dorincourt,' said Mr Havisham solemnly, 'was created an earl four hundred years ago.'

'Well, well!' said Ceddie. 'That was a long time ago! Did you tell Dearest that? It would in'trust her very much. We'll tell her when she comes in. She always likes to hear cur'us things. What else does an earl do besides being created?'

'A great many of them have helped to govern England. Some of them have been brave men and have fought in great battles in the old days.'

'I should like to do that myself,' said Cedric. 'My papa was a soldier, and he was a very brave man – as brave as George Washington. Perhaps that was because he would have been an earl if he hadn't died. I am glad earls are brave. That's a great 'vantage – to be a brave man. Once I used to be rather afraid of things – in the dark, you know; but when I thought about the soldiers in the Revolution and George Washington – it cured me.'

'There is another advantage in being an earl sometimes,' said Mr Havisham slowly, and he fixed his shrewd eyes on the little boy with a rather curious expression. 'Some earls have a great deal of money.'

He was curious because he wondered if his young friend knew what the power of money was.

'That's a good thing to have,' said Ceddie innocently. 'I wish I had a great deal of money.'

'Do you?' said Mr Havisham. 'And why?'

'Well,' explained Cedric, 'there are so many things a person can do with money. You see, there's the apple-woman. If I were very rich I should buy her a little tent to put her stall in, and a little stove, and then I should give her a dollar every morning it rained, so that she could afford to stay at home. And then – oh! I'd give her a shawl. And, you see, her bones wouldn't feel so badly. Her bones are not like our bones, they hurt her when she moves. It's very painful when your bones hurt you. If I were rich enough to do all those things for her I guess her bones would be all right.'

'Ahem!' said Mr Havisham. 'And what else would you do if you were rich?'

'Oh, I'd do a great many things. Of course I should buy Dearest all sorts of beautiful things, needle-books and fans and gold thimbles and rings, and an encyclopaedia, and a carriage, so that she needn't have to wait for the street-cars. If she liked pink silk dresses, I should buy her some, but she likes black best. But I'd take her to the big stores, and tell her to look round and choose for herself. And then Dick –'

'Who is Dick?' asked Mr Havisham.

'Dick is a boot-black,' said his young lordship, quite warming up in his interest in plans so exciting. 'He is one of the nicest boot-blacks you ever knew. He stands at the corner of a street down town. I've known him for years. Once when I was very little I was walking out with Dearest and she bought me a beautiful ball that bounced, and I was carrying it and it bounced into the middle of the street where the carriages and horses were, and I was so disappointed I began to cry – I was very little. I had kilts on, and Dick was blacking a man's shoes, and he said "Hallo!" and he ran in between the horses and caught the ball for me and wiped it off with his coat and gave it to me and said: "It's all right, young 'un." So Dearest admired him very much, and so did I, and ever since then, when we go down town, we talk to him. He says "Hallo!" and I say "Hallo!" and then we talk a little, and he tells me how trade is. It's been bad lately.'

'And what would you like to do for him?' inquired the lawyer, rubbing his chin and smiling a queer smile.

'Well,' said Lord Fauntleroy, settling himself in his chair with a business air, 'I'd buy Jake out.'

'And who is Jake?' Mr Havisham said.

'He's Dick's partner, and he is the worst partner a fellow could have! Dick says so. He isn't a credit to the business, and he isn't square. He cheats, and that makes Dick mad. It would make you mad, you know, if you were blacking boots as hard as you could, and being square all the time, and your partner wasn't square at all. People like Dick, but they don't like Jake, and so sometimes they don't come twice. So if I were rich, I'd buy Jake out and get Dick a "boss" sign – he says a "boss" sign goes a long way; and I'd get him some new clothes and new brushes, and start him out fair. He says all he wants is to start out fair.'

There could have been nothing more confiding and inno-cent than the way in which his small lordship told his little story, quoting his friend Dick's bits of slang in the most candid good faith. He seemed to feel not a shade of a doubt that his elderly companion would be just as interested as he was himself. And in truth Mr Havisham was beginning to be greatly interested; but perhaps not quite so much in Dick and the apple-woman as in this kind little lordling, whose curly head was so busy, under its yellow thatch, with good-natured plans for his friends, and who seemed somehow to have forgotten himself altogether.

'Is there anything –' he began. 'What would you get for yourself if you were rich?'

'Lots of things!' answered Lord Fauntleroy briskly; 'but first I'd give Mary some money for Bridget – that's her sister, with twelve children and a husband out of work. She comes here and cries, and Dearest gives her things in a basket, and then she cries again, and says: "Blessin's be on yez, for a beautiful lady." And I think Mr Hobbs would like a gold watch and chain to remember me by, and a meerschaum pipe. And then I'd like to get up a company.'

'A company!' exclaimed Mr Havisham.

'Like a Republican rally,' explained Cedric, becoming quite excited. 'I'd have torches and uniforms and things for all the boys, and myself too. And we'd march, you know, and drill. That's what I'd like for myself, if I were rich.'

The door opened and Mrs Errol came in.

'I am sorry to have been obliged to leave you so long,' she said to Mr Havisham; 'but a poor woman, who is in great trouble, came to see me.'

'This young gentleman,' said Mr Havisham, 'has been telling me about some of his friends, and what he would do for them if he were rich.'

'Bridget is one of his friends,' said Mrs Errol; 'and it is Bridget to whom I have been talking in the kitchen. She is in great trouble now because her husband has rheumatic fever.'

Cedric slipped down out of his big chair.

'I think I'll go and see her,' he said, 'and ask her how he is. He's a nice man when he is well. I'm obliged to him because he once made me a sword out of wood. He's a very talented man.'

He ran out of the room, and Mr Havisham rose from his chair. He seemed to have something in his mind which he wished to speak of. He hesitated a moment, and then said, looking down at Mrs Errol:

'Before I left Dorincourt Castle I had an interview with the Earl, in which he gave me some instructions. He is desirous that his grandson should look forward with some pleasure to his future life in England, and also to his acquaintance with himself. He said that I must let his lordship know that the change in his life would bring him money and the pleasures children enjoy; if he expressed any wishes I was to gratify them, and to tell him that his grandfather had given him what he wished. I am aware that the Earl did not expect anything quite like this; but if it would give Lord Fauntleroy pleasure to assist this poor woman, I should feel that the Earl would be displeased if he were not gratified.'

For the second time he did not repeat the Earl's exact words. His lordship had indeed said:

'Make the lad understand that I can give him anything he wants. Let him know what it is to be the grandson of the Earl of Dorincourt. Buy him everything he takes a fancy to: let him have money in his pockets, and tell him his grandfather put it there.'

His motives were far from being good, and if he had been dealing with a nature less affectionate and warm-hearted than little Lord Fauntleroy's, great harm might have been done. And Cedric's mother was too gentle to suspect any harm. She thought that perhaps this meant that a lonely, unhappy old man, whose children were dead, wished to be kind to her little boy, and win his love and confidence. And it pleased her very much to think that Ceddie would be able to help Bridget. It made her happier to know that the very first result of the strange fortune which had befallen her little boy was that he could do kind things for those who needed kindness. Quite a warm colour bloomed on her pretty young face.

'Oh,' she said, 'that was very kind of the Earl; Cedric will be so glad! He has always been fond of Bridget and Michael. They are quite deserving. I have often wished I had been able to help them more. Michael is a hard-working man when he is well, but he has been ill a long time and needs expensive medicines and warm clothing and nourishing food. He and Bridget will not be wasteful of what is given them.'

Mr Havisham put his thin hand in his breast pocket and drew forth a large pocket-book. There was a queer look in his keen face. The truth was he was wondering what the Earl of Dorincourt would say when he was told what was the first wish of his grandson that had been granted. He wondered what the cross, worldly, selfish old nobleman would think of it.

'I do not know that you have realized,' he said, 'that the Earl of Dorincourt is an exceedingly rich man. He can afford to gratify any caprice. I think it would please him to know that Lord Fauntleroy had been indulged in any fancy. If you will call him back and allow me, I shall give him five pounds for these people.'

'That would be twenty-five dollars!' exclaimed Mrs Errol. 'It will seem like wealth to them. I can scarcely believe that it is true.'

'It is quite true,' said Mr Havisham with his dry smile. 'A great change has taken place in your son's life, a great deal of power will lie in his hands.'

'Oh,' cried his mother. 'And he is such a little boy – a very little boy. How can I teach him to use it well? It makes me half afraid. My pretty little Ceddie!'

The lawyer slightly cleared his throat. It touched his worldly, hard old heart to see the tender, timid look in her brown eyes.

'I think, madam,' he said, 'that if I may judge from my interview with Lord Fauntleroy this morning, the next Earl of Dorincourt will think for others as well as for his noble self. He is only a child yet, but I think he may be trusted.'

Then his mother went for Cedric and brought him back into the parlour. Mr Havisham heard him talking before he entered the room.

'It's infam-natory rheumatism,' he was saying, 'and that's a kind of rheumatism that's dreadful. And he thinks about the rent not being paid, and Bridget says that makes the inf'ammation worse. And Pat could get a place in a store if he had some clothes.'

His little face looked quite anxious when he came in. He was very sorry for Bridget.

'Dearest said you wanted me,' he said to Mr Havisham. 'I've been talking to Bridget.'

Mr Havisham looked down at him a moment. He felt a

little awkward and undecided. As Cedric's mother had said, he was a very little boy.

'The Earl of Dorincourt –' he began, and then he glanced involuntarily at Mrs Errol.

Little Lord Fauntleroy's mother suddenly kneeled down by him and put her tender arms around his childish body.

'Ceddie,' she said, 'the Earl is your grandpapa, your own papa's father. He is very, very kind, and he loves you and wishes you to love him, because the sons who were his little boys are dead. He wishes you to be happy and to make other people happy. He is very rich, and he wishes you to have everything you would like to have. He told Mr Havisham so, and gave him a great deal of money for you. You can give some to Bridget now; enough to pay her rent and buy Michael everything. Isn't that fine, Ceddie? Isn't he good?' And she kissed the child on his round cheek, where the bright colour suddenly flashed up in his excited amazement.

He looked from his mother to Mr Havisham.

'Can I have it now?' he cried. 'Can I give it to her this minute? She's just going.'

Mr Havisham handed him the money. It was in fresh clean greenbacks and made a neat roll.

Ceddie flew out of the room.

'Bridget!' they heard him shout, as he tore into the kitchen. 'Bridget, wait a minute! Here's some money. It's for you, and you can pay the rent. My grandpapa gave it to me. It's for you and Michael!'

'Oh, Master Ceddie!' cried Bridget, in an awestricken voice. 'It's twenty-foive dollars is here. Where be's the misthress?'

'I think I shall have to go and explain it to her,' Mrs Errol said.

So she too went out of the room, and Mr Havisham was left alone for a while. He went to the window and stood looking out into the street reflectively. He was thinking of the old Earl of Dorincourt, sitting in his great, splendid gloomy library at the castle, gouty and lonely, surrounded by grandeur and luxury, but not really loved by anyone, because in all his long life he had never really loved anyone but himself; he had been selfish and self-indulgent, and arrogant and passionate; he had cared so much for the Earl of Dorincourt and his pleasures that there had been no time for him to think of other people; all his wealth and power, all the benefits from his noble name and high rank, had seemed to him to be things only to be used to amuse and give pleasure to the Earl of Dorincourt; and now that he was an old man, all this excitement and self-indulgence had only brought him ill-health and irritability and a dislike of the world, which certainly disliked him. In spite of all his splendour, there was never a more unpopular old nobleman than the Earl of Dorincourt, and there could scarcely have been a more lonely one. He could fill his castle with guests if he chose. He could give great dinners and splendid hunting parties; but he knew that in secret the people who would accept his invitations were afraid of his frowning old face and sarcastic, biting speeches. He had a cruel tongue and a bitter nature, and he took pleasure in sneering at people and making them feel uncomfortable, when he had the power to do so, because they were sensitive or proud or timid.

Mr Havisham knew his hard, fierce ways by heart, and he was thinking of him as he looked out of the window into the quiet, narrow street. And there rose in his mind, in sharp contrast, the picture of the cheery, handsome little fellow sitting in the big chair and telling his story of his friends, Dick and the apple-woman, in his generous, innocent, honest way. And he thought of the immense income, the beautiful, majestic estates, the wealth, and power for good or evil, which in the course of time would lie in the small, chubby hands little Lord Fauntleroy thrust so deep into his pockets.

'It will make a great difference,' he said to himself. 'It will make a great difference.'

Cedric and his mother came back soon after. Cedric was in high spirits. He sat down in his own chair, between his mother and the lawyer, and fell into one of his quaint attitudes, with his hands on his knees. He was glowing with enjoyment of Bridget's relief and rapture.

'She cried!' he said. 'She said she was crying for joy. I never saw anyone cry for joy before. My grandpapa must be a very good man. I didn't know he was so good a man. It's more – more agreeabler to be an earl than I thought it was. I'm almost glad – I'm almost *quite* glad I'm going to be one.'

CHAPTER 3

Leaving Home

Cedric's good opinion of the advantages of being an earl increased greatly during the next week. It seemed almost impossible for him to realize that there was scarcely anything he might wish to do which he could not do easily; in fact I think it may be said that he did not fully realize it at all. But at least he understood, after a few conversations with Mr Havisham, that he could gratify all his nearest wishes, and he proceeded to gratify them with a simplicity and delight which caused Mr Havisham much diversion. In the week before they sailed for England he did many curious things. The lawyer long after remembered the morning they went down together to pay a visit to Dick, and the afternoon they so amazed the apple-woman of ancient lineage by stopping before her stall and telling her she was to have a tent and a stove and a shawl and a sum of money, which seemed to her quite wonderful.

'For I have to go to England and be a lord,' explained Cedric sweet-temperedly. 'And I shouldn't like to have your bones on my mind every time it rained. My own bones never hurt, so I think I don't know how painful a person's bones can be, but I've sympathized with you a great deal, and I hope you'll be better.'

'She's a very good apple-woman,' he said to Mr Havisham as they walked away, leaving the proprietress of the stall almost gasping for breath, and not at all believing in her great fortune. 'Once, when I fell down and cut my knee, she gave me an apple for nothing. I've always remembered her for it. You know you always remember people who are kind to you.'

It had never occurred to his honest, simple, little mind that there were people who could forget kindnesses.

The interview with Dick was quite exciting. Dick had just been having a great deal of trouble with Jake, and was in low spirits when they saw him. His amazement when Cedric calmly announced that they had come to give him what seemed a very great thing to him, and would set all his troubles right, almost struck him dumb. Lord Fauntleroy's manner of announcing the object of his visit was very simple and unceremonious. Mr Havisham was much impressed by its directness as he stood by and listened. The statement that his old friend had become a lord, and was in danger of being an earl if he lived long enough, caused Dick to so open his eyes and mouth, and start, that his cap fell off. When he picked it up he uttered a rather singular exclamation. Mr Havisham thought it singular, but Cedric had heard it before.

'I soy!' he said, 'what 're yer givin' us?' This plainly embarrassed his lordship a little, but he bore himself bravely.

'Everybody thinks it not true at first,' he said. 'Mr Hobbs thought I'd had a sunstroke. I didn't think I was going to like it myself, but I like it better now I'm used to it. The one who is the earl now – he's my grandpapa; and he wants me to do anything I like. He's very kind, if he *is* an earl; and he sent me a lot of money by Mr Havisham, and I've brought some to you to buy Jake out.'

And the end of the matter was that Dick actually bought Jake out, and found himself the possessor of the business, and some new brushes and a most astonishing sign and outfit.

He could not believe in his good luck any more easily than the apple-woman of ancient lineage could believe in hers; he walked about like a boot-black in a dream; he stared at his young benefactor and felt as if he might wake up at any moment. He scarcely seemed to realize anything until Cedric put out his hand to shake hands with him before going away.

'Well, good-bye,' he said; and though he tried to speak steadily, there was a little trouble in his voice and he winked his big brown eyes. 'And I hope trade'll be good. I'm sorry I'm going away to leave you, but perhaps I shall come back again when I'm an earl. And I wish you'd write to me, because we were always good friends. And if you write to me, here's where you must send your letter.' And he gave him a slip of paper. 'And my name isn't Cedric Errol any more; it's Lord Fauntleroy and – and good-bye, Dick.'

Dick winked his eyes also, and yet they looked rather moist about the lashes. He was not an educated boot-black, and he would have felt it difficult to tell what he felt just then, if he had tried; perhaps that was why he didn't try, and only winked his eyes and swallowed a lump in his throat.

'I wish ye wasn't goin' away,' he said in a husky voice. Then he winked his eyes again. Then he looked at Mr Havisham and touched his cap. 'Thanky, sir, fur bringin' him down here an' fur wot ye've done. He's – he's a queer little feller,' he added. 'I've allers thort a heap of him. He's such a game little feller, an' – an' such a queer little 'un.'

And when they turned away he stood and looked after them in a dazed kind of way, and there was still a mist in his eyes and a lump in his throat, as he watched the gallant little figure marching gaily along by the side of its tall, rigid escort.

Until the day of his departure his lordship spent as much time as possible with Mr Hobbs in the store. Gloom had settled upon Mr Hobbs; he was much depressed in spirits. When his young friend brought to him in triumph the parting gift of a gold watch and chain, Mr Hobbs found it difficult to acknowledge it properly. He laid the case on his stout knee, and blew his nose violently several times.

'There's something written on it,' said Cedric, 'inside the case. I told the man myself what to say. "From his oldest friend, Lord Fauntleroy, to Mr Hobbs. When this you see, remember me." I don't want you to forget me.'

Mr Hobbs blew his nose very loudly again.

'I shan't forget you,' he said, speaking a trifle huskily, as Dick had spoken; 'nor don't you go and forget me when you get among the British arrystocracy.'

'I shouldn't forget you whoever I was among,' answered his lordship. 'I've spent my happiest hours with you; at least, some of my happiest hours. I hope you'll come to see me some time. I'm sure grandpapa would be very much pleased. Perhaps he'll write and ask you when I tell him about you? You – you wouldn't mind his being an earl, would you? I mean you wouldn't stay away just because he was one, if he invited you to come?'

'I'd come to see you,' replied Mr Hobbs graciously.

So it seemed to be agreed that if he received a pressing invitation from the Earl to come and spend a few months at Dorincourt Castle, he was to lay aside his republican prejudices and pack his valise at once.

At last the preparations were complete; the day came when the trunks were taken to the steamer, and the hour arrived when the carriage stood at the door. Then a curious feeling of loneliness came upon the little boy. His mamma had been shut up in her room for some time; when she came down the stairs her eyes looked large and wet, and her sweet mouth was trembling. Cedric went to her, and she bent down to him, and he put his arms around her, and they kissed each other. He knew something made them both sorry, though he scarcely knew what it was; but one tender little thought rose to his lips.

'We liked this little house, Dearest, didn't we?' he said. 'We always will like it, won't we?'

'Yes – yes,' she answered in a low, sweet voice. 'Yes, darling.' And then they went into the carriage and Cedric sat very close to her, and as she looked back out of the window he looked at her, and stroked her hand and held it close.

And then, it seemed almost directly, they were on the steamer in the midst of the wildest bustle and confusion; carriages were driving down and leaving passengers; passengers were getting into a state of excitement about baggage which had not arrived and threatened to be too late; big trunks and cases were being bumped down and dragged about; sailors were uncoiling ropes and hurrying to and fro; officers were giving orders; ladies and gentlemen and children and nurses were coming on board – some were laughing and looked gay, some were silent and sad, here and there two or three were crying and touching their eyes with their handkerchiefs. Cedric found something to interest him on every side; he looked at the piles of rope, at the furled sails, at the tall, tall masts which seemed almost to touch the hot blue sky; he began to make plans for conversing with the sailors and gaining some information on the subject of pirates.

It was just at the very last, when he was standing leaning on the railing of the upper deck and watching the final preparations, enjoying the excitement and the shouts of the sailors and wharfmen, that his attention was called to a slight bustle in one of the groups not far from him. Someone was hurriedly forcing his way through this group and coming towards him. It was a boy, with something red in his hand. It was Dick. He came up to Cedric quite breathless.

'I've run all the way,' he said. 'I've come down to see ye off. Trade's been prime! I bought this for ye out o' what I made yesterday. Ye kin wear it when ye get among the swells. I lost the paper when I was tryin' to get through them fellers downstairs. They didn't want to let me up. It's a handkercher.'

He poured it all forth as if in one sentence. A bell rang and he made a leap away before Cedric had time to speak.

'Good-bye!' he panted. 'Wear it when ye get among the swells.' And he darted off and was gone.

A few seconds later they saw him struggle through the crowd on the lower deck, and rush on shore just before the gang-plank was drawn in. He stood on the wharf and waved his cap.

Cedric held the handkerchief in his hand. It was of bright red silk, ornamented with purple horseshoes and horses' heads.

There was a great straining and creaking and confusion. The people on the wharf began to shout to their friends, and the people on the steamer shouted back:

'Good-bye! Good-bye! Good-bye, old fellow!' Everyone seemed to be saying: 'Don't forget us. Write when you get to Liverpool. Good-bye! Good-bye!'

Little Lord Fauntleroy leaned forward and waved the red handkerchief.

'Good-bye, Dick!' he shouted lustily. 'Thank you! Good-bye, Dick!'

And the big steamer moved away, and the people cheered again, and Cedric's mother drew the veil over her eyes, and on the shore there was left great confusion; but Dick saw nothing save the bright, childish face and the bright hair that the sun shone on and the breeze lifted, and he heard nothing but the hearty childish voice calling 'Good-bye, Dick!' as little Lord Fauntleroy steamed slowly away from the home of his birth to the unknown land of his ancestors.

CHAPTER 4

In England

It was during the voyage that Cedric's mother told him that his home was not to be hers; and when he first understood it his grief was so great that Mr Havisham saw that the Earl had been wise in making the arrangements that his mother should be quite near him, and see him often; for it was very plain he could not have borne the separation otherwise. But his mother managed the little fellow so sweetly and lovingly, and made him feel that she would be so near him, that after a while he ceased to be oppressed by the fear of any real parting.

'My house is not far from the Castle, Ceddie,' she repeated each time the subject was referred to – 'a very little way from yours, and you can always run in and see me every day, and you will have so many things to tell me, and we shall be so happy together! It is a beautiful place. Your papa has often told me about it. He loved it very much; and you will love it too.'

'I should love it better if you were there,' his small lord-ship said with a heavy little sigh.

He could not but feel puzzled by so strange a state of affairs, which could put his 'Dearest' in one house and himself in another.

The fact was that Mrs Errol had thought it better not to tell him why this plan had been made.

'I should prefer he should not be told,' she said to Mr Havisham. 'He would not really understand; he would only be shocked and hurt; and I feel sure that his feeling for the Earl will be a more natural and affectionate one if he does not know that his grandfather dislikes me so bitterly. He has never seen hatred or hardness, and it would be a great blow to him to find out that anyone could hate me. He is so loving himself, and I am so dear to him! It is better for him that he should not be told until he is much older, and it is far better for the Earl. It would make a barrier between them, even though Ceddie is such a child.'

So Cedric only knew that there was some mysterious reason for the arrangement, some reason which he was not old enough to understand, but which would be explained when he was older. He was puzzled; but after all it was not the reason he cared about so much; and after many talks with his mother, in which she comforted him and placed before him the bright side of the picture, the dark side of it gradually began to fade out, though now and then Mr Havisham saw him sitting in some queer little old-fashioned attitude, watching the sea, with a very grave face, and more than once he heard an unchildish sigh rise to his lips.

'I don't like it,' he said once as he was having one of his almost venerable talks with the lawyer. 'You don't know how much I don't like it; but there are a great many troubles in this world, and you have to bear them. Mary says so, and I've heard Mr Hobbs say it too. And Dearest wants me to like to live with my grandpapa, because, you see, all his children are dead, and that's very mournful. It makes you sorry for a man when all his children have died – and one was killed suddenly.'

One of the things which always delighted the people who made the acquaintance of his young lordship was the sage little air he wore at times when he gave himself up to conversation; combined with his occasionally elderly remarks and the extreme innocence and seriousness of his round childish face, it was irresistible. He was such a handsome, blooming, curly-headed little fellow, that, when he sat down and nursed his knee with his chubby hands, and conversed with much gravity, he was a source of great entertainment to his hearers. Gradually Mr Havisham had begun to derive a great deal of private pleasure and amusement from his society.

'And so you are going to try to like the Earl?' he said.

'Yes,' answered his lordship. 'He's my relation, and of course you have to like your relations: and besides, he's been very kind to me. When a person does so many things for you and wants you to have everything you wish for, of course you'd like him if he wasn't your relation; but when he's your relation and does that, why you're very fond of him.'

'Do you think,' suggested Mr Havisham, 'that he will be fond of you?'

'Well,' said Cedric, 'I think he will, because, you see, I'm his relation too, and I'm his boy's little boy besides, and, well, don't you see – of course he must be fond of me now, or he wouldn't want me to have everything that I like, and he wouldn't have sent you for me.'

'Oh,' remarked the lawyer, 'that's it, is it?'

'Yes,' said Cedric, 'that's it. Don't you think that's it too? Of course a man would be fond of his grandson.'

The people who had been seasick had no sooner recovered from their seasickness, and come on deck to recline in their steamer chairs and enjoy themselves, than everyone seemed to know the romantic story of little Lord Fauntleroy, and everyone took an interest in the little fellow, who ran about the ship or walked with his mother or the tall, thin old lawyer, or talked to the sailors. Everyone liked him; he made friends everywhere. He was ever ready to make friends. When the gentlemen walked up and down the deck, and let him walk with them, he stepped out with a manly, sturdy little tramp, and answered all their jokes with much gay enjoyment; when the ladies talked to him there was always laughter in the group of which he was the centre; when he played with the children there was always magnificent fun on hand. Among the sailors he had the heartiest friends; he heard miraculous stories about pirates and shipwrecks and desert islands; he learned to splice ropes and rig toy ships, and gained an amount of information concerning 'tops'ls' and 'mains'ls', quite surprising. His conversations had indeed quite a nautical flavour at times, and on one occasion he raised a shout of laughter in a group of ladies and gentlemen who were sitting on deck, wrapped in shawls and overcoats, by saying sweetly, and with a very engaging expression:

'Shiver my timbers, but it's a cold day!'

It surprised him when they laughed. He had picked up this seafaring remark from an 'elderly naval man' of the name of Jerry, who told him stories in which it occurred frequently. To judge from his stories of his own adventures, Jerry had made some two or three thousand voyages, and had been invariably shipwrecked on each occasion on an island densely populated with bloodthirsty cannibals. Judging also by these same exciting adventures, he had been partially roasted and eaten frequently and had been scalped some fifteen or twenty times.

'That is why he is so bald,' explained Lord Fauntleroy to his mamma. 'After you have been scalped several times the hair never grows again. Jerry's never grew after the last time, when the King of the Parromachaweekins did it with the knife made out of the skull of the Chief of the Wopslemumpkies. He says it was one of the most serious times he ever had. He was so frightened that his hair stood right straight up when the king flourished his knife, and it never would lie down, and the king wears it that way now, and it looks something like a hairbrush. I never heard anything like the asperiences Jerry has had! I should so like to tell Mr Hobbs about them!'

Sometimes, when the weather was very disagreeable and people were kept below decks in the saloon, a party of his grown-up friends would persuade him to tell them some of these 'asperiences' of Jerry's, and, as he sat relating them with great delight and fervour, there was certainly no more popular voyager on any ocean steamer crossing the Atlantic than little Lord Fauntleroy. He was always innocently and good-naturedly ready to do his small best to add to the general entertainment, and there was a charm in the very unconsciousness of his own childish importance.

'Jerry's stories int'rust them very much,' he said to his mamma. 'For my part – you must excuse me, Dearest – but sometimes I should have thought they couldn't be all quite true, if they hadn't happened to Jerry himself; but as they all happened to Jerry – well, it's very strange, you know, and perhaps sometimes he may forget and be a little mistaken, as he's been scalped so often. Being scalped a great many times might make a person forgetful.'

It was eleven days after he had said good-bye to his friend Dick before he reached Liverpool; and it was on the night of the twelfth day that the carriage, in which he and his mother and Mr Havisham had driven from the station, stopped before the gates of Court Lodge. They could not see much of the house in the darkness. Cedric only saw that there was a carriage drive under great arching trees, and after the carriage had rolled down this carriage drive a short distance, he saw an open door and a stream of bright light coming through it.

Mary had come with them to attend her mistress, and she had reached the house before them. When Cedric jumped out of the carriage he saw one or two servants standing in the wide bright hall, and Mary stood in the doorway.

Lord Fauntleroy sprang at her with a gay little shout.

'Did you get here, Mary?' he said. 'Here's Mary, Dearest,' and he kissed the maid on her rough red cheek.

'I am glad you are here, Mary,' Mrs Errol said to her in

a low voice. 'It is such a comfort to me to see you. It takes the strangeness away.' And she held out her little hand, which Mary squeezed encouragingly. She knew how this first 'strangeness' must feel to this little mother who had left her own land and was about to give up her child.

The English servants looked with curiosity at both the boy and his mother. They had heard all sorts of rumours about them both; they knew how angry the old Earl had been, and why Mrs Errol was to live at the Lodge and her little boy at the Castle; they knew all about the great fortune he was to inherit and about the savage old grandfather and his gout and his tempers.

'He'll have no easy time of it, poor little chap,' they had said among themselves.

But they did not know what sort of a little lord had come among them; they did not quite understand the character of the next Earl of Dorincourt.

He pulled off his overcoat quite as if he were used to doing things for himself, and began to look about him. He looked about the broad hall, at the pictures and stags' antlers and curious things that ornamented it. They seemed curious to him because he had never seen such things before in a private house.

'Dearest,' he said, 'this is a very pretty house, isn't it? I am glad you are going to live here. It's quite a large house.'

It was quite a large house compared to the one in the shabby New York street, and it was very pretty and cheerful. Mary led them upstairs to a bright chintz-hung bedroom where a fire was burning, and a large snow-white Persian cat was sleeping luxuriously on the white fur hearthrug.

'It was the housekaper up at the Castle, ma'am, sint her to yez,' explained Mary. 'It's herself is a kind-hearted lady an' has had iverything done to prepar' fur yez. I seen her meself a few minnits, an' she was fond av the Capt'in, ma'am, an' graivs fur him; and she said to say the big cat slapin' on the rug moight make the room same homeloike to yez. She knowed Capt'in Errol whin he was a bye – an' a foine handsum' bye she ses he was, an' a foine young man wid a plisint word fur everyone, great an' shmall. An' ses I to her, ses I, "He's lift a bye that's loike him, ma'am, fur a foiner little felly niver sthipped in shoe-leather".'

When they were ready they went downstairs into another big bright room; its ceiling was low, and the furniture was heavy and beautifully carved, the chairs were deep and had high massive backs, and there were queer shelves and cabinets with strange, pretty ornaments on them. There was a great tiger-skin before the fire, and an armchair on each side of it. The stately white cat had responded to Lord Fauntleroy's stroking and followed him downstairs, and when he threw himself down upon the rug she curled herself up grandly beside him as if she intended to make friends. Cedric was so pleased that he put his head down by hers, and lay stroking her, not noticing what his mother and Mr Havisham were saying.

They were indeed speaking in a rather low tone. Mrs Errol looked a little pale and agitated.

'He need not go tonight?' she said. 'He will stay with me tonight?'

'Yes,' answered Mr Havisham in the same low tone; 'it will not be necessary for him to go tonight. I myself will go to the Castle as soon as we have dined, and inform the Earl of our arrival.'

Mrs Errol glanced down at Cedric. He was lying in a graceful, careless attitude upon the black-and-yellow skin; the fire shone on his handsome, flushed little face, and on the tumbled, curly hair spread out on the rug; the big cat was purring in drowsy content; she liked the caressing touch of the kind little hand on her fur.

Mrs Errol smiled faintly.

'His lordship does not know all that he is taking from

me,' she said rather sadly. Then she looked at the lawyer. 'Will you tell him, if you please,' she said, 'that I should rather not have the money?'

'The money!' Mr Havisham exclaimed. 'You cannot mean the income he proposed to settle upon you?'

'Yes,' she answered quite simply; 'I think I should rather not have it. I am obliged to accept the house, and I thank him for it, because it makes it possible for me to be near my child; but I have a little money of my own – enough to live simply upon – and I should rather not take the other, as he dislikes me so much I should feel a little as if I were selling Cedric to him. I am giving him up only because I love him enough to forget myself for his good, and because his father would wish it to be so.'

Mr Havisham rubbed his chin.

'This is very strange,' he said. 'He will be very angry. He won't understand it.'

'I think he will understand it after he thinks it over,' she said. 'I do not really need the money, and why should I accept luxuries from the man who hates me so much that he takes my little boy from me – his son's child?'

Mr Havisham looked reflective for a few moments.

'I will deliver your message,' he said afterwards.

And then the dinner was brought in and they sat down together, the big cat taking a seat on a chair near Cedric's and purring majestically throughout the meal.

When, later in the evening, Mr Havisham presented himself at the Castle, he was taken at once to the Earl. He found him sitting by the fire in a luxurious easy chair, his foot on a gout-stool. He looked at the lawyer sharply from under his shaggy eyebrows, but Mr Havisham could see that, in spite of his pretence at calmness, he was nervous and secretly excited.

'Well,' he said; 'well, Havisham, come back, have you? What's the news?'

'Lord Fauntleroy and his mother are at Court Lodge,' replied Mr Havisham. 'They bore the voyage very well and are in excellent health.'

The Earl made a half-impatient sound and moved his hand restlessly.

'Glad to hear it,' he said brusquely. 'So far, so good. Make yourself comfortable. Have a glass of wine and settle down. What else?'

'His lordship remains with his mother tonight. Tomorrow I will bring him to the Castle.'

The Earl's elbow was resting on the arm of his chair; he put his hand up and shielded his eyes with it.

'Well?' he said; 'go on. You know I told you not to write to me about the matter, and I know nothing whatever about it. What kind of a lad is he? I don't care about the mother; what sort of lad is he?'

Mr Havisham drank a little of the glass of port he had poured out for himself, and sat holding it in his hand.

'It is rather difficult to judge of the character of a child of seven,' he said cautiously.

The Earl's prejudices were very intense. He looked up quickly and uttered a rough word.

'A fool, is he?' he exclaimed. 'Or a clumsy cub? His American blood tells, does it?'

'I do not think it has injured him, my lord,' replied the lawyer in his dry, deliberate fashion. 'I don't know much about children, but I thought him rather a fine lad.'

His manner of speech was always deliberate and unenthusiastic, but he made it a trifle more so than usual. He had a shrewd fancy that it would be better that the Earl should judge for himself, and be quite unprepared for his first interview with his grandson.

'Healthy and well grown?' asked my lord.

'Apparently very healthy, and quite well grown,' replied the lawyer.

'Straight-limbed and well enough to look at?' demanded the Earl.

A very slight smile touched Mr Havisham's thin lips. There rose up before his mind's eye the picture he had left at Court Lodge – the beautiful, graceful child's body lying upon the tiger-skin in careless comfort – the bright, tumbled hair spread on the rug – the bright, rosy boy's face.

'Rather a handsome boy, I think, my lord, as boys go,' he said, 'though I am scarcely a judge perhaps. But you will find him somewhat different to most English children, I dare say.'

'I haven't a doubt of that,' snarled the Earl, a twinge of gout seizing him. 'A lot of impudent little beggars, those American children; I've heard that often enough.'

'It is not exactly impudence in his case,' said Mr Havisham. 'I can scarcely describe what the difference is. He has lived more with older people than with children, and the difference seems to be a mixture of maturity and childishness.'

'American impudence!' protested the Earl. 'I've heard of it before. They call it precocity and freedom. Beastly, impudent, bad manners; that's what it is!'

Mr Havisham drank some more port. He seldom argued with his lordly patron – never when his lordly patron's noble leg was inflamed by gout. At such times it was always better to leave him alone. So there was a silence of a few moments; it was Mr Havisham who broke it.

'I have a message to deliver from Mrs Errol,' he remarked.

'I don't want any of her messages!' growled his lordship; 'the less I hear of her the better.'

'This is a rather important one,' explained the lawyer. 'She prefers not to accept the income you proposed to settle on her.'

The Earl started visibly.

'What's that?' he cried out. 'What's that?'

Mr Havisham repeated his words.

'She says it is not necessary, and that as the relations between you are not friendly –'

'Not friendly!' ejaculated my lord savagely; 'I should say they were not friendly! I hate to think of her! A mercenary, sharp-voiced American! I don't wish to see her!'

'My lord,' said Mr Havisham, 'you can scarcely call her mercenary. She has asked for nothing. She does not accept the money you offer her.'

'All done for effect!' snapped his noble lordship. 'She wants to wheedle me into seeing her. She thinks I shall admire her spirit. I don't admire it! It's only American independence! I won't have her living like a beggar at my park gates. As she's the boy's mother she has a position to keep up, and she shall keep it up. She shall have the money, whether she likes it or not!'

'She won't spend it,' said Mr Havisham.

'I don't care whether she spends it or not!' blustered my lord. 'She shall have it sent to her. She shan't tell people that she has to live like a pauper because I have done nothing for her! She wants to give the boy a bad opinion of me! I suppose she has poisoned his mind against me already!'

'No,' said Mr Havisham. 'I have another message, which will prove to you that she has not done that.'

'I don't want to hear it!' panted the Earl, out of breath with anger and excitement and gout.

But Mr Havisham delivered it.

'She asks you not to let Lord Fauntleroy hear anything which would lead him to understand that you separate him from her because of your prejudice against her. He is very fond of her, and she is convinced that it would cause a barrier to exist between you. She says he would not comprehend it and it might make him fear you in some measure, or at least cause him to feel less affection for you. She has told him that he is too young to understand the reason, but shall hear it when he is older. She wishes that there should be no shadow on your first meeting.'

The Earl sank back into his chair. His deep-set fierce old eyes gleamed under his beetling brows.

'Come, now!' he said, still breathlessly. 'Come now! You don't mean the mother hasn't told him?'

'Not one word, my lord,' replied the lawyer coolly. 'That I can assure you. The child is prepared to believe you the most amiable and affectionate of grandparents. Nothing – absolutely nothing – has been said to him to give him the slightest doubt of your perfection. And as I carried out your commands in every detail, while in New York, he certainly regards you as a wonder of generosity.'

'He does, eh?' said the Earl.

'I give you my word of honour,' said Mr Havisham, 'that Lord Fauntleroy's impressions of you will depend entirely upon yourself. And if you will pardon the liberty I take in making the suggestion, I think you will succeed better with him if you take the precaution not to speak slightingly of his mother.'

'Pooh, pooh!' said the Earl. 'The youngster's only seven years old!'

'He has spent those seven years at his mother's side,' returned Mr Havisham; 'and she has all his affection.'

CHAPTER 5

At the Castle

It was late in the afternoon when the carriage containing little
Lord Fauntleroy and Mr Havisham drove up the long avenue
which led to the Castle. The Earl had given orders that his
grandson should arrive in time to dine with him, and for some
reason best known to himself he had also ordered that the
child should be sent alone into the room in which he intended
to receive him. As the carriage rolled up the avenue, Lord
Fauntleroy sat leaning comfortably against the luxurious cushions, and regarded the prospect with great interest. He was,
in fact, interested in everything he saw. He had been interested in the carriage, with its large, splendid horses and their
glittering harness; he had been interested in the tall coachman
and footman, with their resplendent livery; and he had been
especially interested in the coronet on the panels, and had
struck up an acquaintance with the footman for the purpose
of inquiring what it meant.

When the carriage reached the great gates of the park,
he looked out of the window to get a good view of the huge
stone lions ornamenting the entrance. The gates were opened
by a motherly, rosy-looking woman, who came out of a pretty
ivy-covered lodge. Two children ran out of the house and
stood looking with round wide-open eyes at the little boy in

the carriage, who looked at them also. Their mother stood curtsying and smiling, and the children, on receiving a sign from her, made bobbing little curtsies too.

'Does she know me?' asked Lord Fauntleroy. 'I think she must think she knows me.' And he took off his black velvet cap to her and smiled.

'How do you do?' he said brightly. 'Good afternoon!'

The woman seemed pleased, he thought. The smile broadened on her rosy face and a kind look came into her blue eyes.

'God bless your lordship!' she said. 'God bless your pretty face! Good luck and happiness to your lordship! Welcome to you!'

Lord Fauntleroy waved his cap and nodded to her again as the carriage rolled by her.

'I like that woman,' he said. 'She looks as if she liked boys. I should like to come here and play with her children. I wonder if she has enough to make up a company?'

Mr Havisham did not tell him that he would scarcely be allowed to make playmates of the gatekeeper's children. The lawyer thought there was time enough for giving him that information.

The carriage rolled on and on between the great beautiful trees which grew on each side of the avenue and stretched their broad swaying branches in an arch across it. Cedric had never seen such trees, they were so grand and stately, and their branches grew so low down on their huge trunks. He did not then know that Dorincourt Castle was one of the most beautiful in all England; that its park was one of the broadest and finest, and its trees and avenue almost without rivals. But he did know that it was all very beautiful. He liked the big, broad-branched trees, with the late afternoon sunlight striking golden lances through them. He liked the perfect stillness which rested on everything. He felt a great, strange pleasure in the beauty of which he caught glimpses under and between the sweeping boughs – the great, beautiful spaces of the park, with still other trees, standing sometimes stately and alone, and sometimes in groups. Now and then they passed places where tall ferns grew in masses, and again and again the ground was azure with the bluebells swaying in the soft breeze. Several times he started up with a laugh of delight as a rabbit leaped up from under the greenery and scudded away with a twinkle of short white tail behind it. Once a covey of partridges rose with a sudden whir and flew away, and then he shouted and clapped his hands.

'It's a beautiful place, isn't it?' he said to Mr Havisham. 'I never saw such a beautiful place. It's prettier even than Central Park.'

He was rather puzzled by the length of time they were on their way.

'How far is it,' he said at length, 'from the gate to the front door?'

'It is between three and four miles,' answered the lawyer.

'That's a long way for a person to live from his gate,' remarked his lordship.

Every few moments he saw something new to wonder at and admire. When he caught sight of the deer, some couched in the grass, some standing with their pretty antlered heads turned with a half-startled air towards the avenue as the carriage wheels disturbed them, he was enchanted.

'Has there been a circus,' he cried, 'or do they live here always? Whose are they?'

'They live here,' Mr Havisham told him. 'They belong to the Earl, your grandfather.'

It was not long after this that they saw the Castle. It rose up before them stately and beautiful and grey, the last rays of the sun casting dazzling lights on its many windows. It had turrets and battlements and towers; a great deal of ivy grew upon its walls; all the broad open space about it was laid out in terraces and lawns and beds of brilliant flowers.

'It's the most beautiful place I ever saw!' said Cedric, his round face flushing with pleasure. 'It reminds anyone of a king's palace. I saw a picture of one once in a fairy-book.'

He saw the great entrance door thrown open and many servants standing in two lines looking at him. He wondered why they were standing there, and admired their liveries very much. He did not know that they were there to do honour to the little boy to whom all this splendour would one day belong – the beautiful Castle like the fairy king's palace, the magnificent park, the grand old trees, the dells full of ferns and bluebells where the hares and rabbits played, the dappled, large-eyed deer couching in the deep grass. It was only a couple of weeks since he had sat with Mr Hobbs among the potatoes and canned peaches, with his legs dangling from the high stool; it would not have been possible for him to realize that he had very much to do with all this grandeur. At the head of the line of servants there stood an elderly woman in a rich, plain, black silk gown; she had grey hair and wore a cap. As he entered the hall she stood nearer than the rest, and the child thought from the look in her eyes that she was going to speak to him. Mr Havisham, who held his hand, paused a moment.

'This is Lord Fauntleroy, Mrs Mellon,' he said. 'Lord Fauntleroy, this is Mrs Mellon, who is the housekeeper.'

Cedric gave her his hand, his eyes lighting up.

'Was it you who sent the cat?' he said. 'I'm much obliged to you, ma'am.'

Mrs Mellon's handsome old face looked as pleased as the face of the lodge-keeper's wife had done.

'I should know his lordship anywhere,' she said to Mr Havisham. 'He has the Captain's face and way. It's a great day, this, sir.'

Cedric wondered why it was a great day. He looked at Mrs Mellon curiously. It seemed to him for a moment as if there were tears in her eyes, and yet it was evident she was not unhappy. She smiled down at him.

'The cat left two beautiful kittens here,' she said: 'they shall be sent up to your lordship's nursery.'

Mr Havisham said a few words to her in a low voice.

'In the library, sir,' Mrs Mellon replied. 'His lordship is to be taken there alone.'

A few minutes later the very tall footman in livery, who had escorted Cedric to the library door, opened it and announced: 'Lord Fauntleroy, my lord,' in quite a majestic tone. If he was only a footman, he felt it was rather a grand occasion when the heir came home to his own land and possessions, and was ushered into the presence of the old Earl, whose place and title he was to take.

Cedric crossed the threshold into the room. It was a very large and splendid room, with massive carven furniture in it, and shelves upon shelves of books; the furniture was so dark, and the draperies so heavy, the diamond-paned windows were so deep, and it seemed such a distance from one end of it to the other, that, since the sun had gone down, the effect of it all was rather gloomy. For a moment Cedric thought there was nobody in the room, but soon he saw that by the fire burning on the wide hearth there was a large easy chair, and that in that chair someone was sitting – someone who did not at first turn to look at him.

But he had attracted attention in one quarter at least. On the floor, by the armchair, lay a dog, a huge tawny mastiff with body and limbs almost as big as a lion's; and this great creature rose majestically and slowly, and marched towards the little fellow with a heavy step.

Then the person in the chair spoke. 'Dougal,' he called, 'come back, sir.'

But there was no more fear in little Lord Fauntleroy's heart than there was unkindness – he had been a brave little fellow all his life. He put his hand on the big dog's collar in the most natural way in the world, and they strayed forward together, Dougal sniffing as he went.

And then the Earl looked up. What Cedric saw was a large old man with shaggy white hair and eyebrows, and a nose like an eagle's beak between his deep fierce eyes. What the Earl saw was a graceful childish figure in a black velvet suit, with a lace collar, and with love-locks waving about the handsome, manly little face, whose eyes met his with a look of innocent good-fellowship. If the Castle was like the palace in a fairy story, it must be owned that little Lord Fauntleroy was himself rather like a small copy of the fairy prince, though he was not at all aware of the fact, and perhaps was rather a sturdy young model of a fairy. But there was a sudden glow of triumph and exultation in the fiery old Earl's heart as he saw what a strong beautiful boy this grandson was, and how unhesitatingly he looked up as he stood with his hand on the big dog's neck. It pleased the grim old nobleman that the child should show no shyness or fear, either of the dog or of himself.

Cedric looked at him just as he had looked at the woman at the lodge and at the housekeeper, and came quite close to him.

'Are you the Earl?' he said. 'I'm your grandson, you know, that Mr Havisham brought. I'm Lord Fauntleroy.'

He held out his hand because he thought it must be the polite and proper thing to do even with earls. 'I hope you are very well,' he continued, with the utmost friendliness. 'I'm very glad to see you.'

The Earl shook hands with him, with a curious gleam in his eyes; just at first he was so astonished that he scarcely knew what to say. He stared at the picturesque little apparition from under his shaggy brows, and took it all in from head to foot.

'Glad to see me, are you?' he said.

'Yes,' answered Lord Fauntleroy, 'very.'

There was a chair near him, and he sat down on it; it was a high-backed, rather tall chair, and his feet did not touch the floor when he had settled himself in it, but he seemed to be quite comfortable as he sat there and regarded his august relative intently and modestly.

'I've kept wondering what you would look like,' he remarked. 'I used to lie in my berth in the ship and wonder if you would be anything like my father.'

'Am I?' asked the Earl.

'Well,' Cedric replied, 'I was very young when he died, and I may not remember exactly how he looked, but I don't think you are like him.'

'You are disappointed, I suppose?' suggested his grandfather.

'Oh no!' responded Cedric politely. 'Of course you would like anyone to look like your father; but of course you would enjoy the way your grandfather looked, even if he wasn't like your father. You know how it is yourself about admiring your relations.'

The Earl leaned back in his chair and stared. He could not be said to know how it was about admiring his relations. He had employed most of his noble leisure in quarrelling violently with them, in turning them out of his house, and applying abusive epithets to them; and they all hated him cordially.

'Any boy would love his grandfather,' continued Lord Fauntleroy, 'especially one that had been as kind to him as you have been.'

Another queer gleam came into the old nobleman's eyes.

'Oh,' he said, 'I have been kind to you, have I?'

'Yes,' answered Lord Fauntleroy brightly; 'I'm ever so much obliged to you about Bridget and the apple-woman and Dick!'

'Bridget!' exclaimed the Earl. 'Dick! The apple-woman!'

'Yes,' explained Cedric; 'the ones you gave me all that money for – the money you told Mr Havisham to give me if I wanted it.'

'Ha!' ejaculated his lordship. 'That's it, is it! The money

you were to spend as you liked. What did you buy with it? I should like to hear something about that.'

He drew his shaggy eyebrows together and looked at the child sharply. He was secretly curious to know in what way the lad had indulged himself.

'Oh,' said Lord Fauntleroy, 'perhaps you didn't know about Dick and the apple-woman and Bridget. I forgot you lived such a long way off from them. They were particular friends of mine. And you see Michael had the fever –'

'Who's Michael?' asked the Earl.

'Michael is Bridget's husband, and they were in great trouble. When a man is sick and can't work and has twelve children you know how it is. And Michael had always been a sober man. And Bridget used to come to our house and cry. And the evening Mr Havisham was there, she was in the kitchen crying because they had almost nothing to eat and couldn't pay the rent; and I went in to see her, and Mr Havisham sent for me and he said you had given him some money for me. And I ran as fast as I could into the kitchen and gave it to Bridget; and that made it all right; and Bridget could scarcely believe her eyes. That's why I'm so obliged to you.'

'Oh,' said the Earl in his deep voice, 'that was one of the things you did for yourself, was it? What else?'

Dougal had been sitting by the tall chair; the great dog had taken its place there when Cedric sat down. Several times it had turned and looked up at the boy as if interested in the conversation. Dougal was a solemn dog, who seemed to feel altogether too big to take life's responsibilities lightly. The old Earl, who knew the dog well, had watched it with secret interest. Dougal was not a dog whose habit it was to make acquaintances rashly, and the Earl wondered somewhat to see how quietly the brute sat under the touch of the childish hand. And, just at this moment, the big dog gave little Lord Fauntleroy one more look of dignified scrutiny, and deliberately laid its huge, lion-like head on the boy's black-velvet knee.

The small hand went on stroking this new friend as Cedric answered:

'Well, there was Dick,' he said. 'You'd like Dick, he's so square.'

This was an Americanism the Earl was not prepared for.

'What does that mean?' he inquired.

Lord Fauntleroy paused a moment to reflect. He was not very sure himself what it meant. He had taken it for granted as meaning something very creditable because Dick had been fond of using it.

'I think it means that he wouldn't cheat anyone,' he exclaimed, 'or hit a boy who was under his size, and that he blacks people's boots very well and makes them shine as much as he can. He's a professional boot-black.'

'And he's one of your acquaintances, is he?' said the Earl.

'He's an old friend of mine,' replied his grandson. 'Not quite as old as Mr Hobbs, but quite old. He gave me a present before the ship sailed.'

He put his hand into his pocket and drew forth a neatly folded red object and opened it with an air of affectionate pride. It was the red silk handkerchief with the large purple horseshoes and heads on it.

'He gave me this,' said his young lordship. 'I shall keep it always. You can wear it round your neck or keep it in your pocket. He bought it with the first money he earned after I bought Jake out and gave him the new brushes. It's a keepsake. I put some poetry in Mr Hobbs's watch. It was, "When this you see, remember me". When this I see I shall always remember Dick.'

The sensations of the Right Honourable the Earl of Dorincourt could scarcely be described. He was not an old nobleman who was very easily bewildered, because he had seen a great deal of the world; but here was something he found so novel that it almost took his lordly breath away, and caused him some singular emotions. He had never cared for children; he had been so occupied with his own pleasures that he had never had time to care for them. His own sons had not interested him when they were very young – though sometimes he remembered having thought Cedric's father a handsome and strong little fellow. He had been so selfish himself that he had missed the pleasure of seeing unselfishness in others, and he had not known how tender and faithful and affectionate a kind-hearted little child can be, and how innocent and unconscious are its simple, generous impulses. A boy had always seemed to him a most objectionable little animal, selfish and greedy and boisterous when not under strict restraint; his own two eldest sons had given their tutors constant trouble and annoyance, and of the younger one he fancied he had heard few complaints because the boy was of no particular importance. It had never once occurred to him that he should like his grandson; he had sent for the little Cedric because his pride impelled him to do so. If the boy was to take his place in the future, he did not wish his name to be ridiculous by descending to an uneducated boor. He had been convinced the boy would be a clownish fellow if he were brought up in America. He had no feeling of affection for the lad, his only hope was that he should find him decently well featured and with a respectable share of sense; he had been so disappointed in his other sons, and had been made so furious by Captain Errol's American marriage, that he had never once thought that anything creditable could come of it. When the footman had announced Lord Fauntleroy he had almost dreaded to look at the boy lest he should find him all he had feared. It was because of this feeling that he had ordered that the child should be sent to him alone. His pride could not endure that others should see his disappointment if he was to be disappointed. His proud, stubborn old heart therefore had leaped within him when the boy came forward with his graceful easy carriage, his fearless hand on the big dog's neck. Even in the moments when he had hoped the most, the Earl had never hoped that his grandson would look like that. It seemed almost too good to be true that this should be the boy he had dreaded to see – the child of the woman he so disliked – this little fellow with so much beauty and such a brave, childish grace! The Earl's stern composure was quite shaken by this startling surprise.

And then their talk began; and he was still more curiously moved and more and more puzzled. In the first place he was so used to seeing people rather afraid and embarrassed before him, that he had expected nothing else but that his grandson would be timid or shy. But Cedric was no more afraid of the Earl than he had been of Dougal. He was not bold; he was only innocently friendly, and he was not conscious that there should be any reason why he should be awkward or afraid. The Earl could not help seeing that the little boy took him for a friend and treated him as one, without having any doubt of him at all. It was quite plain as the little fellow sat there in his tall chair and talked in his friendly way that it had never occurred to him that this large, fierce-looking old man could be anything but kind to him, and rather pleased to see him there. And it was plain, too, that in his childish way he wished to please and interest his grandfather. Cross and hardhearted and worldly as the old Earl was, he could not help feeling a secret and novel pleasure in this very confidence. After all, it was not disagreeable to meet someone who did not distrust or shrink from him, or seem to detect the ugly part of his nature; someone who looked at him with clear, unsuspecting eyes – if it was only a little boy in a black-velvet suit.

So the old man leaned back in his chair, and led his young companion on to telling him still more of himself, and with that odd gleam in his eyes watched the little fellow as he talked. Lord Fauntleroy was quite willing to answer all his questions and chatted on in his genial little way quite composedly. He told him all about Dick and Jerry and the apple-woman and Mr Hobbs; he described the Republican rally in all the glory of its banners and transparencies, torches and rockets. In the course of the conversation he reached the Fourth of July and the Revolution, and was just becoming enthusiastic, when he suddenly remembered something and stopped very abruptly.

'What is the matter?' demanded his grandfather. 'Why don't you go on?'

Lord Fauntleroy moved rather uneasily in his chair. It was evident to the Earl that Lord Fauntleroy was embarrassed by the thought which had just occurred to him.

'I was just thinking that perhaps you mightn't like it,' he replied. 'Perhaps someone belonging to you might have been there. I forgot you were an Englishman.'

'You can go on,' said my lord. 'No one belonging to me was there. You forgot you were an Englishman too.'

'Oh no,' said Cedric quickly. 'I'm an American!'

'You are an Englishman,' said the Earl grimly. 'Your father was an Englishman.'

It amused him a little to say this, but it did not amuse Cedric. The lad had never thought of such a development as this. He felt himself grow quite hot up to the roots of his hair.

'I was born in America,' he protested. 'You have to be an American if you are born in America. I beg your pardon,' with serious politeness and delicacy, 'for contradicting you. Mr Hobbs told me, if there was another war, you know, I should have to – to be an American!'

The Earl gave a grim half-laugh – it was short and grim, but it was a laugh.

'You would, would you?' he said.

He hated America and Americans, but it amused him to see how serious and interested this small patriot was. He thought that so good an American might make a rather good Englishman when he was a man.

They had not time to go very deep into the Revolution again – and indeed Lord Fauntleroy felt some delicacy about returning to the subject – before dinner was announced.

Cedric left his chair and went to his noble kinsman. He looked down at his gouty foot.

'Would you like me to help you?' he said politely. 'You could lean on me, you know. Once when Mr Hobbs hurt his foot with a potato barrel rolling on it, he used to lean on me.'

The big footman almost perilled his reputation and his situation by smiling. He was an aristocratic footman who had always lived in the best of noble families, and he had never smiled, indeed he would have felt himself a disgraced and vulgar footman if he had allowed himself to be led by any circumstance whatever into such an indiscretion as a smile. But he had a very narrow escape. He only just saved himself by staring straight over the Earl's head at a very ugly picture.

The Earl looked his valiant young relative over from head to foot.

'Do you think you could do it?' he asked gruffly.

'I *think* I could,' said Cedric. 'I'm strong. I'm seven, you know. You could lean on your stick on one side, and on me on the other. Dick says I've a good deal of muscle for a boy that's only seven.'

He shut his hand and moved it upwards to his shoulder, so that the Earl might see the muscle Dick had kindly approved of, and his face was so grave and earnest that the footman found it necessary to look very hard indeed at the ugly picture.

'Well,' said the Earl, 'you may try.'

Cedric gave him his stick, and began to assist him to rise. Usually the footman did this, and was violently sworn at when his lordship had an extra twinge of gout. The Earl was not a very polite person as a rule, and many a time the huge footmen about him quaked inside their imposing liveries.

But this evening he did not swear, though his gouty foot gave him more twinges than one. He chose to try an experiment. He got up slowly and put his hand on the small shoulder presented to him with so much courage. Little Lord Fauntleroy made a careful step forward, looking down at the gouty foot.

'Just lean on me,' he said with encouraging good cheer. 'I'll walk very slowly.'

If the Earl had been supported by the footman he would have rested less on his stick and more on his assistant's arm. And yet it was part of his experiment to let his grandson feel his burden as no light weight. It was quite a heavy weight indeed, and after a few steps his young lordship's face grew quite hot, and his heart beat rather fast, but he braced himself sturdily, remembering his muscle and Dick's approval of it.

'Don't be afraid of leaning on me,' he panted. 'I'm all right – if – if it isn't a very long way.'

It was not really very far to the dining-room, but it seemed rather a long way to Cedric before they reached the chair at the head of the table. The hand on his shoulder seemed to grow heavier at every step, and his face grew redder and hotter, and his breath shorter, but he never thought of giving up; he stiffened his childish muscles, held his head erect and encouraged the Earl as he limped along.

'Does your foot hurt very much when you stand on it?' he asked. 'Did you ever put it in hot water and mustard? Mr Hobbs used to put his in hot water. Arnica is a very nice thing, they tell me.'

The big dog stalked slowly beside them, and the big footman followed; several times he looked very queer as he watched the little figure making the very most of all its strength, and bearing its burden with such goodwill. The Earl too looked rather queer, once, as he glanced sideways down at the flushed little face.

When they entered the room where they were to dine, Cedric saw it was a very large and imposing one, and that the footman who stood behind the chair at the head of the table stared very hard as they came in.

But they reached the chair at last. The hand was removed from his shoulder and the Earl was fairly seated.

Cedric took out Dick's handkerchief and wiped his forehead.

'It's a warm night, isn't it?' he said. 'Perhaps you need a fire because – because of your foot, but it seems just a little warm to me.'

His delicate consideration for his noble relative's feelings was such that he did not wish to seem to intimate that any of his surroundings were unnecessary.

'You have been doing some rather hard work,' said the Earl.

'Oh no!' said Lord Fauntleroy, 'it wasn't exactly hard, but I got a little warm. A person will get warm in summer time.'

And he rubbed his damp curls rather vigorously with the gorgeous handkerchief. His own chair was placed at the other end of the table, opposite his grandfather's. It was a chair with arms, and intended for a much larger individual than himself; indeed everything he had seen so far – the great rooms, with their high ceilings, the massive furniture, the big footman, the big dog, the Earl himself – were all of proportions calculated to make this little lad feel that he was very small indeed. But that did not trouble him; he had never thought himself very large or important, and he was quite willing to accommodate himself even to circumstances which rather overpowered him.

Perhaps he had never looked so little a fellow as when seated now in his great chair, at the end of the table. Notwithstanding his solitary existence, the Earl chose to live in considerable state. He was fond of his dinner, and he dined in a formal style. Cedric looked at him across a glitter of splendid glass and plate, which to his unaccustomed eyes seemed quite dazzling. A stranger looking on might well have smiled at the picture – the great stately room, the big liveried servants, the bright lights, the glittering silver and glass, the fierce-looking old nobleman at the head of the table and the very small boy at the foot. Dinner was usually a very serious matter with the Earl – and it was a very serious matter with the cook, if his lordship was not pleased or had an indifferent appetite. Today, however, his appetite seemed a trifle better than usual, perhaps because he had something to think of besides the flavour of the *entrées* and the management of the gravies. His grandson gave him something to think of. He kept looking at him across the table. He did not say very much himself, but he managed to make the boy talk. He had never imagined that he could be entertained by hearing a child talk, but Lord Fauntleroy at once puzzled and amused him, and he kept remembering how he had let the childish shoulder feel his weight just for the sake of trying how far the boy's courage and endurance would go, and it pleased him to know that his grandson had not quailed and had not seemed to think even for a moment of giving up what he had undertaken to do.

'You don't wear your coronet all the time?' remarked Lord Fauntleroy respectfully.

'No,' replied the Earl with his grim smile; 'it is not becoming to me.'

'Mr Hobbs said you always wore it,' said Cedric; 'but after he thought it over, he said he supposed you must sometimes take it off to put your hat on.'

'Yes,' said the Earl, 'I take it off occasionally.'

And one of the footmen suddenly turned aside and gave a singular little cough behind his hand.

Cedric finished his dinner first, and then he leaned back in his chair and took a survey of the room.

'You must be very proud of your house,' he said, 'it's such a beautiful house. I never saw anything so beautiful; but of course as I'm only seven, I haven't seen much.'

'And you think I must be proud of it, do you?' said the Earl.

'I should think anyone would be proud of it,' replied Lord Fauntleroy. 'I should be proud of it if it were my house. Everything about it is beautiful. And the park, and those trees, how beautiful they are and how the leaves rustle!'

Then he paused an instant and looked across the table rather wistfully.

'It's a very big house for just two people to live in, isn't it?' he said.

'It is quite large enough for two,' answered the Earl. 'Do you find it too large?'

His little lordship hesitated a moment.

'I was only thinking,' he said, 'that if two people lived in it who were not very good companions, they might feel lonely sometimes.'

'Do you think I shall make a good companion?' inquired the Earl.

'Yes,' replied Cedric, 'I think you will. Mr Hobbs and I were great friends. He was the best friend I had except Dearest.'

The Earl made a quick movement of his bushy eyebrows. 'Who is Dearest?'

'She is my mother,' said Lord Fauntleroy in a rather low, quiet little voice.

Perhaps he was a trifle tired, as his bedtime was nearing, and perhaps after the excitement of the last few days it was natural he should be tired, so perhaps too the feeling of weariness brought to him a vague sense of loneliness in the remembrance that tonight he was not to sleep at home, watched over by the loving eyes of that 'best friend' of his. They had always been 'best friends', this boy and his young mother. He could not help thinking of her, and the more he thought of her the less he was inclined to talk, and by the time the dinner was at an end the Earl saw that there was a faint shadow on his face. But Cedric bore himself with excellent courage, and when they went back to the library, though the tall footman walked on one side of his master, the Earl's hand rested on his grandson's shoulder, though not so as before.

When the footman left them alone, Cedric sat down upon the hearthrug near Dougal. For a few minutes he stroked the dog's ears in silence and looked at the fire.

The Earl watched him. The boy's eyes looked wistful and thoughtful, and once or twice he gave a little sigh. The Earl sat still, and kept his eyes fixed on his grandson.

'Fauntleroy,' he said at last, 'what are you thinking of?'

Fauntleroy looked up with a manful effort at a smile.

'I was thinking about Dearest,' he said; 'and – and I think I'd better get up and walk up and down the room.'

He rose up, and put his hands in his small pockets, and began to walk to and fro. His eyes were very bright and his lips were pressed together, but he kept his head up and walked firmly. Dougal moved lazily and looked at him, and then stood up. He walked over to the child, and began to follow him uneasily. Fauntleroy drew one hand from his pocket and laid it on the dog's head.

'He's a very nice dog,' he said. 'He's my friend. He knows how I feel.'

'How do you feel?' asked the Earl.

It disturbed him to see the struggle the little fellow was having with his first feeling of homesickness, but it pleased him to see that he was making so brave an effort to bear it well. He liked this childish courage.

'Come here,' he said.

Fauntleroy went to him.

'I never was away from my own house before,' said the boy, with a troubled look in his brown eyes. 'It makes a person feel a strange feeling when he has to stay all night in another person's castle instead of in his own house. But Dearest is

71

not very far away from me. She told me to remember that
– and – and I'm seven – and I can look at the picture she
gave me.'

He put his hand in his pocket, and brought out a small
violet velvet-covered case.

'This is it,' he said. 'You see, you press this spring and
it opens, and she is in there!'

He had come close to the Earl's chair, and, as he drew
forth the little case, he leaned against the arm of it, and against
the old man's arm too, as confidingly as if children had always
leaned there.

'There she is,' he said, as the case opened; and he looked
up with a smile.

The Earl knitted his brows; he did not wish to see the
picture, but he looked at it in spite of himself; and there
looked up at him from it such a pretty young face – a face so
like the child's at his side – that it quite startled him.

'I suppose you think you are very fond of her?' he said.

'Yes,' answered Lord Fauntleroy, in a gentle tone, and
with simple directness; 'I do think so, and I think it's true.
You see Mr Hobbs was my friend, and Dick and Bridget and
Mary and Michael, they were my friends too; but Dearest –
well, she is my *close* friend, and we always tell each other
everything. My father left her to me to take care of, and when
I am a man I am going to work and earn money for her.'

'What do you think of doing?' inquired his
grandfather.

His young lordship slipped down upon the hearthrug,
and sat there with the picture still in his hand. He seemed
to be reflecting seriously before he answered.

'I did think perhaps I might go into business with Mr
Hobbs,' he said; 'but I should *like* to be a president.'

'We'll send you to the House of Lords instead,' said his
grandfather.

'Well,' remarked Lord Fauntleroy, 'if I *couldn't* be a

president, and if that is a good business, I shouldn't mind. The grocery business is dull sometimes.'

Perhaps he was weighing the matter in his mind, for he sat very quiet after this, and looked at the fire for some time.

The Earl did not speak again. He leaned back in his chair and watched him. A great many strange new thoughts passed through the old nobleman's mind. Dougal had stretched himself out and gone to sleep with his head on his huge paws. There was a long silence.

In about half an hour's time Mr Havisham was ushered in. The great room was very still when he entered. The Earl was still leaning back in his chair. He moved as Mr Havisham approached and held up his hand in a gesture of warning – it seemed as if he had scarcely intended to make the gesture – as if it were almost involuntary. Dougal was still asleep, and close beside the great dog, sleeping also, with his curly head upon his arm, lay little Lord Fauntleroy.

CHAPTER 6

The Earl and His Grandson

When Lord Fauntleroy wakened in the morning – he had not wakened at all when he had been carried to bed the night before – the first sounds he was conscious of were the crackling of a wood fire and the murmur of voices.

'You will be careful, Dawson, not to say anything about it,' he heard someone say. 'He does not know why she is not to be with him, and the reason is to be kept from him.'

'If them's his lordship's orders, mem,' another voice answered, 'they'll have to be kep', I suppose. But, if you'll excuse the liberty, mem, as it's between ourselves, servant or no servant, all I have to say is, it's a cruel thing – parting that poor, pretty, young widdered cre'tur from her own flesh and blood, and him such a little beauty and a nobleman born. James and Thomas, mem, last night in the servants' hall, they both of 'em say as they never see anythink in their two lives – nor yet no other gentleman in livery – like that little fellow's ways, as innercent an' polite an' interested as if he'd been sitting there dining with his best friend – and the temper of a' angel, instead of one (if you'll excuse me, mem), as it's well known is enough to curdle your blood in your veins at times. And as to looks, mem, when we was rung for, James and me, to go into the library and bring him upstairs, and James lifted

him up in his arms, what with his little innercent face all red
and rosy, and his little head on James's shoulder and his hair
hanging down, all curly an' shinin', a prettier, takiner sight
you'd never wish to see. An' it's my opinion, my lord wasn't
to it neither, for he looked at him, and he says to James, "See
you don't wake him!" he says.'

Cedric moved on his pillow, and turned over, opening
his eyes.

There were two women in the room. Everything was
bright and cheerful with gay-flowered chintz. There was a
fire on the hearth, and the sunshine was streaming in
through the ivy-entwined windows. Both women came
towards him, and he saw that one of them was Mrs Mellon,
the housekeeper, and the other a comfortable, middle-aged
woman, with a face as kind and good-humoured as a face
could be.

'Good morning, my lord,' said Mrs Mellon. 'Did you
sleep well?'

His lordship rubbed his eyes and smiled.

'Good morning,' he said. 'I didn't know I was here.'

'You were carried upstairs when you were asleep,' said
the housekeeper. 'This is your bedroom, and this is Dawson,
who is to take care of you.'

Fauntleroy sat up in bed and held out his hand to Dawson
as he had held it out to the Earl.

'How do you do, ma'am?' he said. 'I'm much obliged to
you for coming to take care of me.'

'You can call her Dawson, my lord,' said the housekeeper
with a smile. 'She is used to being called Dawson.'

'*Miss* Dawson or *Mrs* Dawson?' inquired his lordship.

'Just Dawson, my lord,' said Dawson herself, beaming
all over. 'Neither Miss nor Missis, bless your little heart! Will
you get up now, and let Dawson dress you, and then have
your breakfast in the nursery?'

'I learned to dress myself many years ago, thank you,'

answered Fauntleroy. 'Dearest taught me. "Dearest" is my mamma. We had only Mary to do all the work – washing and all – and so of course it wouldn't do to give her so much trouble. I can take my bath, too, pretty well, if you'll just be kind enough to 'zamine the corners after I'm done.'

Dawson and the housekeeper exchanged glances.

'Dawson will do anything you ask her to,' said Mrs Mellon.

'That I will, bless him,' said Dawson, in her comforting, good-humoured voice. 'He shall dress himself if he likes, and I'll stand by, ready to help him if he wants me.'

'Thank you,' responded Lord Fauntleroy; 'it's a little hard sometimes about the buttons, you know, and then I have to ask somebody.'

He thought Dawson a very kind woman, and before the bath and the dressing were finished they were excellent friends, and he had found out a great deal about her. He had discovered that her husband had been a soldier and had been killed in a real battle, and that her son was a sailor, and was away on a long cruise, and that he had seen pirates and cannibals and Chinese people and Turks, and that he brought home strange shells, and pieces of coral which Dawson was ready to show at any moment, some of them being in her trunk. All this was very interesting. He also found out that she had taken care of little children all her life, and that she had just come from a great house in another part of England, where she had been taking care of a beautiful little girl whose name was Lady Gwyneth Vaughan.

'And she is a sort of relation of your lordship's,' said Dawson. 'And perhaps some time you may see her.'

'Do you think I shall?' said Fauntleroy. 'I should like that. I never knew any little girls, but I always like to look at them.'

When he went into the adjoining room to take his breakfast and saw what a great room it was, and found there was another adjoining it, which Dawson told him was his also; the feeling that he was very small indeed came over him again so strongly that he confided it to Dawson, as he sat down to the table on which the pretty breakfast service was arranged.

'I am a very little boy,' he said rather wistfully, 'to live in such a large castle, and have so many big rooms – don't you think so?'

'Oh, come,' said Dawson, 'you feel just a little strange at first, that's all; but you'll get over that very soon, and then you'll like it here. It's such a beautiful place, you know.'

'It's a very beautiful place of course,' said Fauntleroy with a little sigh, 'but I should like it better if I didn't miss Dearest so. I always had my breakfast with her in the morning, and put the sugar and cream in her tea for her, and handed her the toast. That made it very sociable of course.'

'Oh well,' answered Dawson comfortably, 'you know you can see her every day, and there's no knowing how much you'll have to tell her. Bless you, wait till you've walked about a bit and seen things – the dogs, and the stables with all the horses in them. There's one of them I know you'll like to see –'

'Is there?' exclaimed Fauntleroy. 'I'm very fond of horses. I was very fond of Jim. He was the horse that belonged to Mr Hobbs's grocery wagon. He was a beautiful horse when he wasn't balky.'

'Well,' said Dawson, 'you just wait till you've seen what's in the stables. And, deary me, you haven't looked even into the very next room yet!'

'What is there?' asked Fauntleroy.

'Wait until you've had your breakfast, and then you shall see,' said Dawson.

At this he naturally began to grow curious, and he applied himself assiduously to his breakfast. It seemed to him that there must be something worth looking at in the next room; Dawson had such a consequential, mysterious air.

'Now then,' he said, slipping off his seat a few minutes later; 'I've had enough. Can I go and look at it?'

Dawson nodded and led the way, looking more mysterious and important than ever. He began to be very much interested indeed.

When she opened the door of the room, he stood upon the threshold and looked about him in amazement. He did not speak; he only put his hands in his pockets and stood there flushing up to his forehead and looking in.

He flushed up because he was so surprised and, for the moment, excited. To see such a place was enough to surprise any ordinary boy.

The room was a large one too, as all the rooms seemed to be, and it appeared to him more beautiful than the rest, only in a different way. The furniture was not so massive and antique as was that in the rooms he had seen downstairs; the draperies and rugs and walls were brighter; there were shelves full of books, and on the tables were numbers of toys – beautiful, ingenious things – such as he had looked at with wonder and delight through the shop windows in New York.

'It looks like a boy's room,' he said at last, catching his breath a little. 'Who do they belong to?'

'Go and look at them,' said Dawson. 'They belong to you!'

'To me!' he cried. 'To me! Why do they belong to me? Who gave them to me?' And he sprang forward with a gay little shout. It seemed almost too much to be believed. 'It was Grandpapa!' he said, with his eyes as bright as stars. 'I know it was Grandpapa!'

'Yes, it was his lordship,' said Dawson, 'and if you will be a nice little gentleman, and not fret about things, and will enjoy yourself, and be happy all the day, he will give you anything you ask for.'

It was a tremendously exciting morning. There were so many things to be examined, so many experiments to be tried;

each novelty was so absorbing that he could scarcely turn from it to look at the next. And it was so curious to know that all this had been prepared for himself alone; that, even before he had left New York, people had come down from London to arrange the rooms he was to occupy, and had provided the books and playthings most likely to interest him.

'Did you ever know anyone,' he said to Dawson, 'who had such a kind grandfather?'

Dawson's face wore an uncertain expression for a moment. She had not a very high opinion of his lordship the Earl. She had not been in the house many days, but she had been there long enough to hear the old nobleman's peculiarities discussed very freely in the servants' hall.

'An' of all the wicious, savage, hill-tempered hold fellows it was ever my hill-luck to wear livery hunder,' the tallest footman had said, 'he's the wiolentest and wust by a long shot.'

And this particular footman, whose name was Thomas, had also repeated to his companions below stairs some of the Earl's remarks to Mr Havisham, when they had been discussing these very preparations.

'Give him his own way and fill his rooms with toys,' my lord had said. 'Give him what will amuse him, and he'll forget about his mother quickly enough. Amuse him, and fill his mind with other things, and we shall have no trouble. That's boy nature.'

So perhaps, having had this truly amiable object in view, it did not please him so very much to find it did not seem to be exactly this particular boy's nature. The Earl had passed a bad night and had spent the morning in his room; but at noon, after he had lunched, he sent for his grandson.

Fauntleroy answered the summons at once. He came down the broad staircase with a bounding step; the Earl heard him run across the hall, and then the door opened and he came in with red cheeks and sparkling eyes.

'I was waiting for you to send for me,' he said. 'I was ready a long time ago. I'm *ever* so much obliged to you for all those things! I'm *ever* so much obliged to you! I have been playing with them all the morning.'

'Oh,' said the Earl, 'you like them, do you?'

'I like them so much – well, I couldn't tell you how much!' said Fauntleroy, his face glowing with delight. 'There's one that's like baseball, only you play it on a board with black and white pegs, and you keep your score with some counters on a wire. I tried to teach Dawson, but she couldn't quite understand it just at first – you see she never played baseball, being a lady; and I'm afraid I wasn't very good at explaining it to her. But you know all about it, don't you?'

'I'm afraid I don't,' replied the Earl. 'It's an American game, isn't it? Is it something like cricket?'

'I never saw cricket,' said Fauntleroy, 'but Mr Hobbs took me several times to see baseball. It's a splendid game. You get so excited! Would you like me to go and get my game and show it to you? Perhaps it would amuse you and make you forget about your foot. Does your foot hurt you very much this morning?'

'More than I enjoy,' was the answer.

'Then perhaps you couldn't forget it,' said the little fellow anxiously. 'Perhaps it would bother you to be told about the game. Do you think it would amuse you, or do think it would bother you?'

'Go and get it,' said the Earl.

It certainly was a novel entertainment this – making a companion of a child who offered to teach him to play games, but the very novelty of it amused him. There was a smile lurking about the Earl's mouth when Cedric came back with the box containing the game in his arms, and an expression of the most eager interest on his face.

'May I pull that little table over here to your chair?' he asked.

'Ring for Thomas,' said the Earl. 'He will place it for you.'

'Oh, I can do it myself,' answered Fauntleroy. 'It's not very heavy.'

'Very well,' replied his grandfather. The lurking smile deepened on the old man's face as he watched the little fellow's preparations; there was such an absorbed interest in them. The small table was dragged forward and placed by his chair, and the game taken from its box and arranged upon it.

'It's very interesting when you once begin,' said Fauntleroy. 'You see, the black pegs can be your side and the white ones mine. They're men, you know, and once round the field is a home run and counts one – and these are the outs – and here is the first base and that's the second and that's the third and that's the home-base.'

He entered into the details of explanation with the greatest animation. He showed all the attitudes of pitcher and catcher and batter in the real game, and gave a dramatic description of a wonderful 'hot ball' he had seen caught on the glorious occasion on which he had witnessed a match in company with Mr Hobbs. His vigorous, graceful little body, his eager gestures, his simple enjoyment of it all were pleasant to behold.

When at last the explanations and illustrations were at an end and the game began in good earnest, the Earl still found himself entertained. His young companion was wholly absorbed; he played with all his childish heart; his gay little laughs when he made a good throw, his enthusiasm over a 'home run', his impartial delight over his own good luck or his opponent's, would have given a flavour to any game.

If a week before anyone had told the Earl of Dorincourt that on that particular morning he would be forgetting his gout and his bad temper in a child's game, played with black and white wooden pegs, on a gaily painted board, with a curly-headed small boy for a companion, he would without doubt have made himself very unpleasant; and yet he certainly had forgotten himself when the door opened and Thomas announced a visitor.

The visitor in question, who was an elderly gentleman in black, and no less a person than the clergyman of the parish, was so startled by the amazing scene which met his eye that he almost fell back a pace, and ran some risk of colliding with Thomas.

There was in fact no part of his duty that the Reverend Mr Mordaunt found so decidedly unpleasant as that part which compelled him to call upon his noble patron at the Castle. His noble patron indeed usually made these visits as disagreeable as it lay in his lordly power to make them. He abhorred churches and charities, and flew into violent rages when any of his tenantry took the liberty of being poor and ill and needed assistance. When his gout was at its worst, he did not hesitate to announce that he would not be bored and irritated by being told stories of their miserable fortunes; when his gout troubled him less and he was in a somewhat more humane frame of mind, he would perhaps give the rector some money, after having bullied him in the most painful manner, and berated the whole parish for its shiftlessness and imbecility. But, whatsoever his mood, he never failed to make as many sarcastic and embarrassing speeches as possible, and to cause the Reverend Mr Mordaunt to wish it were proper and Christian-like to throw something heavy at him. During all the years in which Mr Mordaunt had been in charge of Dorincourt parish, the rector certainly did not remember having seen his lordship, of his own free will, do anyone a kindness, or, under any circumstances whatever, show that he thought of anyone but himself.

He had called today to speak to him of a specially pressing case, and as he had walked up the avenue, he had, for two reasons, dreaded his visit more than usual. In the first place, he knew that his lordship had for several days been suffering from the gout, and had been in so villainous a humour that rumours of it had even reached the village – carried there by one of the young women servants to her sister, who kept a little shop and retailed darning-needles and cotton and peppermints and gossip, as a means of earning an honest living. What Mrs Dibble did not know about the Castle and its inmates, and the farmhouses and their inmates, and the village and its population, was really not worth being talked about. And of course she knew everything about the Castle, because her sister Jane Shorts was one of the upper house-maids, and was very friendly and intimate with Thomas.

'And the way his lordship do go on!' said Mrs Dibble, over the counter, 'and the way he do use language, Mr Thomas told Jane herself, no flesh or blood as is in livery could stand – for throw a plate of toast at Mr Thomas hisself, he did, not more than two days since, and if it weren't for other things being agreeable and the society below stairs most genteel, warning would have been gave within a' hour!'

And the rector heard all this, for somehow the Earl was a favourite black sheep in the cottages and farmhouses, and his bad behaviour gave many a good woman something to talk about when she had company to tea.

And the second reason was even worse, because it was a new one and had been talked about with the most excited interest.

Who did not know of the old nobleman's fury when his handsome son the Captain had married the American lady? Who did not know how cruelly he had treated the Captain, and how the big, gay, sweet-smiling young man, who was the only member of the grand family anyone liked, had died in a foreign land, poor and unforgiven? Who did not know how fiercely his lordship had hated the poor young creature who had been this son's wife, and how he had hated the thought of her child and never meant to see the boy – until his two sons died and left him without an heir? And then, who did not know that he had looked forward without any affection or pleasure to his grandson's coming, and that he had made up his mind that he should find the boy a vulgar, awkward, pert American lad, more likely to disgrace his noble name than to honour it?

The proud, angry old man thought he had kept all his thoughts secret. He did not suppose anyone had dared to guess at, even less talk over what he felt, and dreaded; but his servants watched him, and read his face and his ill-humours and fits of gloom, and discussed them in the servants' hall. And while he thought himself quite secure from the common herd, Thomas was telling Jane and the cook and the butler and the housemaids and the other footmen that it was his opinion that 'the hold man was wuss than usual a-thinkin' hover the Captin's boy, an' hanticipatin' as he won't be no credit to the fambly. An' serve him right,' added Thomas; 'hit's 'is hown fault. Wot can he iggspect from a child brought up in pore circumstances in that there low Hamerica?'

And as the Reverend Mr Mordaunt walked under the great trees he remembered that this questionable little boy had arrived at the Castle only the evening before, and that there were nine chances to one that his lordship's worst fears were realized, and twenty-two chances to one that if the poor little fellow had disappointed him, the Earl was even now in a tearing rage, and ready to vent all his rancour on the first person who called – which it appeared probable would be his reverend self.

Judge then of his amazement when, as Thomas opened the library door, his ears were greeted by a delightful ring of childish laughter.

'That's two out!' almost shouted an excited, clear little voice. 'You see it's two out!'

And there was the Earl's chair, and the gout-stool, and his foot on it; and by him a small table and a game on it; and quite close to him, actually leaning against his arm and his ungouty knee, was a little boy with face glowing, and eyes dancing with excitement. 'It's two out!' the little stranger cried. 'You hadn't any luck that time, had you?' And then they both recognized at once that someone had come in.

The Earl glanced around, knitted his shaggy eyebrows as he had a trick of doing, and when he saw who it was, Mr Mordaunt was still more surprised to see that he looked even less disagreeable than usual instead of more so. In fact, he looked almost as if he had forgotten for the moment how disagreeable he was, and how unpleasant he really could make himself when he tried.

'Ah,' he said in his harsh voice, but giving his hand rather graciously, 'good morning, Mordaunt. I've found a new employment, you see.'

He put his other hand on Cedric's shoulder – perhaps deep down in his heart there was a stir of gratified pride that it was such an heir he had to present; there was a spark of something like pleasure in his eyes as he moved the boy slightly forward.

'This is the new Lord Fauntleroy,' he said. 'Fauntleroy, this is Mr Mordaunt, the rector of the parish.'

Fauntleroy looked up at the gentleman in the clerical garments, and gave him his hand.

'I am very glad to make your acquaintance, sir,' he said, remembering the words he had heard Mr Hobbs use on one or two occasions when he had been greeting a new customer with ceremony. Cedric felt quite sure that one ought to be more than usually polite to a minister.

Mr Mordaunt held the small hand in his a moment as he looked down at the child's face, smiling involuntarily. He liked the little fellow from that instant – as in fact people always did like him. And it was not the boy's beauty and grace which most appealed to him; it was the simple, natural kindliness in the little lad which made any words he uttered, however quaint and unexpected, sound pleasant and sincere.

As the rector looked at Cedric, he forgot to think of the Earl at all. Nothing in the world is so strong as a kind heart, and somehow this kind little heart, though it was only the heart of a child, seemed to clear all the atmosphere of the big gloomy room and make it brighter.

'I am delighted to make your acquaintance, Lord Fauntleroy,' said the rector. 'You made a long journey to come to us. A great many people will be glad to know you made it safely.'

'It *was* a long way,' answered Fauntleroy; 'but Dearest, my mother, was with me, and I wasn't lonely. Of course you are never lonely if your mother is with you; and the ship was beautiful.'

'Take a chair, Mordaunt,' said the Earl. Mr Mordaunt sat down. He glanced from Fauntleroy to the Earl.

'Your lordship is greatly to be congratulated,' he said warmly. But the Earl plainly had no intention of showing his feelings on the subject.

'He is like his father,' he said rather gruffly. 'Let us hope he'll conduct himself more creditably.' And then he added. 'Well, what is it this morning, Mordaunt? Who is in trouble now?'

This was not as bad as Mr Mordaunt had expected, but he hesitated a second before he began.

'It is Higgins,' he said; 'Higgins of Edge Farm. He has been very unfortunate. He was ill himself last autumn, and his children had scarlet fever. I can't say that he is a very good manager, but he has had ill-luck, and of course he is behindhand in many ways. He is in trouble about his rent now. Newick tells him if he doesn't pay it he must leave the place; and of course that would be a very serious matter. His wife is ill, and he came to me yesterday to beg me to see you about it, and ask you for time. He thinks if you would give him time he could catch up again.'

'They all think that,' said the Earl, looking rather black.

Fauntleroy made a movement forward. He had been standing between his grandfather and the visitor, listening with all his might. He had begun to be interested in Higgins at once. He wondered how many children there were, and if the scarlet fever had hurt them very much. His eyes were wide open and were fixed upon Mr Mordaunt with intense interest as that gentleman went on with the conversation.

'Higgins is a well-meaning man,' said the rector, making an effort to strengthen his plea.

'He is a bad enough tenant,' replied his lordship. 'And he is always behindhand, Newick tells me.'

'He is in great trouble now,' said the rector. 'He is very fond of his wife and children, and if the farm is taken from him they may literally starve. He cannot give them the nour-ishing things they need. Two of the children were left very low after the fever, and the doctor orders for them wine and luxuries that Higgins cannot afford.'

At this Fauntleroy moved a step nearer.

'That was the way with Michael,' he said.

The Earl slightly started. 'I forgot *you*!' he said. 'I forgot we had a philanthropist in the room. Who was Michael?' And the gleam of queer amusement came back into the old man's deep-set eyes.

'He was Bridget's husband, who had the fever,' answered Fauntleroy; 'and he couldn't pay the rent or buy wine and things. And you gave me that money to help him.'

The Earl drew his brows together into a curious frown, which somehow was scarcely grim at all. He glanced across at Mr Mordaunt.

'I don't know what sort of a landed proprietor he will make,' he said. 'I told Havisham the boy was to have what he wanted – and what he wanted, it seems, was money to give to beggars.'

'Oh, but they weren't beggars,' said Fauntleroy eagerly. 'Michael was a splendid bricklayer! They all worked.'

'Oh,' said the Earl, 'they were not beggars. They were splendid bricklayers and boot-blacks and apple-women.'

He bent his gaze on the boy for a few seconds in silence. The fact was that a new thought was coming to him, and though perhaps it was not promoted by the noblest emotions, it was not a bad thought. 'Come here,' he said at last.

Fauntleroy went and stood as near to him as possible without encroaching on the gouty foot.

'What would *you* do in this case?' his lordship asked.

It must be confessed that Mr Mordaunt experienced for the moment a curious sensation. Being a man of great thoughtfulness, and having spent so many years on the estate of Dorincourt, knowing the tenantry, rich and poor, the people of the village, honest and industrious, dishonest and lazy, he realized very strongly what power for good or evil would be given in the future to this one small boy standing there, his brown eyes wide open, his hands deep in his pockets; and the thought came to him also that a great deal of power might perhaps, through the caprice of a proud, self-indulgent old man, be given to him now, and that if his young nature were not a simple and generous one, it might be the worst thing that could happen, not only for others, but for himself.

'And what would *you* do in such a case?' demanded the Earl. Fauntleroy drew a little nearer, and laid one hand on his knee, with the most confiding air of good comradeship.

'If I were very rich,' he said, 'and not only just a little boy, I should let him stay, and give him the things for his children; but then, I am only a boy.' Then, after a second's pause, in which his face brightened visibly: '*You* can do anything, can't you?' he said.

'Humph!' said my lord, staring at him. 'That's your opinion, is it?' And he was not displeased either.

'I mean you can give anyone anything,' said Fauntleroy. 'Who's Newick?'

'He is my agent,' answered the Earl, 'and some of my tenants are not overfond of him.'

'Are you going to write him a letter now?' inquired Fauntleroy. 'Shall I bring you the pen and ink? I can take the game off this table.'

It plainly had not for an instant occurred to him that Newick would be allowed to do his worst.

The Earl paused a moment, still looking at him. 'Can you write?' he asked.

'Yes,' answered Cedric, 'but not very well.'

'Move the things from the table,' commanded my lord, 'and bring the pen and ink, and a sheet of paper from my desk.'

Mr Mordaunt's interest began to increase. Fauntleroy did as he was told very deftly. In a few moments the sheet of paper, the big inkstand and the pen were ready.

'There,' he said gaily, 'now you can write it.'

'You are to write it,' said the Earl.

'I!' exclaimed Fauntleroy, and a flush overspread his forehead. 'Will it do if I write it? I don't always spell quite right when I haven't a dictionary and nobody tells me.'

'It will do,' answered the Earl. 'Higgins will not complain of the spelling. I'm not the philanthropist; you are. Dip your pen in the ink.'

Fauntleroy took up the pen and dipped it in the ink-bottle, then he arranged himself in position, leaning on the table.

'Now,' he inquired, 'what must I say?'

'You may say, "Higgins is not to be interfered with for the present", and sign it "Fauntleroy",' said the Earl.

Fauntleroy dipped his pen in the ink again, and, resting his arm, began to write. It was rather a slow and serious process, but he gave his whole soul to it. After a while, however, the manuscript was complete, and he handed it to his grandfather with a smile slightly tinged with anxiety.

'Do you think it will do?' he asked.

The Earl looked at it, and the corners of his mouth twitched a little.

'Yes,' he answered; 'Higgins will find it entirely satisfactory.' And he handed it to Mr Mordaunt.

What Mr Mordaunt found written was this:

Dear mr Newik if you pleas mr higins is not to be inturfeared with for the present and oblige

Yours rispecferly

Fauntleroy

'Mr Hobbs always signed his letters that way,' said Fauntleroy; 'and I thought I'd better say "please". Is that exactly the right way to spell "interfered"?'

'It's not exactly the way it is spelled in the dictionary,' answered the Earl.

'I was afraid of that,' said Fauntleroy. 'I ought to have asked. You see that's the way with words of more than one syllable; you have to look in the dictionary. It's always safest. I'll write it over again.'

And write it over again he did, making quite an imposing copy, and taking precautions in the matter of spelling by consulting the Earl himself.

'Spelling is a curious thing,' he said. 'It's so often different from what you expect it to be. I used to think "please" was spelled p-l-e-e-s, but it isn't, you know; and you'd think "dear" was spelled d-e-r-e, if you didn't inquire. Sometimes it almost discourages you.'

When Mr Mordaunt went away he took the letter with him, and he took something else with him also – namely, a pleasanter feeling and a more hopeful one than he had ever carried home with him down that avenue on any previous visit he had made at Dorincourt Castle.

When he was gone Fauntleroy, who had accompanied him to the door, went back to his grandfather.

'May I go to Dearest now?' he said. 'I think she will be waiting for me.'

The Earl was silent for a moment.

'There is something in the stable for you to see first,' he said. 'Ring the bell.'

'If you please,' said Fauntleroy, with his quick little flush, 'I'm very much obliged; but I think I'd better see it tomorrow. She will be expecting me all the time.'

'Very well,' answered the Earl. 'We will order the carriage.' Then he added dryly: 'It's a pony.'

Fauntleroy drew a long breath.

'A pony!' he exclaimed. 'Whose pony is it?'

'Yours,' replied the Earl.

'Mine?' cried the little fellow. 'Mine – like the things upstairs?'

'Yes,' said his grandfather. 'Would you like to see it? Shall I order it to be brought round?'

Fauntleroy's cheeks grew redder and redder.

'I never thought I should have a pony!' he said. 'I never thought that! How glad Dearest will be. You give me *every thing*, don't you?'

'Do you wish to see it?' inquired the Earl.

Fauntleroy drew a long breath. 'I *want* to see it,' he said. 'I want to see it so much I can hardly wait. But I'm afraid there isn't time.'

'You *must* go and see your mother this afternoon?' asked the Earl. 'You think you can't put it off?'

'Why,' said Fauntleroy, 'she has been thinking about me all the morning, and I have been thinking about her.'

'Oh,' said the Earl, 'you have, have you? Ring the bell.'

As they drove down the avenue, under the arching trees, he was rather silent. But Fauntleroy was not. He talked about the pony. What colour was it? How big was it? What was its name? What did it like to eat best? How old was it? How early in the morning might he get up and see it?

'Dearest will be so glad!' he kept saying. 'She will be so much obliged to you for being so kind to me! She knows I always liked ponies so much, but we never thought I should have one. There was a little boy on Fifth Avenue who had one, and he used to ride out every morning and we used to take a walk past his house to see him.'

He leaned back against the cushions and regarded the Earl with rapt interest for a few minutes and in entire silence.

'I think you must be the best person in the world,' he burst forth at last. 'You are always doing good, aren't you? – and thinking about other people. Dearest says that is the best kind of goodness; not to think about yourself, but to think about other people. That is just the way you are, isn't it?'

His lordship was so dumbfounded to find himself presented in such agreeable colours that he did not know exactly what to say. He felt that he needed time for reflection. To see each of his ugly, selfish motives changed into a good and generous one by the simplicity of a child was a singular experience.

Fauntleroy went on, still regarding him with admiring eyes – those great, clear, innocent eyes!

'You make so many people happy,' he said. 'There's Michael and Bridget and their twelve children, and the apple-woman and Dick and Mr Hobbs, and Mr Higgins and Mrs Higgins and their children, and Mr Mordaunt – because of course he was glad – and Dearest and me, about the pony and all the other things. Do you know, I've counted it up on my fingers and in my mind, and it's twenty-seven people you've been kind to. That's a good many – twenty-seven!'

'And I was the person who was kind to them, was I?' said the Earl.

'Why, yes, you know,' answered Fauntleroy. 'You made them all happy. Do you know,' with some delicate hesitation, 'that people are sometimes mistaken about earls when they don't know them. Mr Hobbs was. I am going to write to him and tell him about it.'

'What was Mr Hobbs's opinion of earls?' asked his lordship.

'Well, you see, the difficulty was,' replied his young companion, 'that he didn't know any, and he'd only read about them in books. He thought – you mustn't mind it – that they were gory tyrants; and he said he wouldn't have them hanging around his store. But if he'd known *you*, I'm sure he would have felt quite different. I shall tell him about you.'

'What shall you tell him?'

'I shall tell him,' said Fauntleroy, glowing with enthusiasm, 'that you are the kindest man I ever heard of. And you are always thinking of other people, and making them happy, and – and I hope when I grow up I shall be just like you.'

'Just like me!' repeated his lordship, looking at the little kindling face. And a dull red crept up under his withered skin, and he suddenly turned his eyes away and looked out of the carriage window at the great beech trees, with the sun shining on their glossy, red-brown leaves.

'*Just* like you,' said Fauntleroy, adding modestly: 'If I can. Perhaps I'm not good enough, but I'm going to try.'

The carriage rolled on down the stately avenue under the beautiful, broad-branched trees, through the spaces of green shade and lanes of golden sunlight. Fauntleroy saw again the lovely places where the ferns grew high and the bluebells swayed in the breeze; he saw the deer, standing or lying in the deep grass, turn their large startled eyes as the carriage passed, and caught glimpses of the brown rabbits as they scurried away. He heard the whir of the partridges and the calls and songs of the birds, and it all seemed even more beautiful to him than before. All his heart was filled with pleasure and happiness in the beauty that was on every side. But the old Earl saw and heard very different things, though he was apparently looking out too. He saw a long life, in which there had been neither generous deeds nor kind thoughts; he saw years in which a man who had been young and strong and rich and powerful had used his youth and strength and wealth and power only to please himself and kill time as the days and years succeeded each other; he saw this man, when the time had been killed and old age had come, solitary and without real friends in the midst of all his splendid wealth; he saw people who disliked or feared him, and people who would flatter and cringe to him, but no one who really cared whether he lived or died, unless they had something to gain or lose by it. He looked out on the broad acres which belonged to him, and he knew what Fauntleroy did not – how far they extended, what wealth they represented and how many people had homes on their soil. And he knew too – another thing Fauntleroy did not – that in all those homes, humble or well to do, there was probably not one person, however much he envied the wealth and stately name and power, and however willing he would have been to possess them, who would for an instant have thought of calling the noble owner 'good', or wishing, as this simple-souled little boy had, to be like him.

And it was not exactly pleasant to reflect upon, even for a cynical, worldly old man, who had been sufficient unto himself for seventy years and who had never deigned to care what opinion the world held of him so long as it did not interfere with his comfort or entertainment. And the fact was, indeed, that he had never before condescended to reflect upon it at all, and he only did so now because a child had believed him better than he was and by wishing to follow in his illustrious footsteps and imitate his example, had suggested to him the curious question whether he was exactly the person to take as a model.

Fauntleroy thought the Earl's foot must be hurting him, his brows knitted themselves together so, as he looked out at the park; and thinking this, the considerate little fellow tried not to disturb him, and enjoyed the trees and the ferns and the deer in silence. But at last the carriage, having passed the gates and bowled through the green lanes for a short distance, stopped. They had reached Court Lodge; and Fauntleroy was out upon the ground almost before the big footman had time to open the carriage door.

The Earl wakened from his reverie with a start.

'What!' he said. 'Are we here?'

'Yes,' said Fauntleroy. 'Let me give you your stick. Just lean on me when you get out.'

'I am not going to get out,' replied his lordship brusquely.

'Not – not to see Dearest?' exclaimed Fauntleroy with astonished face.

'"Dearest" will excuse me,' said the Earl dryly. 'Go to her and tell her that not even a new pony would keep you away.'

'She will be disappointed,' said Fauntleroy. 'She will want to see you very much.'

'I am afraid not,' was the answer. 'The carriage will call for you as we come back. Tell Jefferies to drive on, Thomas.'

Thomas closed the carriage door: and, after a puzzled look, Fauntleroy ran up the drive. The Earl had the opportunity – as Mr Havisham once had – of seeing a pair of handsome, strong little legs flash over the ground with astonishing rapidity. Evidently their owner had no intention of losing any time. The carriage rolled slowly away, but his lordship did not at once lean back; he still looked out. Through a space in the trees he could see the house door; it was wide open. The little figure dashed up the steps; another figure – a little figure too, slender and young, in its black gown – ran to meet it. It seemed as if they flew together, as Fauntleroy leaped into his mother's arms, hanging about her neck and covering her sweet young face with kisses.

CHAPTER 7

At Church

On the following Sunday morning Mr Mordaunt had a large congregation. Indeed he could scarcely remember any Sunday on which the church had been so crowded. People appeared upon the scene who seldom did him the honour of coming to hear his sermons. There were even people from Hazelton, which was the next parish. There were hearty, sunburned farmers; stout, comfortable, apple-cheeked wives in their best bonnets and most gorgeous shawls, and half a dozen children or so to each family. The doctor's wife was there, with her four daughters. Mrs Kimsey and Mr Kimsey, who kept the druggist's shop, and made pills, and did up powders for everybody within ten miles, sat in their pew; Mrs Dibble in hers, Miss Smiff, the village dressmaker, and her friend Miss Perkins, the milliner, sat in theirs; the doctor's young man was present, and the druggist's apprentice; in fact, almost every family in the countryside was represented in one way or another.

In the course of the preceding week, many wonderful stories had been told of little Lord Fauntleroy. Mrs Dibble had been kept so busy attending to customers who came in to buy a pennyworth of needles or a ha'p'orth of tape and to hear what she had to relate, that the little shop-bell over the door had nearly twinkled itself to death over the coming and going. Mrs Dibble knew exactly how his small lordship's rooms had been furnished for him, what expensive toys had been bought, how there was a beautiful brown pony awaiting him and a small groom to attend it, and a little dog-cart, with silver-mounted harness. And she could tell, too, what all the servants had said when they had caught glimpses of the child on the night of his arrival; and how every female below stairs had said it was a shame, so it was, to part the poor pretty dear from his mother; and had all declared their hearts came into their mouths when he went alone into the library to see his grandfather, for there was no knowing how he'd be treated, and his lordship's temper was enough to fluster them with old heads on their shoulders, let alone a child.

'But if you'll believe me, Mrs Jennifer, mum,' Mrs Dibble had said, 'fear that child does not know – so Mr Thomas hisself says; an' set an' smile he did, an' talked to his lordship as if they'd been friends ever since his first hour. An' the Earl so took aback, Mr Thomas says, that he couldn't do nothing but listen and stare from under his eyebrows. An' it's Mr Thomas's opinion, Mrs Bates, mum, that bad as he is, he was pleased in his secret soul, an' proud too; for a handsomer little fellow, or with better manners, though so old-fashioned, Mr Thomas says, he'd never wish to see.'

And then there had come the story of Higgins. The Reverend Mr Mordaunt had told it at his own dinner table, and the servant who had heard it had told it in the kitchen, and from there it had spread like wildfire.

And on market-day, when Higgins had appeared in town, he had been questioned on every side, and Newick had been questioned too, and in response had shown to two or three people the note signed 'Fauntleroy'.

And so the farmers' wives had found plenty to talk of over their tea and their shopping, and they had done the subject full justice and made the most of it. And on Sunday they had either walked to church or had been driven in their gigs by their husbands, who were perhaps a trifle curious themselves about the new little lord who was to be in time the owner of the soil.

It was by no means the Earl's habit to attend church, but he chose to appear on this first Sunday – it was his whim to present himself in the huge family pew, with Fauntleroy at his side.

There were many loiterers in the churchyard and many lingerers in the lane that morning. There were groups at the gates and in the porch, and there had been much discussion as to whether my lord would really appear or not. When this discussion was at its height, one good woman suddenly uttered an exclamation.

'Eh,' she said, 'that must be the mother, pretty young thing.'

All who had heard turned and looked at the slender figure in black coming up the path. The veil was thrown back from her face and they could see how fair and sweet it was, and how the bright hair curled as softly as a child's under the little widow's cap.

She was not thinking of the people about; she was thinking of Cedric, and of his visits to her, and his joy over his new pony, on which he had actually ridden to her door the day before, sitting very straight and looking very proud and happy. But soon she could not help being attracted by the fact that she was being looked at and that her arrival had created some sort of sensation. She first noticed it because an old woman in a red cloak made a bobbing curtsy to her, and then another did the same thing and said, 'God bless you, my lady!' and one man after another took off his hat as she passed. For a moment she did not understand, and then she realized that it was because she was little Lord Fauntleroy's mother that they did so, and she flushed rather shyly, and smiled and bowed too, and said, 'Thank you,' in a gentle voice to the old woman who had blessed her. To a person who had always lived in a bustling, crowded American city this simple deference was very novel, and at first just a little embarrassing; but after all, she could not help liking and being touched by the friendly warmheartedness of which it seemed to speak. She had scarcely passed through the stone porch into the church before the great event of the day happened. The carriage from the Castle with its handsome horses and tall, liveried servants, bowled round the corner and down the green lane.

'Here they come!' went from one looker-on to another.

And then the carriage drew up, and Thomas stepped down and opened the door, and a little boy, dressed in black velvet, and with a splendid mop of bright waving hair jumped out.

Every man, woman and child looked curiously upon him.

'He's the Captain over again!' said those of the onlookers who remembered his father. 'He's the Captain's self to the life!'

He stood there in the sunlight looking up at the Earl, as Thomas helped that nobleman out, with the most affectionate interest that could be imagined. The instant he could help, he put out his hand and offered his shoulder as if he had been seven feet high. It was plain enough to everyone that however it might be with other people, the Earl of Dorincourt struck no terror into the breast of his grandson.

'Just lean on me,' they heard him say. 'How glad the people are to see you, and how well they all seem to know you!'

'Take off your cap, Fauntleroy,' said the Earl. 'They are bowing to you.'

'To me!' cried Fauntleroy, whipping off his cap in a moment, baring his bright head to the crowd and turning shining, puzzled eyes on them as he tried to bow to everyone at once.

'God bless your lordship!' said the curtsying, red-cloaked old woman who had spoken to his mother; 'long life to you!'

'Thank you, ma'am,' said Fauntleroy. And then they went into the church, and were looked at there, on their way up the aisle to the square red-cushioned and curtained pew. When Fauntleroy was fairly seated he made two discoveries which pleased him: the first was that, across the church, where he could look at her, his mother sat and smiled at him; the second, that at one end of the pew against the wall knelt two quaint figures, carven in stone, facing each other as they kneeled on either side of a pillar supporting two stone missals, their pointed hands folded as if in prayer, their dress very antique and strange. On the tablet by them was written something of which he could only read the curious words:

Here lyeth ye bodye of Gregorye Arthure Fyrst Earle
of Dorincort allsoe of Alisone Hildegarde hys wyfe.

'May I whisper?' inquired his lordship, devoured by curiosity.

'What is it?' said his grandfather.

'Who are they?'

'Some of your ancestors,' answered the Earl, 'who lived a few hundred years ago.'

'Perhaps,' said Lord Fauntleroy, regarding them with respect, 'perhaps I got my spelling from them.' And then he proceeded to find his place in the church service. When the music began he stood up and looked across at his mother, smiling. He was very fond of music, and his mother and he often sang together, so he joined in with the rest, his pure, sweet, high voice rising as clear as the song of a bird. He quite forgot himself in his pleasure in it. The Earl forgot himself a little too, as he sat in his curtain-shielded corner of the pew and watched the boy. Cedric stood with the big psalter open in his hands, singing with all his childish might, his face a little uplifted, happily; and as he sang a long ray of sunshine crept in and slanting through a golden pane of a stained-glass window brightened the falling hair about his young head. His mother, as she looked at him across the church, felt a thrill pass through her heart, and a prayer rose in it too; a prayer that the pure, simple happiness of his childish soul might last, and that the strange, great fortune which had fallen to him might bring no wrong or evil with it. There were many soft anxious thoughts in her tender heart in those new days.

'Oh, Ceddie,' she had said to him the evening before, as she hung over him in saying goodnight before he went away, 'oh, Ceddie dear, I wish for your sake I was very clever and could say a great many wise things! But only be good, dear, only be brave, only be kind and true always, and then you will never hurt anyone so long as you live, and you may help many, and the big world may be better because my little child was born. And that is best of all, Ceddie – it is better than everything else, that the world should be a little better because a man has lived – even ever so little better, dearest.'

And on his return to the Castle Fauntleroy had repeated her words to his grandfather.

'And I thought about you when she said that,' he ended; 'and I told her that was the way the world was because you had lived, and I was going to try if I could be like you.'

'And what did she say to that?' asked his lordship a trifle uneasily.

'She said that was right, and we must always look for good in people and try to be like it.'

Perhaps it was this the old man remembered as he glanced through the divided folds of the red curtain of his pew. Many times he looked over the people's heads to where his son's wife sat alone, and he saw the fair face the unforgiven dead had loved, and the eyes which were so like those of the child at his side; but what his thoughts were, and whether they were hard and bitter, or softened a little, it would have been hard to discover.

As they came out of the church, many of those who had

attended the service stood waiting to see them pass. As they neared the gate a man who stood with his hat in his hand made a step forward and then hesitated. He was a middle-aged farmer, with a careworn face.

'Well, Higgins,' said the Earl.

Fauntleroy turned quickly to look at him.

'Oh,' he exclaimed, 'is it Mr Higgins?'

'Yes,' answered the Earl dryly; 'and I suppose he came to take a look at his new landlord.'

'Yes, my lord,' said the man, his sunburned face reddening. 'Mr Newick told me his young lordship was kind enough to speak for me, and I thought I'd like to say a word of thanks, if I might be allowed.'

Perhaps he felt some wonder when he saw what a little fellow it was who had innocently done so much for him, and who stood there looking up just as one of his own less fortunate children might have done – apparently not realizing his own importance in the least.

'I've a great deal to thank your lordship for,' he said; 'a great deal. I –'

'Oh,' said Fauntleroy, 'I only wrote the letter. It was my grandfather who did it. But you know how he is about always being good to everybody. Is Mrs Higgins well now?'

Higgins looked a trifle taken aback. He also was somewhat startled at hearing his noble landlord presented in the character of a benevolent being, full of engaging qualities.

'I – well, yes, your lordship,' he stammered; 'the missus is better since the trouble was took off her mind. It was worrying broke her down.'

'I'm glad of that,' said Fauntleroy. 'My grandfather was very sorry about your children having the scarlet fever, and so was I. He has had children himself. I'm his son's little boy, you know.'

Higgins was on the verge of being panic-stricken. He felt it would be the safer and more discreet plan not to look at the Earl, as it had been well known that his fatherly affection for his sons had been such that he had seen them about twice a year, and that when they had been ill he had promptly departed for London, because he would not be bored with doctors and nurses. It was a little trying therefore to his lordship's nerves to be told, while he looked on, his eyes gleaming from under his shaggy eyebrows, that he felt an interest in scarlet fever.

'You see, Higgins,' broke in the Earl with a fine grim smile, 'you people have been mistaken in me. Lord Fauntleroy understands me. When you want reliable information on the subject of my character, apply to him. Get into the carriage, Fauntleroy.'

And Fauntleroy jumped in, and the carriage rolled away down the green lane, and even when it turned the corner into the high road the Earl was still grimly smiling.

CHAPTER 8

Learning to Ride

Lord Dorincourt had occasion to wear his grim smile many a time as the days passed by. Indeed, as his acquaintance with his grandson progressed, he wore the smile so often that there were moments when it almost lost its grimness. There is no denying that before Lord Fauntleroy had appeared on the scene the old man had been growing very tired of his loneliness and his gout and his seventy-years. After so long a life of excitement and amusement, it was not agreeable to sit alone even in the most splendid room, with one foot on a gout-stool, and with no other diversion than flying into a rage, and shouting at a frightened footman who hated the sight of him. The old Earl was too clever a man not to know perfectly well that his servants detested him, and that even if he had visitors, they did not come for love of him – though some found a sort of amusement in his sharp, sarcastic talk, which spared no one. So long as he had been strong and well, he had gone from one place to another, pretending to amuse himself, though he had not really enjoyed it; and when his health began to fail, he felt tired of everything and shut himself up at Dorincourt with his gout and his newspapers and his books. But he could not read all the time, and he became more and more 'bored', as he called it. He hated the long nights and days, and he grew more and more savage and irritable. And then Fauntleroy came; and when the Earl saw the lad, fortunately for the little fellow, the secret pride of the grandfather was gratified at the outset. If Cedric had been a less handsome little fellow the old man might have taken so strong a dislike to the boy that he would not have given himself the chance to see his grandson's finer qualities. But he chose to think that Cedric's beauty and fearless spirit were the results of Dorincourt blood and a credit to the Dorincourt rank. And then when he heard the lad talk, and saw what a well-bred little fellow he was, notwithstanding his boyish ignorance of all that his new position meant, the old Earl liked his grandson more, and actually began to find himself rather entertained. It had amused him to give into those childish hands the power to bestow a benefit on poor Higgins. My lord cared nothing for poor Higgins, but it pleased him a little that his grandson would be talked about by the country people and would begin to be popular with the tenantry, even in his childhood. Then it had gratified him to drive to church with Cedric and to see excitement and interest caused by the arrival. He knew how the people would speak of the beauty of the little lad; of his fine, strong, straight little body; of his erect bearing, his handsome face and his bright hair, and how they would say (as the Earl had heard one woman exclaim to another) that the boy was 'every inch a lord'. My lord of Dorincourt was an arrogant old man, proud of his name, proud of his rank, and therefore proud to show the world that at last the House of Dorincourt had an heir who was worthy of the position he was to fill.

The morning the new pony had been tried the Earl had been so pleased that he had almost forgotten his gout. When the groom had brought out the pretty creature, which arched its brown glossy neck and tossed its fine head in the sun, the Earl had sat at the open window of the library and had looked on while Fauntleroy took his first riding lesson. He wondered if the boy would show signs of timidity. It was not a very small pony, and he had often seen children lose courage in making their first essay at riding.

Fauntleroy mounted in great delight. He had never been on a pony before, and he was in the highest spirits. Wilkins, the groom, led the animal by the bridle up and down before the library window.

'He's a well plucked 'un, he is,' Wilkins remarked in the stable afterwards with many grins. 'It weren't no trouble to put *him* up. An' a old 'un wouldn't ha' sat any straighter when he *were* up. He ses – ses he to me, "Wilkins," he ses, "am I sitting up straight? They sit up straight at the circus," ses he. And I ses, "As straight as a arrer, your lordship!" – an' he laughs, as pleased as could be, an' he ses, "That's right," he ses, "you tell me if I don't sit up straight, Wilkins."'

But sitting up straight and being led at a walk were not altogether and completely satisfactory. After a few minutes Fauntleroy spoke to his grandfather – watching him from the window.

'Can't I go by myself?' he asked. 'And can't I go faster? The boy on Fifth Avenue used to trot and canter!'

'Do you think you could trot and canter?' said the Earl.

'I should like to try,' answered Fauntleroy.

His lordship made a sign to Wilkins, who at the signal brought up his own horse and mounted it and took Fauntleroy's pony by the leading-rein.

'Now,' said the Earl, 'let him trot.'

The next few minutes were rather exciting to the small equestrian. He found that trotting was not so easy as walking, and the faster the pony trotted, the less easy it was.

'It j-jolts a g-goo-good deal – do-doesn't it?' he said to Wilkins. 'D-does it j-jolt y-you?'

'No, my lord,' answered Wilkins. 'You'll get used to it in time. Rise in your stirrups.'

'I'm ri-rising all the t-time,' said Fauntleroy.

He was both rising and falling rather uncomfortably and with many shakes and bounces. He was out of breath and his face grew red, but he held on with all his might, and sat as straight as he could. The Earl could see that from his window. When the riders came back within speaking distance, after they had been hidden by the trees a few minutes, Fauntleroy's hat was off, his cheeks were like poppies, and his lips were set, but he was still trotting manfully.

'Stop a minute!' said his grandfather. 'Where's your hat?'

Wilkins touched his. 'It fell off, your lordship,' he said with evident enjoyment. 'Wouldn't let me stop to pick it up, my lord.'

'Not much afraid, is he?' asked the Earl dryly.

'Him, your lordship!' exclaimed Wilkins. 'I shouldn't say as he knowed what it meant. I've taught young gen'lemen to ride afore, an' I never see one stick on more determiner.'

'Tired?' said the Earl to Fauntleroy. 'Want to get off?'

'It jolts you more than you think it will,' admitted his young lordship frankly. 'And it tires you a little too; but I don't want to get off. I want to learn how. As soon as I've got my breath I want to go back for the hat.'

The cleverest person in the world, if he had undertaken to teach Fauntleroy how to please the old man who watched him, could not have taught him anything which would have succeeded better. As the pony trotted off again towards the avenue, a faint colour crept up in the fierce old face, and the eyes, under the shaggy brows, gleamed with a pleasure such as his lordship had scarcely expected to know again. And he sat and watched quite eagerly until the sound of the horses' hoofs returned. When they did come, which was after some time, they came at a faster pace. Fauntleroy's hat was still off, Wilkins was carrying it for him; his cheeks were redder than before, and his hair was flying about his ears, but he came at quite a brisk canter.

'There,' he panted as they drew up, 'I c-can-tered. I

didn't do it as well as the boy on Fifth Avenue, but I did it, and I stayed on!'

He and Wilkins and the pony were close friends after that. Scarcely a day passed on which the country people did not see them out together, cantering gaily on the high road or through the green lanes. The children in the cottages would run to the door to look at the proud little brown pony with the gallant little figure sitting so straight in the saddle, and the young lord would snatch off his cap and swing it at them, and shout, 'Hallo! Good morning!' in a very unlordly manner, though with great heartiness. Sometimes he would stop and talk with the children, and once Wilkins came back to the Castle with a story of how Fauntleroy had insisted on dismounting near the village school, so that a boy who was lame and tired might ride home on his pony.

'An' I'm blessed,' said Wilkins, in telling the story at the stables, 'I'm blessed if he'd hear of anything else! He wouldn't let me get down, because he said the boy mightn't feel comfortable on a big horse. An' ses he, "Wilkins," ses he, "that boy's lame and I'm not, and I want to talk to him too." And up the lad has to get, and my lord trudges alongside of him with his hands in his pockets, and his cap on the back of his head, a-whistling and talking as easy as you please! And when we come to the cottage, an' the boy's mother come out all in a taking to see what's up, he whips off his cap an' ses he, "I've brought your son home, ma'am," ses he, "because his leg hurt him, and I don't think that stick is enough for him to lean on; and I'm going to ask my grandfather to have a pair of crutches made for him." An' I'm blessed if the woman wasn't struck all of a heap, as well she might be! I thought I should 'a' hexplodid, myself!'

When the Earl heard the story he was not angry, as Wilkins had been half afraid that he would be; on the contrary, he laughed outright, and called Fauntleroy up to him, and made him tell all about the matter from beginning to end, and then he laughed again. And actually, a few days later, the Dorincourt carriage stopped in the green lane before the cottage where the lame boy lived, and Fauntleroy jumped out and walked up to the door, carrying a pair of strong, light, new crutches, shouldered like a gun, and presented them to Mrs Hartle (the lame boy's name was Hartle) with these words: 'My grandfather's compliments, and if you please, these are for your boy, and we hope he will get better.'

'I said your compliments,' he explained to the Earl when he returned to the carriage. 'You didn't tell me to, but I thought perhaps you forgot. That was right, wasn't it?'

And the Earl laughed again, and did not say it was not. In fact, the two were becoming more intimate every day, and every day Fauntleroy's faith in his lordship's benevolence and virtue increased. He had no doubt whatever that his grandfather was the most amiable and generous of elderly gentlemen. Certainly he himself found his wishes gratified almost before they were uttered; and such gifts and pleasures were lavished upon him, that he was sometimes almost bewildered by his own possessions. Apparently he was to have everything he wanted, and to do everything he wished to do. And though this would certainly not have been a very wise plan to pursue with all small boys, his young lordship bore it amazingly well. Perhaps, notwithstanding his sweet nature, he might have been somewhat spoiled by it, if it had not been for the hours he spent with his mother at Court Lodge. That 'best friend' of his watched over him very closely and tenderly. The two had many long talks together, and he never went back to the Castle with her kisses on his cheeks without carrying in his heart some simple, pure words worth remembering.

There was one thing, it is true, which puzzled the little fellow very much. He thought over the mystery of it much oftener than anyone supposed; even his mother did not know how often he pondered on it; the Earl for a long time never suspected that he did so at all. But being quick to observe, the little boy could not help wondering why it was that his mother and grandfather never seemed to meet. He had noticed that they never did meet. When the Dorincourt carriage stopped at Court Lodge the Earl never alighted, and on the rare occasions of his lordship's going to church, Fauntleroy was always left to speak to his mother in the porch alone, or perhaps to go home with her. And yet, every day, fruit and flowers were sent to Court Lodge from the hothouses at the Castle. But the one virtuous action of the Earl's which had set him upon the pinnacle of perfection in Cedric's eyes, was what he had done soon after that first Sunday when Mrs Errol had walked home from church unattended. About a week later, when Cedric was going one day to visit his mother, he found at the door, instead of the large carriage and prancing pair, a pretty little brougham and a handsome bay horse.

'That is a present from you to your mother,' the Earl said abruptly. 'She cannot go walking about the country. She needs a carriage. The man who drives will take charge of it. It is a present from *you*.'

Fauntleroy's delight could but feebly express itself. He could scarcely contain himself until he reached the lodge. His mother was gathering roses in the garden. He flung himself out of the little brougham and flew to her.

'Dearest!' he cried. 'Could you believe it? This is yours! He says it is a present from me. It is your own carriage to drive everywhere in!'

He was so happy that she did not know what to say. She could not have borne to spoil his pleasure by refusing to accept the gift, even though it came from the man who chose to consider himself her enemy. She was obliged to step into the carriage, roses and all, and let herself be taken for a drive, while Fauntleroy told her stories of his grandfather's goodness and amiability. They were such innocent stories that sometimes she could not help laughing a little, and then she would draw her little boy closer to her side and kiss him, feeling glad that he could see only good in the old man who had so few friends.

The very next day after that, Fauntleroy wrote to Mr Hobbs. He wrote quite a long letter, and after the first copy was written, he brought it to his grandfather to be inspected.

'Because,' he said, 'it's so uncertain about the spelling. And if you'll tell me the mistakes, I'll write it out again.'

This was what he had written:

My dear mr hobbs I want to tell you about my
granfarther he is the best earl you ever new it is a
mistake about earls being tirents he is not a tirent
at all i wish you new him you would be good
friends i am sure you would he has the gout in
his foot and is a grate sufrer but he is so pashent i
love him more every day becaus no one could
help loving an earl that who is kind to every one
in this world i wish you could talk to him he
knows everything in the world you can ask him
any question but he has never plaid base ball he
has given me a pony and cart and my mamma a
bewtifle carige and i have three rooms and toys of
all kinds it would serprise you you would like the
castle and the park it is such a large castle you
could lose yourself wilkins tells me wilkins is my
groom he says there is a dungon under the castle
it is so pretty every thing in the park would
serprise you there are such big trees and there are
deers and rabbits and games flying about in the
cover my grandfather is very rich but he is not
proud and orty as you thought earls always were i
like to be with him the people are so polite and
kind they take of their hats to you and the
women make curtsies and sometimes say god
bless you i can ride now but at first it shook me

when i troted my grandfather let a poor man stay
on his farm when he could not pay his rent and
mrs mellon went to take wine and things to his
sick children i should like to see you and i wish
dearest could live at the castle but i am very
happy when i don't miss her too much and i love
my grandfarther every one does plees write soon.

your afechshnet old friend
Cedric Errol

ps no one is in the dungon my granfarther never
had any one langwishin in there
ps he is such a good earl he reminds me of you he
is a unerversle favrit

'Do you miss your mother very much?' asked the Earl
when he had finished reading this.

'Yes,' said Fauntleroy, 'I miss her all the time.'

He went and stood before the Earl and put his hand on
his knee looking up at him.

'*You* don't miss her, do you?' he said.

'I don't know her,' answered his lordship rather crustily.

'I know that,' said Fauntleroy, 'and that's what makes
me wonder. She told me not to ask you any questions, and
– and I won't, but sometimes I can't help thinking, you know,
and it makes me all puzzled. But I'm not going to ask any
questions. And when I miss her very much, I go and look out
of my window to where I see her light shine for me every
night through an open place in the trees. It is a long way off,
but she puts it in her window as soon as it is dark and I can
see it twinkle far away, and I know what it says.'

'What does it say?' asked my lord.

'It says, "Good night, God keep you all the night!" –
just what she used to say when we were together. Every
night she used to say that to me, and every morning she said,

"God bless you all the day!" So you see I am quite safe all the time –'

'Quite, I have no doubt,' said his lordship dryly. And he drew down his beetling eyebrows and looked at the little boy so fixedly and so long that Fauntleroy wondered what he could be thinking of.

CHAPTER 9

The Poor Cottages

The fact was, his lordship the Earl of Dorincourt thought in those days of many things of which he had never thought before, and all his thoughts were in one way or another connected with his grandson. His pride was the strongest part of his nature, and the boy gratified it at every point. Through this pride he began to find a new interest in life. He began to take pleasure in showing his heir to the world. The world had known of his disappointment in his sons; so there was an agreeable touch of triumph in exhibiting this new Lord Fauntleroy, who could disappoint no one. He wished the child to appreciate his own power and to understand the splendour of his position; he wished that others should realize it too. He made plans for his future. Sometimes in secret he actually found himself wishing that his own past life had been a better one, and that there had been less in it than this pure, childish heart would shrink from if it knew the truth. It was not agreeable to think how the beautiful innocent face would look if its owner should be made by any chance to understand that his grandfather had been called for many a year 'the wicked Earl of Dorincourt'. The thought even made him feel a trifle nervous. He did not wish the boy to find it out. Sometimes in this new interest he forgot his gout, and after a while his doctor was surprised to find his noble patient's health growing better than he had expected it ever would be again. Perhaps the Earl grew better because the time did not pass so slowly for him, and he had something to think of besides his pains and infirmities.

One fine morning people were amazed to see little Lord Fauntleroy riding his pony with another companion than Wilkins. This new companion rode a tall, powerful, grey horse, and was no other than the Earl himself. It was in fact Fauntleroy who had suggested this plan. As he had been on the point of mounting his pony he had said rather wistfully to his grandfather:

'I wish you were going with me. When I go away I feel lonely because you are left all by yourself in such a big castle. I wish you could ride too.'

And the greatest excitement had been aroused in the stables a few minutes later by the arrival of an order that Selim was to be saddled for the Earl. After that Selim was saddled almost every day; and the people became accustomed to the sight of the tall grey horse carrying the tall grey old man with his handsome, fierce, eagle face, by the side of the brown pony which bore little Lord Fauntleroy. And in their rides together through the green lanes and pretty country roads, the two riders became more intimate than ever. And gradually the old man heard a great deal about 'Dearest' and her life. As Fauntleroy trotted by the big horse he chatted gaily. There could not well have been a brighter little comrade, his nature was so happy. It was he who talked the most. The Earl often was silent, listening and watching the joyous, glowing face. Sometimes he would tell his young companion to set the pony off at a gallop, and when the little fellow dashed off, sitting so straight and fearless, he would watch the boy with a gleam of pride and pleasure in his eyes; and Fauntleroy when, after such a dash, he came back waving his cap with a laughing shout, always felt that he and his grandfather were very good friends indeed.

One thing that the Earl discovered was that his son's wife did not lead an idle life. It was not long before he learned that the poor people knew her very well indeed. When there was sickness or sorrow or poverty in any house, the little brougham often stood before the door.

'Do you know,' said Fauntleroy once, 'they all say, "God bless you!" when they see her, and the children are glad. There are some who go to her house to be taught to sew. She says she feels so rich now that she wants to help the poor ones.'

It had not displeased the Earl to find that the mother of his heir had a beautiful young face and looked as much like a lady as if she had been a duchess, and in one way it did not displease him to know that she was popular and beloved by the poor. And yet he was often conscious of a hard, jealous pang when he saw how she filled her child's heart and how the boy clung to her as his best beloved. The old man would have desired to stand first himself and have no rival.

That same morning he drew up his horse on an elevated point of the moor over which they rode, and made a gesture with his whip, over the broad, beautiful landscape spread before them.

'Do you know that all that land belongs to me?' he said to Fauntleroy.

'Does it?' answered Fauntleroy. 'How much it is to belong to one person, and how beautiful!'

'Do you know that some day it will all belong to you – that and a great deal more?'

'To me!' exclaimed Fauntleroy in rather an awestricken voice. 'When?'

'When I am dead,' his grandfather answered.

'Then I don't want it,' said Fauntleroy. 'I want you to live always.'

'That's kind,' answered the Earl in his dry way; 'nevertheless some day it will all be yours – some day you will be the Earl of Dorincourt.'

Little Lord Fauntleroy sat very still in his saddle for a few moments. He looked over the broad moors, the green farms, the beautiful copses, the cottages in the lanes, the pretty villages, and over the trees to where the turrets of the great castle rose, grey and stately. Then he gave a queer little sigh.

'What are you thinking of?' asked the Earl.

'I am thinking,' replied Fauntleroy, 'what a little boy I am, and of what Dearest said to me.'

'What was it?' inquired the Earl.

'She said that perhaps it was not so easy to be very rich; that if anyone had so many things always, one might sometimes forget that everyone else was not so fortunate, and that one who is rich should always be careful and try to remember. I was talking to her about how good you were, and she said that was such a good thing, because an earl had so much power, and if he cared only about his own pleasure and never thought about the people who lived on his lands, they might have trouble that he could help – and there were so many people, and it would be such a hard thing. And I was just looking at all those houses, and thinking how I should have to find out about the people when I was an earl. How did you find out about them?'

As his lordship's knowledge of his tenantry consisted in finding out which of them paid their rent promptly, and in turning out those who did not, this was rather a hard question. 'Newick finds out for me,' he said, and he pulled his great grey moustache, and looked at his small questioner rather uneasily.

'We will go home now,' he added; 'and when you are an earl, see to it that you are a better one than I have been!'

He was very silent as they rode home. He felt it to be almost incredible that he, who had never really loved anyone in his life, should find himself growing so fond of this little fellow – as without doubt he was. At first he had only been pleased and proud of Cedric's beauty and bravery, but there was something more than pride in his feeling now. He laughed a grim, dry laugh all to himself sometimes, when he thought how he liked to have the boy near him, how he liked to hear his voice, and how in secret he really wished to be liked and thought well of by his small grandson.

'I'm an old fellow in my dotage, and I have nothing else to think of,' he would say to himself; and yet he knew it was not that altogether. And if he allowed himself to admit the truth, he would perhaps have found himself obliged to own that the very things which attracted him, in spite of himself, were the qualities he had never possessed – the frank, true, kindly nature, the affectionate trustfulness which could never think evil.

It was only about a week after that ride when, after a visit to his mother, Fauntleroy came into the library with a troubled, thoughtful face. He sat down in that high-backed chair in which he had sat on the evening of his arrival, and for a while he looked at the embers on the hearth. The Earl watched him in silence, wondering what was coming. It was evident that Cedric had something on his mind. At last he looked up. 'Does Newick know all about the people?' he asked.

'It is his business to know about them,' said his lordship. 'Been neglecting it – has he?'

Contradictory as it may seem, there was nothing which entertained and edified him more than the little fellow's interest in his tenantry. He had never taken any interest in them himself, but it pleased him well enough that, with all his childish habits of thought and in the midst of all his childish amusements and high spirits, there should be such a quaint seriousness working in the curly head.

'There is a place,' said Fauntleroy, looking up at him with wide-open, horror-stricken eyes. 'Dearest has seen it; it is at the other end of the village. The houses are close together, and almost falling down; you can scarcely breathe; and the people are so poor, and everything is dreadful! Often they have fever and the children die; and it makes them wicked to live like that, and be so poor and miserable! It is worse than Michael and Bridget! The rain comes in at the roof! Dearest went to see a poor woman who lived there. She would not let me come near her until she had changed all her things. The tears ran down her cheeks when she told me about it!'

The tears had come into his own eyes, but he smiled through them.

'I told her you didn't know, and I would tell you,' he said. He jumped down and came and leaned against the Earl's chair. 'You can make it all right,' he said, 'just as you made it all right for Higgins. You always make it all right for everybody. I told her you would, and that Newick must have forgotten to tell you.'

The Earl looked down at the hand on his knee. Newick had not forgotten to tell him; in fact, Newick had spoken to him more than once of the desperate condition of the end of the village known as Earl's Court. He knew all about the tumbledown, miserable cottages, and the bad drainage, and the damp walls and broken windows and leaking roofs, and all about the poverty, the fever and the misery. Mr Mordaunt had painted it all to him in the strongest words he could use, and his lordship had used violent language in response; and, when his gout had been at the worst, he had said that the sooner the people of Earl's Court died and were buried by the parish the better it would be – and there was an end of the matter. And yet, as he looked at the small hand on his knee, and from the small hand to the honest, earnest, frank-eyed face, he was actually a little ashamed both of Earl's Court and of himself.

'What!' he said. 'You want to make a builder of model cottages of me, do you?' And he positively put his own hand upon the childish one and stroked it.

'Those must be pulled down,' said Fauntleroy with great

eagerness. 'Dearest says so. Let us – let us go and have them pulled down tomorrow. The people will be so glad when they see you! They'll know you have come to help them!' And his eyes shone like stars in his glowing face.

The Earl rose from his chair and put his hand on the child's shoulder. 'Let us go out and take our walk on the terrace,' he said with a short laugh, 'and we can talk it over.'

And though he laughed two or three times again, as they walked to and fro on the broad stone terrace, where they walked together almost every fine evening, he seemed to be thinking of something which did not displease him, and still he kept his hand on his small companion's shoulder.

CHAPTER 10

The Earl Alarmed

The truth was that Mrs Errol had found a great many sad things in the course of her work among the poor of the little village that appeared so picturesque when it was seen from the moor-sides. Everything was not as picturesque when seen near by, as it looked from a distance. She had found idleness and poverty and ignorance where there should have been comfort and industry. And she had discovered after a while that Erlesboro was considered to be the worst village in that part of the country. Mr Mordaunt had told her a great many of his difficulties and discouragements, and she had found out a great deal by herself. The agents who had managed the property had always been chosen to please the Earl, and had cared nothing for the degradation and wretchedness of the poor tenants. Many things, therefore, had been neglected which should have been attended to, and matters had gone from bad to worse.

As to Earl's Court, it was a disgrace, with its dilapidated houses and miserable, careless, sickly people. When first Mrs Errol went to the place, it made her shudder. Such ugliness and slovenliness and want seemed worse in a country place than in a city. It seemed as if there it might be helped. And as she looked at the squalid, uncared-for children growing up in the midst of vice and brutal indifference, she thought of her own little boy spending his days in the great, splendid castle, guarded and served like a young prince, having no wish ungratified, and knowing nothing but luxury and ease and beauty. And a bold thought came into her wise little mother-heart. Gradually she had begun to see, as had others, that it had been her boy's good fortune to please the Earl very much, and that he would scarcely be likely to be denied anything for which he expressed a desire.

'The Earl would give him everything,' she said to Mr Mordaunt. 'He would indulge his every whim. Why should not that indulgence be used for the good of others? It is for me to see that this shall come to pass.'

She knew she could trust the kind, childish heart; so she told the little fellow the story of Earl's Court, feeling sure that he would speak of it to his grandfather, and hoping that some good results would follow.

And strange as it appeared to everyone, good results did follow. The fact was that the strongest power to influence the Earl was his grandson's perfect confidence in him – the fact that Cedric always believed that his grandfather was going to do what was right and generous. He could not quite make up his mind to let him discover that he had no inclination to be generous at all, and that he wanted his own way on all occasions, whether it was right or wrong. It was such a novelty to be regarded with admiration as a benefactor of the entire human race and the soul of nobility, that he did not enjoy the idea of looking into the affectionate brown eyes and saying 'I am a violent, selfish old rascal; I never did a generous thing in my life, and I don't care about Earl's Court or the poor people' – or something which would amount to the same thing. He actually had learned to be fond enough of that small boy with the mop of yellow love-locks, to feel that he himself would prefer to be guilty of an amiable action now and then. And so – though he laughed at himself – after some reflection, he sent for Newick, and had quite a long interview with him on the subject of the Court, and it was decided that the wretched hovels should be pulled down and new houses should be built.

'It is Lord Fauntleroy who insists on it,' he said dryly; 'he thinks it will improve the property. You can tell the tenants that it's his idea.' And he looked down at his small lordship, who was lying on the hearthrug playing with Dougal. The great dog was the lad's constant companion, and followed him about everywhere, stalking solemnly after him when he walked, and trotting majestically behind when he rode or drove.

Of course both the country people and the town people heard of the proposed improvement. At first many of them would not believe it; but when a small army of workmen arrived and commenced pulling down the crazy, squalid cottages, people began to understand that little Lord Fauntleroy had done them a good turn again, and that through his innocent interference the scandal of Earl's Court had at last been removed. If he had only known how they talked about him and praised him everywhere, and prophesied great things for him when he grew up, how astonished he would have been! But he never suspected it. He lived his simple, happy child life, frolicking about in the park; chasing the rabbits to their burrows; lying under the trees on the grass, or on the rug in the library, reading wonderful books and talking to the Earl about them, and then telling the stories again to his mother; writing long letters to Dick and Mr Hobbs, who responded in characteristic fashion; riding out at his grandfather's side, or with Wilkins as escort. As they rode through the market town he used to see the people turn and look, and he noticed that as they lifted their hats their faces often brightened very much, but he thought it was all because his grandfather was with him.

'They are so fond of you,' he once said, looking up at his

lordship with a bright smile. 'Do you see how glad they are when they see you? I hope they will some day be as fond of me. It must be nice to have *every*body like you.'

And he felt quite proud to be the grandson of so greatly admired and beloved an individual.

When the cottages were being built, the lad and his grandfather used to ride over to Earl's Court together to look at them, and Fauntleroy was full of interest. He would dismount from his pony and go and make acquaintance with the workmen, asking them questions about building and brick-laying, and telling them things about America. After two or three such conversations, he was able to enlighten the Earl on the subject of brickmaking as they rode home.

'I always like to know about things like those,' he said, 'because you never know what you are coming to.'

When he left them the workmen used to talk him over among themselves, and laugh at his odd, innocent speeches; but they liked him and liked to see him stand among them, talking away, with his hands in his pockets, his hat pushed back on his curls, and his small face full of eagerness. 'He's a rare 'un,' they used to say. 'An' a noice little outspoken chap too. Not much o' th' bad stock in him.' And they would go home and tell their wives about him, and the women would tell each other, and so it came about that almost everyone talked of, or knew some story of, little Lord Fauntleroy; and gradually almost everyone knew that the 'wicked Earl' had found something he cared for at last – something which had touched and even warmed his hard, bitter old heart.

But no one knew quite how much it had been warmed, and how day by day the old man found himself caring more and more for the child, who was the only creature that had ever trusted him. He found himself looking forward to the time when Cedric would be a young man, strong and beautiful, with life all before him, but having still that kind heart and the power to make friends everywhere; and the Earl wondered what the lad would do, and how he would use his gifts. Often as he watched the little fellow lying upon the hearth, conning some big book, the light shining on the bright young head, his old eyes would gleam and his cheek would flush.

'The boy can do anything,' he would say to himself, 'anything!'

He never spoke to anyone else of his feeling for Cedric; when he spoke of him to others it was always with the same grim smile. But Fauntleroy soon knew that his grandfather loved him and always liked him to be near – near to his chair if they were in the library, opposite to him at table or by his side when he rode or drove or took his evening walk on the broad terrace.

'Do you remember,' Cedric said once, looking up from his book as he lay on the rug, 'do you remember what I said to you that first night about our being good companions? I don't think any people could be better friends than we are, do you?'

'We are pretty good companions, I should say,' replied his lordship. 'Come here.'

Fauntleroy scrambled up and went to him.

'Is there anything you want?' the Earl asked. 'Anything you have not?'

The little fellow's brown eyes fixed themselves on his grandfather with a rather wistful look.

'Only one thing,' he answered.

'What is that?' inquired the Earl.

Fauntleroy was silent a second. He had not thought matters over to himself so long for nothing.

'What is it?' my lord repeated.

Fauntleroy answered.

'It is Dearest,' he said.

The old Earl winced a little.

'But you see her almost every day,' he said. 'Is not that enough?'

'I used to see her all the time,' said Fauntleroy. 'She used to kiss me when I went to sleep at night, and in the morning she was always there, and we could tell each other things without waiting.'

The old eyes and young ones looked into each other through a moment of silence. Then the Earl knitted his brows.

'Do you *never* forget about your mother?' he said.

'No,' answered Fauntleroy, 'never; and she never forgets about me. I shouldn't forget about *you* you know, if I didn't live with you. I should think about you all the more.'

'Upon my word,' said the Earl, after looking at him a moment longer, 'I believe you would!'

The jealous pang that came when the boy spoke so of his mother seemed even stronger than it had been before – it was stronger because of this old man's increasing affection for the boy.

But it was not long before he had other pangs, so much harder to face that he almost forgot, for the time, he had ever hated his son's wife at all. And in a strange and startling way it happened. One evening, just before the Earl's Court cottages were completed, there was a grand dinner party at Dorincourt. There had not been such a party at the Castle for a long time. A few days before it took place, Sir Harry Lorridaile and Lady Lorridaile, who was the Earl's only sister, actually came for a visit – a thing which caused the greatest excitement in the village and set Mrs Dibble's shop-bell tinkling madly again, because it was well known that Lady Lorridaile had only been to Dorincourt once since her marriage, thirty-five years before. She was a handsome old lady with white curls and dimpled, peachy cheeks, and she was as good as gold, but she had never approved of her brother any more than did the rest of the world, and having a strong will of her own and not being at all afraid to speak her mind frankly, she had, after several lively quarrels with his lordship, seen very little of him since her young days.

She had heard a great deal of him that was not pleasant through the years in which they had been separated. She had heard about his neglect of his wife, and of the poor lady's death; and of his indifference to his children; and of the two weak, vicious, unprepossessing elder boys who had been no credit to him or to anyone else. Those two elder sons, Bevis and Maurice, she had never seen; but once there had come to Lorridaile Park a tall, stalwart, beautiful young fellow about eighteen years old who had told her that he was her nephew Cedric Errol, and that he had come to see her because he was passing near the place and wished to look at his Aunt Constantia, of whom he had heard his mother speak. Lady Lorridaile's kind heart had warmed through and through at the sight of the young man, and she had made him stay with her a week, and petted him and made much of him and admired him immensely. He was so sweet-tempered, light-hearted, spirited a lad, that when he went away she had hoped to see him often again; but she never did, because the Earl had been in a bad humour when he went back to Dorincourt, and had forbidden him ever to go to Lorridaile Park again. But Lady Lorridaile had always remembered him tenderly, and though she feared he had made a rash marriage in America, she had been very angry when she heard how he had been cast off by his father and that no one really knew where or how he lived. At last there came a rumour of his death, and then Bevis had been thrown from his horse and killed, and Maurice had died in Rome of the fever; and soon after came the story of the American child who was to be found and brought home as Lord Fauntleroy.

'Probably to be ruined as the others were,' she said to her husband, 'unless his mother is good enough and has a will of her own to help her to take care of him.'

But when she heard that Cedric's mother had been parted from him she was almost too indignant for words.

'It is disgraceful, Harry!' she said. 'Fancy a child of that age being taken from his mother, and made the companion of a man like my brother! The old Earl will either be brutal to the boy or indulge him until he is a little monster. If I thought it would do any good to write –'

'It wouldn't, Constantia,' said Sir Harry.

'I know it wouldn't,' she answered. 'I know his lordship the Earl of Dorincourt too well; but it is outrageous.'

Not only the poor people and farmers heard about little Lord Fauntleroy; others knew of him. He was talked about so much and there were so many stories of him – of his beauty, his sweet temper, his popularity and his growing influence over the Earl his grandfather – that rumours of him reached the gentry at their country places and he was heard of in more than one county of England. People talked about him at the dinner tables, ladies pitied his young mother, and wondered if the boy were as handsome as he was said to be, and men who knew the Earl and his habits laughed heartily at the stories of the little fellow's belief in his lordship's amiability. Sir Thomas Asshe of Asshaine Hall, being in Erlesboro one day, met the Earl and his grandson riding together and stopped to shake hands with my lord and congratulate him on his change of looks and on his recovery from the gout. 'And d'ye know,' he said, when he spoke of the incident afterwards, 'the old man looked as proud as a turkey-cock; and upon my word I don't wonder, for a handsomer, finer lad than his grandson I never saw! As straight as a dart, and sat his pony like a young trooper!'

And so by degrees Lady Lorridaile, too, heard of the child; she heard about Higgins, and the lame boy, and the cottages at Earl's Court, and a score of other things – and she began to wish to see the little fellow. And just as she was wondering how it might be brought about, to her utter astonishment she received a letter from her brother inviting her to come with her husband to Dorincourt.

'It seems incredible!' she exclaimed. 'I have heard it said

that the child has worked miracles, and I begin to believe it. They say my brother adores the boy and can scarcely endure to have him out of sight. And he is so proud of him! Actually I believe he wants to show him to us.' And she accepted the invitation at once.

When she reached Dorincourt Castle with Sir Harry, it was late in the afternoon, and she went to her room at once before seeing her brother. Having dressed for dinner she entered the drawing-room. The Earl was there standing near the fire and looking very tall and imposing; and at his side stood a little boy in black velvet, and a large Vandyke collar of rich lace – a little fellow whose round bright face was so handsome, and who turned upon her such beautiful, candid brown eyes, that she almost uttered an exclamation of pleasure and surprise at the sight.

As she shook hands with the Earl, she called him by the name she had not used since her girlhood.

'What, Molyneux,' she said, 'is this the child?'

'Yes, Constantia,' answered the Earl, 'this is the boy. Fauntleroy, this is your grand-aunt, Lady Constantia Lorridaile.'

'How do you do, grand-aunt?' said Fauntleroy.

Lady Lorridaile put her hand on his shoulder, and after looking down into his upraised face a few seconds, kissed him warmly.

'I am your Aunt Constantia,' she said, 'and I loved your poor papa, and you are very like him.'

'It makes me glad when I am told I am like him,' answered Fauntleroy, 'because it seems as if everyone liked him – just like Dearest, eszackly – Aunt Constantia' (adding the two words after a second's pause).

Lady Lorridaile was delighted. She bent and kissed him again, and from that moment they were warm friends.

'Well, Molyneux,' she said aside to the Earl afterwards, 'it could not possibly be better than this!'

'I think not,' answered his lordship dryly. 'He is a fine

little fellow. We are great friends. He believes me to be the most charming and sweet-tempered of philanthropists. I will confess to you, Constantia – as you would find it out if I did not – that I am in some slight danger of becoming rather an old fool about him.'

'What does his mother think of you?' asked Lady Lorridaile, with her usual straight-forwardness.

'I have not asked her,' answered the Earl, slightly scowling.

'Well,' said Lady Lorridaile, 'I will be frank with you at the outset, Molyneux, and tell you I don't approve of your course, and that it is my intention to call on Mrs Errol as soon as possible; so if you wish to quarrel with me you had better mention it at once. What I hear of the young creature makes me quite sure that the child owes her everything. We were told even at Lorridaile Park that your poorer tenants adore her already.'

'They adore *him*,' said the Earl, nodding towards Fauntleroy. 'As to Mrs Errol, you'll find her a pretty little woman. I'm rather in debt to her for giving some of her beauty to the boy, and you can go to see her if you like. All I ask is that she will remain at Court Lodge, and that you will not ask me to go and see her,' and he scowled a little again.

'But he doesn't hate her as much as he used to, that is plain enough to me,' her ladyship said to Sir Harry afterwards. 'And he is a changed man in a measure, and, incredible as it may seem, Harry, it is my opinion that he is being made into a human being, through nothing more or less than his affection for that innocent, affectionate little fellow. Why, the child actually loves him – leans on his chair and against his knees. My lord's own children would as soon have thought of nestling up to a tiger.'

The very next day she went to call upon Mrs Errol. When she returned she said to her brother:

'Molyneux, she is the loveliest little woman I ever saw!

She has a voice like a silver bell, and you may thank her for making the boy what he is. She has given him more than her beauty, and you make a great mistake in not persuading her to come and take charge of you. I shall invite her to Lorridaile.'

'She'll not leave the boy,' replied the Earl.

'I must have the boy too,' said Lady Lorridaile, laughing.

But she knew Fauntleroy would not be given up to her, and each day she saw more clearly how closely those two had grown to each other, and how all the proud, grim old man's ambition and hope and love centred themselves in the child, and how the warm, innocent nature returned his affection with most perfect trust and faith.

She knew too that the prime reason for the great dinner party was the Earl's secret desire to show the world his grandson and heir; and to let people see that the boy who had been so much spoken of and described was even a finer little specimen of boyhood than rumour had made him.

'Bevis and Maurice were such a bitter humiliation to him,' she said to her husband. 'Everyone knew it. He actually hated them. His pride has full sway here.' Perhaps there was not one person who accepted the invitation without feeling some curiosity about little Lord Fauntleroy, and wondering if he would be on view.

And when the time came he was on view.

'The lad has good manners,' said the Earl. 'He will be in no one's way. Children are usually idiots or bores – mine were both – but he can actually answer when he's spoken to, and be silent when he is not. He is never offensive.'

But he was not allowed to be silent very long. Everyone had something to say to him. The fact was they wished to make him talk. The ladies petted him and asked him questions and the men asked him questions too, and joked with him, as the men on the steamer had done when he crossed the Atlantic. Fauntleroy did not quite understand why they laughed so sometimes when he answered them, but he was so used to seeing people amused when he was quite serious, that he did not mind. He thought the whole evening delightful. The magnificent rooms were so brilliant with lights, there were so many flowers, the gentlemen seemed so gay, and the ladies wore such beautiful, wonderful dresses, and such sparkling ornaments in their hair and on their necks. There was one young lady who, he heard them say, had just come down from London, where she had spent 'the season'; and she was so charming that he could not keep his eyes from her. She was a rather tall young lady, with a proud little head and very soft hair, and large eyes the colour of purple pansies, and the colour of her cheeks and lips was like that of a rose. She was dressed in a beautiful white dress, and had pearls around her throat. There was one strange thing about this young lady. So many gentlemen stood near her, and seemed anxious to please her, that Fauntleroy thought she must be something like a princess. He was so much interested in her that without knowing it he drew nearer and nearer to her and at last she turned and spoke to him.

'Come here, Lord Fauntleroy,' she said, smiling; 'and tell me why you look at me so.'

'I was thinking how beautiful you are,' his young lordship replied.

Then all the gentlemen laughed outright, and the young lady laughed a little too, and the rose colour in her cheeks brightened.

'Ah, Fauntleroy,' said one of the gentlemen who had laughed most heartily, 'make the most of your time! When you are older you will not have the courage to say that.'

'But nobody could help saying it,' said Fauntleroy sweetly. 'Could you help it? Don't *you* think she is pretty too?'

'We are not allowed to say what we think,' said the gentleman, while the rest laughed more than ever.

But the beautiful young lady – her name was Miss Vivian Herbert – put out her hand and drew Cedric to her side, looking prettier than before, if possible.

'Lord Fauntleroy shall say what he thinks,' she said; 'and I am much obliged to him. I am sure he thinks what he says.' And she kissed him on his cheek.

'I think you are prettier than anyone I ever saw,' said Fauntleroy, looking at her with innocent, admiring eyes, 'except Dearest. Of course, I couldn't think anyone *quite* as pretty as Dearest. I think she is the prettiest person in the world.'

'I am sure she is,' said Miss Vivian Herbert. And she laughed and kissed his cheek again.

She kept him by her side a great part of the evening, and the group of which they were the centre was very gay. He did not know how it happened, but before long he was telling them all about America, and the Republican rally, and Mr Hobbs and Dick, and in the end he proudly produced from his pocket Dick's parting gift – the red silk handkerchief.

'I put it in my pocket tonight because it was a party,' he said. 'I thought Dick would like me to wear it at a party.'

And queer as the big, flaming, spotted thing was, there was a serious, affectionate look in his eyes, which prevented his audience from laughing very much.

'You see I like it,' he said, 'because Dick is my friend.'

But though he was talked to so much, as the Earl had said, he was in no one's way. He could be quiet and listen when others talked, and so no one found him tiresome. A slight smile crossed more than one face when several times he went and stood near his grandfather's chair, or sat on a stool close to him, watching him and absorbing every word he uttered with the most charmed interest. Once he stood so near the chair's arm that his cheek touched the Earl's shoulder, and his lordship, detecting the general smile, smiled a little himself. He knew what the lookers-on were thinking, and he felt some secret amusement in their seeing what a good friend he was to this youngster, who might have been expected to share the popular opinion of him.

Mr Havisham had been expected to arrive in the afternoon, but, strange to say, he was late. Such a thing had really never been known to happen before during all the years in which he had been a visitor at Dorincourt Castle. He was so late that the guests were on the point of rising to go in to dinner when he arrived. When he approached his host the Earl regarded him with amazement. He looked as if he had been hurried or agitated; his dry, keen old face was actually pale.

'I was detained,' he said, in a low voice to the Earl, 'by – an extraordinary event.'

It was as unlike the methodic old lawyer to be agitated by anything as it was to be late, but it was evident that he had been disturbed. At dinner he ate scarcely anything, and two or three times, when he was spoken to, he started as if his thoughts were far away. At dessert, when Fauntleroy came in, he looked at him more than once, nervously and uneasily. Fauntleroy noted the look and wondered at it. He and Mr Havisham were on friendly terms, and they usually exchanged smiles.

The lawyer seemed to have forgotten to smile that evening.

The fact was he forgot everything but the strange and painful news he knew he must tell the Earl before the night was over – the strange news which he knew would be so terrible a shock, and which would change the face of everything. As he looked about at the splendid rooms and the brilliant company – at the people gathered together, he knew, more that they might see the bright-haired little fellow near the Earl's chair than for any other reason – as he looked at the proud old man and at little Lord Fauntleroy smiling at his side, he really felt quite shaken, notwithstanding that he was a hardened old lawyer. What a blow it was that he must deal them!

He did not exactly know how the long superb dinner ended. He sat through it as if he were in a dream, and several times he saw the Earl glance at him in surprise.

But it was over at last, and the gentlemen joined the ladies in the drawing-room. They found Fauntleroy sitting on a sofa with Miss Vivian Herbert – the great beauty of the last London season; they had been looking at some pictures, and he was thanking his companion, as the door opened.

'I'm ever so much obliged to you for being so kind to me!' he was saying; 'I never was at a party before, and I've enjoyed myself so much!'

He had enjoyed himself so much that when the gentlemen gathered about Miss Herbert again and began to talk to her, as he listened and tried to understand their laughing speeches his eyelids began to droop. They drooped until they covered his eyes two or three times, and then the sound of Miss Herbert's low, pretty laugh would bring him back, and he would open them again for about two seconds. He was quite sure he was not going to sleep, but there was a large, yellow satin cushion behind him and his head sank against it, and after a while his eyelids drooped for the last time. They did not even quite open when, as it seemed a long time after, someone kissed him lightly on the cheek. It was Miss Vivian Herbert, who was going away, and she spoke to him softly.

'Good night, little Lord Fauntleroy,' she said. 'Sleep well.'

And in the morning he did not know that he had tried to open his eyes and had murmured sleepily:

'Good night – I'm so – glad – I saw you – you are so – pretty –'

He only had a very faint recollection of hearing the gentlemen laugh again and of wondering why they did it.

* * *

No sooner had the last guest left the room than Mr Havisham turned from his place by the fire, and stepped nearer the sofa, where he stood looking down at the sleeping occupant. Little Lord Fauntleroy was taking his ease luxuriously. One leg crossed the other and swung over the edge of the sofa; one arm was flung easily above his head; the warm flush of healthy, happy, childish sleep was on his quiet face; his waving tangle of bright hair strayed over the yellow satin cushion. He made a picture well worth looking at.

As Mr Havisham looked at it, he put his hand up and rubbed his shaven chin, with a harassed countenance.

'Well, Havisham,' said the Earl's harsh voice behind him. 'What is it? It is evident something has happened. What was the extraordinary event, if I may ask?'

Mr Havisham turned from the sofa, still rubbing his chin.

'It was bad news,' he answered, 'distressing news, my lord – the worst of news. I am sorry to be the bearer of it.'

The Earl had been uneasy for some time during the evening, as he glanced at Mr Havisham, and when he was uneasy he was always ill-tempered.

'Why do you look so at the boy!' he exclaimed irritably. 'You have been looking at him all the evening as if – See here now, why should you look at the boy, Havisham, and hang over him like some bird of ill-omen! What has your news to do with Lord Fauntleroy?'

'My lord,' said Mr Havisham, 'I will waste no words. My news has everything to do with Lord Fauntleroy. And if we are to believe it – it is not Lord Fauntleroy who lies sleeping before us, but only the son of Captain Errol. And the present Lord Fauntleroy is the son of your son Bevis, and is at this moment in a lodging-house in London.'

The Earl clutched the arms of his chair with both his hands until the veins stood out upon them; the veins stood out on his forehead too; his fierce old face was almost livid.

'What do you mean!' he cried out. 'You are mad! Whose lie is this?'

'If it is a lie,' answered Mr Havisham, 'it is painfully like the truth. A woman came to my chambers this morning. She said your son Bevis married her six years ago in London. She showed me her marriage certificate. They quarrelled a year after the marriage, and he paid her to keep away from him. She has a son five years old. She is an American of the lower class – an ignorant person – and until lately she did not fully understand what her son could claim. She consulted a lawyer, and found out that the boy was really Lord Fauntleroy and the heir to the earldom of Dorincourt; and she, of course, insists on his claims being acknowledged.'

There was a movement of the curly head on the yellow satin cushion. A soft, long, sleepy sigh came from the parted lips, and the little boy stirred in his sleep, but not at all restlessly or uneasily. Not at all as if his slumber were disturbed by the fact that he was being proved a small impostor and that he was not Lord Fauntleroy at all and never would be the Earl of Dorincourt. He only turned his rosy face more on its side as if to enable the old man who stared at it so solemnly to see it better.

The handsome, grim old face was ghastly. A bitter smile fixed itself upon it.

'I should refuse to believe a word of it,' he said, 'if it were not such a low, scoundrelly piece of business that it becomes quite possible in connection with the name of my son Bevis. It is quite like Bevis. He was always a disgrace to us. Always a weak, untruthful, vicious young brute with low tastes – my son and heir, Bevis, Lord Fauntleroy. The woman is an ignorant, vulgar person, you say?'

'I am obliged to admit that she can scarcely spell her own name,' answered the lawyer. 'She is absolutely uneducated and openly mercenary. She cares for nothing but the money. She is very handsome in a coarse way, but –'

The fastidious old lawyer ceased speaking and gave a sort of shudder.

The veins on the old Earl's forehead stood out like purple cords. Something else stood out upon it too – cold drops of moisture. He took out his handkerchief and swept them away. His smile grew even more bitter.

'And I,' he said, 'I objected to – to the other woman, the mother of this child' – pointing to the sleepy form on the sofa – 'I refused to recognize her. And yet she could spell her own name. I suppose this is retribution.'

Suddenly he sprang up from his chair and began to walk up and down the room. Fierce and terrible words poured forth from his lips. His rage and hatred and cruel disappointment shook him as a storm shakes a tree. His violence was something dreadful to see, and yet Mr Havisham noticed that at the very worst of his wrath he never seemed to forget the little sleeping figure on the yellow satin cushions, and that he never once spoke loud enough to awaken it.

'I might have known it,' he said. 'They were a disgrace to me from their first hour! I hated them both; and they hated me! Bevis was the worst of the two. I will not believe this yet though! I will contend against it to the last. But it is like Bevis – it is like him!'

And then he raged again and asked questions about the woman, about her proofs, and pacing the room, turned first white and then purple in his repressed fury.

When at last he had learned all there was to be told, and knew the worst, Mr Havisham looked at him with a feeling of anxiety. He looked broken and haggard and changed. His rages had always been bad for him, but this one had been worse than the rest because there had been something more than rage in it.

He came slowly back to the sofa, at last, and stood near it.

'If anyone had told me I could be fond of a child,' he said, his harsh voice low and unsteady, 'I should not have believed them. I always detested children – my own more than the rest. I am fond of this one; he is fond of me' (with a bitter smile). 'I am not popular; I never was. But he is fond of me. He never was afraid of me – he always trusted me. He would have filled my place better than I have filled it. I know that. He would have been an honour to the name.'

He bent down and stood a minute or so looking at the happy, sleeping face. His shaggy eyebrows were knitted fiercely, and yet somehow he did not seem fierce at all. He put up his hand, pushed the bright hair back from the fore-head, and then turned away and rang the bell.

When the largest footman appeared, he pointed to the sofa.

'Take,' he said, and then his voice changed a little, 'take Lord Fauntleroy to his room.'

CHAPTER 11

Anxiety in America

When Mr Hobbs's young friend left him to go to Dorincourt Castle and become Lord Fauntleroy, and the grocery-man had time to realize that the Atlantic Ocean lay between himself and the small companion who had spent so many agreeable hours in his society, he really began to feel very lonely indeed. The fact was, Mr Hobbs was not a clever man, nor even a bright one; he was indeed rather a slow and heavy person, and he had never made many acquaintances. He was not mentally energetic enough to know how to amuse himself, and in truth he never did anything of an entertaining nature but read the newspapers and add up his accounts. It was not very easy for him to add up his accounts, and sometimes it took him a long time to bring them out right; and in the old days little Lord Fauntleroy, who had learned how to add up quite nicely with his fingers and a slate and pencil, had sometimes even gone to the length of trying to help him; and then too he had been so good a listener and had taken such an interest in what the newspaper said, and he and Mr Hobbs had held such long conversations about the Revolution and the British and the elections and the Republican party, that it was no wonder his going left a blank in the grocery store. At first it seemed to Mr Hobbs that Cedric was not really far away, and would come back again; that some day he would look up from his paper and see the lad standing in the doorway, in his white suit and red stockings, and with his straw hat on the back of his head, and would hear him say in his cheerful little voice: 'Hallo, Mr Hobbs! This is a hot day – isn't it?' But as the days passed on and this did not happen, Mr Hobbs felt very dull and uneasy. He did not even enjoy his newspaper as much as he used to. He would put the paper down on his knee after reading it, and sit and stare at the high stool for a long time. There were some marks on the long legs which made him feel quite dejected and melancholy. They were marks made by the heels of the next Earl of Dorincourt, when he kicked and talked at the same time. It seems that even youthful earls kick the legs of things they sit on; noble blood and lofty lineage do not prevent it. After looking at those marks Mr Hobbs would take out his gold watch and open it and stare at the inscription: 'From his oldest friend, Lord Fauntleroy, to Mr Hobbs. When this you see, remember me.' And after staring at it awhile he would shut it up with a loud snap, and sigh and get up and go and stand in the doorway – between the box of potatoes and the barrel of apples – and look up the street. At night, when the store was closed, he would light his pipe and walk slowly along the pavement until he reached the house where Cedric had lived, on which there was a sign that read, 'This House to Let'; and he would stop near it and look up and shake his head, and puff at his pipe very hard, and after a while walk mournfully back again.

This went on for two or three weeks before any new idea came to him. Being slow and ponderous, it always took him a long time to reach a new idea. As a rule he did not like new ideas, but preferred old ones. After two or three weeks, however, during which, instead of getting better, matters really grew worse, a novel plan slowly and deliberately dawned upon him. He would go to see Dick. He smoked a great many pipes before he arrived at the conclusion, but finally he did arrive at it. He would go to see Dick. He knew all about Dick. Cedric had told him, and his idea was that perhaps Dick might be some comfort to him in the way of talking things over.

So one day when Dick was very hard at work blacking a customer's boots, a short stout man with a heavy face and a bald head stopped on the pavement and stared for two or three minutes at the boot-black's sign, which read:

PROFESOR DICK TIPTON
CAN'T BE BEAT.

He stared at it so long that Dick began to take a lively interest in him, and when he had put the finishing touch to his customer's boots he said:

'Want a shine, sir?'

The stout man came forward deliberately and put his foot on the rest.

'Yes,' he said.

Then, when Dick fell to work, the stout man looked from Dick to the sign and from the sign to Dick.

'Where did you get that?' he asked.

'From a friend o' mine,' says Dick, 'a little feller. He guv' me the whole outfit. He was the best little feller ye ever saw. He's in England now. Gone to be one of those lords.'

'Lord – Lord,' asked Mr Hobbs, with ponderous slowness, 'Lord Fauntleroy – goin' to be Earl of Dorincourt?'

Dick almost dropped his brush.

'Why, boss,' he exclaimed, 'd'ye know him yerself?'

'I've known him,' answered Mr Hobbs, wiping his warm forehead, 'ever since he was born. We were lifetime acquaintances – that's what *we* were.'

It really made him feel quite agitated to speak of it. He pulled the splendid gold watch out of his pocket and opened it, and showed the inside of the case to Dick.

'"When this you see, remember me",' he read. 'That was his parting keepsake to me. "I don't want you to forget me" – those were his words – I'd ha' remembered him,' he went on, shaking his head, 'if he hadn't given me a thing, an' I hadn't seen hide nor hair on him again. He was a companion as *any* man would remember.'

'He was the nicest little feller I ever see,' said Dick. 'An' as to sand – I never ha' seen so much sand to a little feller. I thought a heap o' him, I did – an' we was friends too – we was sort o' chums frum the fust, that little 'un an' me. I grabbed his ball from under a stage fur him, an' he never forgot it; an' he'd come down here, he would, with his mother or his nuss, an' he'd holler: "Hallo, Dick!" at me, as friendly as if he was six feet high, when he warn't knee high to a grasshopper, and was dressed in gal's clo'es. He was a gay little chap, and when you was down on your luck it did you good to talk to him.'

'That's so,' said Mr Hobbs. 'It was a pity to make an earl out of him. He would have *shone* in the grocery business – or dry goods either; he would have *shone*!' And he shook his head with deeper regret than ever.

It proved that they had so much to say to each other that it was not possible to say it all at one time, and so it was agreed that the next night Dick should make a visit to the store and keep Mr Hobbs company. The plan pleased Dick well enough. He had been a street waif nearly all his life, but he had never been a bad boy, and he had always had a private yearning for a more respectable kind of existence. Since he had been in business for himself, he had made enough money to enable him to sleep under a roof instead of out in the streets, and he had begun to hope he might reach even a higher plane in time. So, to be invited to call on a stout, respectable man who owned a corner store, and even had a horse and wagon, seemed to him quite an event.

'Do you know anything about earls and castles?' Mr Hobbs inquired. 'I'd like to know more of the particulars.'

'There's a story on some of 'em in the *Penny Story Gazette*,' said Dick. 'It's called the "Crime of a Coronet; or, the Revenge of the Countess May". It's a boss thing too. Some of us boys're takin' it to read.'

'Bring it up when you come,' said Mr Hobbs, 'an' I'll pay for it. Bring all you can find that have any earls in 'em. If there aren't earls, markises'll do, or dooks – though *he* never made mention of any dooks or markises. We did go over coronets a little, but I never happened to see any. I guess they don't keep 'em 'round here.'

'Tiffany'd have 'em if anybody did,' said Dick, 'but I don't know as I'd know one if I saw it.'

Mr Hobbs did not explain that he would not have known one if he saw it. He merely shook his head ponderously.

'I s'pose there is very little call for 'em,' he said, and that ended the matter.

This was the beginning of quite a substantial friendship. When Dick went up to the store Mr Hobbs received him with great hospitality. He gave him a chair tilted against the door, near a barrel of apples, and after his young visitor was seated, he made a jerk at them with the hand in which he held his pipe, saying:

'Help yerself.'

Then he looked at the story papers, and after that they read and discussed the British aristocracy; and Mr Hobbs smoked his pipe very hard and shook his head a great deal. He shook it most when he pointed out the high stool with the marks on its legs.

'There's his very kicks,' he said impressively; 'his very kicks. I sit and look at 'em by the hour. This is a world of ups an' it's a world of downs. Why, he'd set there, and eat

biscuits out of a box, an' apples out of a barrel, an' pitch
his cores into the street; an' now he's a lord a-livin' in a
castle. Those are a lord's kicks; they'll be an earl's kicks
some day. Sometimes I says to myself, says I, "Well, I'll be
jiggered!"'

He seemed to derive a great deal of comfort from his
reflections and Dick's visit. Before Dick went home they had
a supper in the small back room; they had biscuits and cheese
and sardines, and other canned things out of the store, and
Mr Hobbs solemnly opened two bottles of ginger ale, and
pouring out two glasses, proposed a toast.

'Here's to *him*!' he said, lifting his glass, 'an' may he
teach 'em a lesson – earls an' markises an' dooks an' all!'

After that night the two saw each other often, and
Mr Hobbs was much more comfortable and less desolate.
They read the *Penny Story Gazette* and other interesting
things, and gained a knowledge of the habits of the nobility
and gentry which would have surprised those despised
classes if they had realized it. One day Mr Hobbs made
a pilgrimage to a bookstore down town for the express
purpose of adding to their library. He went to a clerk and
leaned over the counter to speak to him.

'I want,' he said, 'a book about earls.'

'What!' exclaimed the clerk.

'A book,' repeated the grocery-man, 'about earls.'

'I'm afraid,' said the clerk, looking rather queer, 'that
we haven't what you want.'

'Haven't?' said Mr Hobbs anxiously. 'Well, say markises
then – or dooks.'

'I know of no such book,' answered the clerk.

Mr Hobbs was much disturbed. He looked down at the
floor, then he looked up.

'None about female earls?' he inquired.

'I'm afraid not,' said the clerk with a smile.

'Well,' exclaimed Mr Hobbs, 'I'll be jiggered!'

He was just going out of the store, when the clerk called him back and asked him if a story in which the nobility were chief characters would do. Mr Hobbs said it would – if he could not get an entire volume devoted to earls. So the clerk sold him a book called *The Tower of London*, written by Mr Harrison Ainsworth, and he carried it home.

When Dick came they began to read it. It was a very wonderful and exciting book, and the scene was laid in the reign of the famous English queen who is called by some people Bloody Mary. And as Mr Hobbs heard of Queen Mary's deeds and the habit she had of chopping people's heads off, putting them to the torture and burning them alive he became very much excited. He took his pipe out of his mouth and stared at Dick, and at last he was obliged to mop the perspiration from his brow with his red pocket-handkerchief.

'Why, he ain't safe!' he said. 'He ain't safe! If the women folks can sit up on their thrones an' give the word for things like that to be done, who's to know what's happening to him this very minute? He's no more safe than nothing! Just let a woman like that get mad, an' no one's safe!'

'Well,' said Dick, though he looked rather anxious himself, 'ye see this 'ere 'un isn't the one that's bossin' things now. I know her name's Victohry, an' this 'un here in the book – her name's Mary.'

'So it is,' said Mr Hobbs, still mopping his forehead, 'so it is. An' the newspapers are not sayin' anything about any racks, thumbscrews or stake-burnin's – but still it doesn't seem as if 'twas safe for him over there with those queer folks. Why, they tell me they don't keep the Fourth o' July!'

He was privately uneasy for several days; and it was not until he received Fauntleroy's letter and had read it several times, both to himself and to Dick, and had also read the letter Dick got about the same time, that he became composed again.

But they both found great pleasure in their letters. They read and reread them, and talked them over and enjoyed every word of them. And they spent days over the answers they sent, and read them over almost as often as the letters they had received.

It was rather a labour for Dick to write his. All his knowledge of reading and writing he had gained during a few months when he had lived with his elder brother, and had gone to a night school; but, being a sharp boy, he had made the most of that brief education, and had spelled out things in newspapers since then, and practised writing with bits of chalk on pavements or walls or fences. He told Mr Hobbs all about his life and about his elder brother, who had been rather good to him after their mother died, when Dick was quite a little fellow. Their father had died some time before. The brother's name was Ben, and he had taken care of Dick as well as he could, until the boy was old enough to sell newspapers and run errands. They had lived together, and as he grew older Ben had managed to get along until he had quite a decent place in a store.

'And then,' exclaimed Dick with disgust, 'blest if he didn't go an' marry a gal! Just went and got spoony, an' hadn't any more sense left! Married her, an' set up house-keepin' in two back rooms. An' a hefty 'un she was, a regular tiger-cat. She'd tear things to pieces when she got mad – and she was mad *all* the time. Had a baby just like her – yell day 'n' night! An' if I didn't have to 'tend it, an' when it screamed, she'd fire things at me. She fired a plate at me one day an' hit the baby – cut its chin. Doctor said he'd carry the mark till he died. A nice mother she was! Crackey! but didn't we have a time – Ben 'n' mehself 'n' the young 'un. She was mad at Ben because he didn't make money faster; 'n' at last he went out West with a man to set up a cattle ranch. An' he hadn't been gone a week 'fore, one night, I got home from sellin' my papers, 'n' the rooms wus locked up 'n' empty, 'n' the woman o' the house, she told me Minna'd gone – shown a clean pair o' heels. Some 'un else said she'd gone across the water to be nuss to a lady as had a little baby too. Never heard a word of her since – nuther has Ben. If I'd ha' bin him, I wouldn't ha' fretted a bit – 'n' I guess he didn't. But he thought a heap o' her at the start. Tell you, he was spoons on her. She was a daisy-lookin' gal, too, when she was dressed up 'n' not mad. She'd big black eyes 'n' black hair downs too her knees; she'd make it into a rope as big as your arm, and twist it 'round 'n' round her head; 'n' I tell you her eyes'd snap! Folks used to say she was part Itali-un – said her mother or father'd come from there, 'n' it made her queer. I tell ye she was one of 'em – she was!'

He often told Mr Hobbs stories of her and of his brother Ben, who, since his going out West, had written once or twice to Dick. Ben's luck had not been good, and he had wandered from place to place; but at last he had settled on a ranch in California, where he was at work at the time when Dick became acquainted with Mr Hobbs.

'That gal,' said Dick one day, 'she took all the grit out o' him. I couldn't help feeling sorry for him sometimes.'

They were sitting in the store doorway together, and Mr Hobbs was filling his pipe.

'He oughtn't to 'ave married,' he said solemnly as he rose to get a match. 'Women – I never could see any use in 'em myself.'

As he took the match from its box, he stopped and looked down on the counter.

'Why,' he said, 'if here isn't a letter! I didn't see it afore. The postman must have laid it down when I wasn't noticin', or the newspaper slipped over it.'

He picked it up and looked at it carefully.

'It's from *him*!' he exclaimed. 'That's the very one it's from!'

He forgot his pipe altogether. He went back to his chair

quite excited, and took his pocket-knife and opened the envelope.

'I wonder what news there is this time,' he said.

And then he unfolded the letter and read as follows:

Dorincourt Castle

My dear Mr Hobbs, – i write this in a great hury becaus i have something curous to tell you i know you will be very much suprised my dear frend when i tel you. It is all a mistake and i am not a lord and i shall not have to be an earl there is a lady whitch was marid to my uncle bevis who is dead and she has a little boy and he is lord fauntleroy because that is the way it is in England the earls eldest sons little boy is the earl if every body is dead i mean if his farther and grandfarther are dead my grandfarther is not dead but my uncle bevis is and so his boy is lord Fauntleroy and i am not becaus my papa was the youngest son and my name is Cedric Errol like it was when i was in New York and all the things will belong to the other boy i thought at first i should have to give him my pony and cart but my grandfarther says i need not my grandfarther is very sorry and i think he does not like the lady but preaps he thinks dearest and i are sorry becaus i shall not be an earl i would like to be an earl now better than i thout i would at first becaus this is a beautifle castle and i like every body so and when you are rich you can do so many things i am not rich now becaus when your papa is only the youngest son he is not very rich i am going to learn to work so that I can take care of dearest i have been asking Wilkins about grooming horses preaps i might be a groom or a coachman, the lady brought her

little boy to the castle and my grandfarther and
Mr Havisham talked to her i think she was angry
she talked loud and my grandfarther was angry
too i never saw him angry before i wish it did not
make them all mad i thort i would tell you and
Dick right away becaus you would be intrusted so
no more at present with love from

your old frend
Cedric Errol (Not lord Fauntleroy)

Mr Hobbs fell back in his chair, the letter dropped on
his knee, his penknife slipped to the floor and so did the
envelope.

'Well,' he ejaculated, 'I am jiggered!'

He was so dumbfounded that he actually changed his
exclamation. It had always been his habit to say, 'I *will* be
jiggered,' but this time he said, 'I *am* jiggered.' Perhaps he
really *was* jiggered. There is no knowing.

'Well,' said Dick, 'the whole thing's bust up, hasn't it?'

'Bust!' said Mr Hobbs. 'It's my opinion it's all a put-up
job o' the British 'ristycrats to rob him of his rights because
he's an American. They've had a spite agin us ever since the
Revolution, an' they're takin' it out on him. I told you he
wasn't safe, an' see what's happened! Like as not, the whole
government's got together to rob him of his lawful ownin's.'
He was very much agitated. He had not approved of the
change in his young friend's circumstances at first, but lately
he had become more reconciled to it, and after the receipt
of Cedric's letter he had perhaps even felt some secret pride
in his young friend's magnificence. He might not have a good
opinion of earls, but he knew that even in America money
was considered rather an agreeable thing, and if all the wealth
and grandeur were to go with the title, it must be rather
hard to lose it.

'They're trying to rob him,' he said, 'that's what they're doing, and folks that have money ought to look after him.'

And he kept Dick with him until quite a late hour to talk it over, and when that young man left he went with him to the corner of the street; and on his way back he stopped opposite the empty house for some time, staring at the 'To Let', and smoking his pipe in much disturbance of mind.

CHAPTER 12

The Rival Claimants

A very few days after the dinner party at the Castle, almost everybody in England who read the newspapers at all knew the romantic story of what had happened at Dorincourt. It made a very interesting story when it was told with all the details. There was the little American boy who had been brought to England to be Lord Fauntleroy, and who was said to be so fine and handsome a little fellow, and to have already made people fond of him; there was the old Earl, his grandfather, who was so proud of his heir; there was the pretty young mother who had never been forgiven for marrying Captain Errol; and there was the strange marriage of Bevis, the dead Lord Fauntleroy, and the strange wife, of whom no one knew anything, suddenly appearing with her son, and saying that he was the real Lord Fauntleroy and must have his rights. All these things were talked about and written about, and caused a tremendous sensation. And then there came the rumour that the Earl of Dorincourt was not satisfied with the turn affairs had taken, and would perhaps contest the claim by law, and the matter might end with a wonderful trial.

There never had been such excitement before in the county in which Erlesboro was situated. On market-days people stood in groups and talked and wondered what would be done; the farmers' wives invited one another to tea that they might tell one another all they had heard and all they thought and all they thought other people thought. They related wonderful anecdotes about the Earl's rage and his determination not to acknowledge the new Lord Fauntleroy, and his hatred of the woman who was the claimant's mother. But of course it was Mrs Dibble who could tell the most, and who was more in demand than ever.

'An' a bad look-out it is,' she said. 'An' if you were to ask me, ma'am, I should say as it was a judgement on him for the way he's treated that sweet young cre'tur as he parted from her child – for he's got that fond of him an' that set on him an' that proud on him as he's a'most drove mad by what's happened. An' what's more, this new one's no lady, as his little lordship's ma is. She's a bold-faced, black-eyed thing, as Mr Thomas says no gentleman in livery 'u'd bemean hisself to be guv orders by; an' let her come into the house, he says, an' he goes out of it. An' the boy don't no more compare with the other one than nothin' you could mention. An' mercy knows what's goin' to come of it all, an' where it's to end, an' you might have knocked me down with a feather when Jane brought the news.'

In fact there was excitement everywhere; at the Castle, in the library, where the Earl and Mr Havisham sat and talked; in the servants' hall, where Mr Thomas and the butler and the other men and women servants gossiped and exclaimed at all times of the day; and in the stables, where Wilkins went about his work in a quite depressed state of mind, and groomed the brown pony more beautifully than ever, and said mournfully to the coachman that he 'never taught a young gen'leman to ride as took to it more nat'ral or was a better-plucked one than he was. He was a one as it were some pleasure to ride behind.'

But in the midst of all this disturbance there was one

person who was quite calm and untroubled. That person was the little Lord Fauntleroy who was said not to be Lord Fauntleroy at all. When first the state of affairs had been explained to him, he had felt some little anxiousness and perplexity, it is true, but its foundation was not in baffled ambition.

While the Earl told him what had happened, he had sat on a stool holding on to his knee, as he so often did when he was listening to anything interesting; and by the time the story was finished he looked quite sober.

'It makes me feel very queer,' he said; 'it makes me feel – queer.'

The Earl looked at the boy in silence. It made him feel queer too – queerer than he had ever felt in his whole life. And he felt more queer still when he saw that there was a troubled expression on the small face which was usually so happy.

'Will they take Dearest's house away from her – and her carriage?' Cedric asked in a rather unsteady, anxious little voice.

'No!' said the Earl decidedly – in quite a loud voice in fact. 'They can take nothing from her.'

'Ah,' said Cedric with evident relief. 'Can't they?'

Then he looked up at his grandfather, and there was a wistful shade in his eyes, and they looked very big and soft.

'That other boy,' he said rather tremulously, 'he will have to – to be your boy now – as I was – won't he?'

'No!' answered the Earl – and he said it so fiercely and loudly that Cedric jumped.

'No?' he exclaimed in wonderment. 'Won't he? I thought –'

He stood up from his stool quite suddenly.

'Shall I be your boy, even if I'm not going to be an earl?' he said. 'Shall I be your boy, just as I was before?' And his flushed little face was all alight with eagerness.

How the old Earl did look at him from his head to foot, to be sure! How his great shaggy brows did draw themselves together, and how queerly his deep eyes shone under them – how very queerly!

'My boy!' he said – and, if you'll believe it, his very voice was queer, almost shaky and a little broken and hoarse, not at all what you would expect an earl's voice to be, though he spoke more decidedly and peremptorily even than before. 'Yes, you'll be my boy as long as I live; and by George, sometimes I feel as if you were the only boy I had ever had.'

Cedric's face turned red to the roots of his hair; it turned red with relief and pleasure. He put both his hands deep into his pockets and looked squarely into his noble relative's eyes.

'Do you?' he said. 'Well then, I don't care about the earl part at all. I don't care whether I'm an earl or not. I thought – you see, I thought the one that was going to be the earl would have to be your boy, too, and – and I couldn't be. That was what made me feel so queer.'

The Earl put his hand on his shoulder and drew him nearer.

'They shall take nothing from you that I can hold for you,' he said, drawing his breath hard. 'I won't believe yet that they can take anything from you. You were made for the place, and – well, you may fill it still. But whatever comes, you shall have all that I can give you – all!'

It scarcely seemed as if he were speaking to a child, there was such determination in his face and voice; it was more as if he were making a promise to himself – and perhaps he was.

He had never before known how deep a hold upon him his fondness for the boy and his pride in him had taken. He had never seen his strength and good qualities and beauty as he seemed to see them now. To his obstinate nature it seemed impossible – more than impossible – to give up what he had so set his heart upon. And he had determined that he would not give it up without a fierce struggle.

Within a few days after she had seen Mr Havisham, the woman who claimed to be Lady Fauntleroy presented herself at the Castle, and brought her child with her. She was sent away. The Earl would not see her, she was told by the footman at the door; his lawyer would attend to her case. It was Thomas who gave the message, and who expressed his opinion of her freely afterward, in the servants' hall. He 'hoped', he said, 'as he had wore livery in 'igh famblies long enough to know a lady when he see one, an' if that was a lady he was no judge of females'.

'The one at the Lodge,' added Thomas loftily, ''Merican or no 'Merican, she's one o' the right sort, as any gentleman u'd reckinize with 'alf a heye. I remarked it myself to Henery when fust we called there.'

The woman drove away; the look on her handsome common face half frightened, half fierce. Mr Havisham had noticed, during his interviews with her, that though she had a passionate temper and a coarse, insolent manner, she was neither so clever nor so bold as she meant to be; seemed sometimes to be almost overwhelmed by the position in which she had placed herself. It was as if she had not expected to meet with such opposition.

'She is evidently,' the lawyer said to Mrs Errol, 'a person from the lower walks of life. She is uneducated and untrained in everything, and quite unused to meeting people like ourselves on any terms of equality. She does not know what to do. Her visit to the Castle quite cowed her. She was infuriated, but she was cowed. The Earl would not receive her, but I advised him to go with me to the Dorincourt Arms, where she is staying. When she saw him enter the room, she turned white, though she flew into a rage at once, and threatened and demanded in one breath.'

The fact was that the Earl had stalked into the room and stood, looking like a venerable aristocratic giant, staring at the woman from under his beetling brows, and not condescending a word. He simply stared at her, taking her in from head to foot as if she were some repulsive curiosity. He let her talk and demand until she was tired without himself uttering a word, and then he said:

'You say you are my eldest son's wife. If that is true, and if the proof you offer is too much for us, the law is on your side. In that case your boy is Lord Fauntleroy. The matter will be sifted to the bottom, you may rest assured. If your claims are proved, you will be provided for. I want to see nothing either of you or the child as long as I live. The place will unfortunately have enough of you after my death. You are exactly the kind of person I should have expected my son Bevis to choose.'

And then he turned his back upon her and stalked out of the room as he had stalked into it.

Not many days after that a visitor was announced to Mrs Errol, who was writing in her little morning-room. The maid who brought the message looked rather excited; her eyes were quite round with amazement, in fact, and being young and inexperienced, she regarded her mistress with nervous sympathy.

'It's the Earl hisself, ma'am!' she said in tremulous awe.

When Mrs Errol entered the drawing-room a very tall, majestic-looking old man was standing on the tiger-skin rug. He had a handsome, grim old face, with an aquiline profile, a long white moustache and an obstinate look.

'Mrs Errol, I believe?' he said.

'Mrs Errol,' she answered.

'I am the Earl of Dorincourt,' he said.

He paused a moment, almost unconsciously, to look into her uplifted eyes. They were so like the big, affectionate, childish eyes he had seen uplifted to his own so often every day during the last few months, that they gave him a quite curious sensation.

'The boy is very like you,' he said abruptly.

'It has been often said so, my lord,' she replied, 'but I have been glad to think him like his father also.'

As Lady Lorridaile had told him, her voice was very sweet, and her manner was very simple and dignified. She did not seem in the least troubled by his sudden coming.

'Yes,' said the Earl, 'he is like – my son – too.' He put his hand up to his big white moustache and pulled it fiercely. 'Do you know,' he said, 'why I have come here?'

'I have seen Mr Havisham,' Mrs Errol began, 'and he has told me of the claims which have been made –'

'I have come to tell you,' said the Earl, 'that they will be investigated and contested, if a contest can be made. I have come to tell you that the boy shall be defended with all the power of the law. His rights –'

The soft voice interrupted him.

'He must have nothing that is *not* his by right, even if the law can give it to him,' she said.

'Unfortunately the law cannot,' said the Earl. 'If it could it should. This outrageous woman and her child –'

'Perhaps she cares for him as much as I care for Cedric, my lord,' said little Mrs Errol. 'And if she was your eldest son's wife, her son is Lord Fauntleroy, and mine is not.'

She was no more afraid of him than Cedric had been, and she looked at him just as Cedric would have looked, and he, having been an old tyrant all his life, was privately pleased by it. People so seldom dared to differ from him that there was an entertaining novelty in it.

'I suppose,' he said, scowling slightly, 'that you would much prefer that he should not be the Earl of Dorincourt?'

Her fair young face flushed.

'It is a very magnificent thing to be the Earl of Dorincourt, my lord,' she said. 'I know that, but I care most that he should be what his father was – brave and just and true always.'

'In striking contrast to what his grandfather was, eh?' said his lordship sardonically.

'I have not had the pleasure of knowing his grandfather,' replied Mrs Errol, 'but I know my little boy believes –' She stopped short a moment, looking quietly into his face, and then she added: 'I know that Cedric loves you.'

'Would he have loved me,' said the Earl dryly, 'if you had told him why I did not receive you at the Castle?'

'No,' answered Mrs Errol; 'I think not. That was why I did not wish him to know.'

'Well,' said my lord brusquely, 'there are few women who would not have told him.'

He suddenly began to walk up and down the room, pulling his great moustache more violently than ever.

'Yes, he is fond of me,' he said, 'and I am fond of him. I can't say I ever was fond of anything before. I am fond of him. He pleased me from the first. I am an old man, and was tired of my life. He has given me something to live for, I am proud of him. I was satisfied to think of his taking his place some day as the head of the family.'

He came back and stood before Mrs Errol.

'I am miserable,' he said. 'Miserable!'

He looked as if he was. Even his pride could not keep his voice steady or his hands from shaking. For a moment it almost seemed as if his deep, fierce eyes had tears in them. 'Perhaps it is because I am miserable that I have come to you,' he said, quite glaring down at her. 'I used to hate you; I have been jealous of you. This wretched, disgraceful business has changed that. After seeing that repulsive woman who calls herself the wife of my son Bevis, I actually felt it would be a relief to look at you. I have been an obstinate old fool, and I suppose I have treated you badly. You are like the boy, and the boy is the first object in my life. I am miserable, and I came to you merely because you are like the boy, and he cares for you, and I care for him. Treat me as well as you can, for the boy's sake.'

He said it all in his harsh voice, and almost roughly, but

somehow he seemed so broken down for the time that Mrs Errol was touched to the heart. She got up and moved an armchair a little forward.

'I wish you would sit down,' she said in a soft, pretty, sympathetic way. 'You have been so much troubled that you are very tired, and you need all your strength.'

It was just as new to him to be spoken to and cared for in that gentle, simple way as it was to be contradicted. He was reminded of 'the boy' again, and he actually did as she asked him. Perhaps his disappointment and wretchedness were good discipline for him; if he had not been wretched he might have continued to hate her, but just at present he found her a little soothing. Almost anything would have seemed pleasant by contrast with Lady Fauntleroy; and this one had so sweet a face and voice, and a pretty dignity when she spoke or moved. Very soon, by the quiet magic of these influences, he began to feel less gloomy, and then he talked still more.

'Whatever happens,' he said, 'the boy shall be provided for. He shall be taken care of, now and in the future.'

Before he went away he glanced around the room.

'Do you like the house?' he demanded.

'Very much,' she answered.

'This is a cheerful room,' he said. 'May I come here again and talk this matter over?'

'As often as you wish, my lord,' she replied.

And then he went out to his carriage and drove away, Thomas and Henry almost stricken dumb upon the box at the turn affairs had taken.

CHAPTER 13

Dick to the Rescue

Of course as soon as the story of Lord Fauntleroy and the difficulties of the Earl of Dorincourt were discussed in the English newspapers, they were discussed in the American newspapers. The story was too interesting to be passed over lightly, and it was talked of a great deal. There were so many versions of it that it would have been an edifying thing to buy all the papers and compare them. Mr Hobbs read so much about it that he became quite bewildered. One paper described his young friend Cedric as an infant in arms – another as a young man at Oxford, winning all the honours, and distinguishing himself by writing Greek poems; one said he was engaged to a young lady of great beauty, who was the daughter of a duke; another said he had just been married; the only thing, in fact, which was not said was that he was a little boy between seven and eight, with handsome legs and curly hair. One said he was no relation to the Earl of Dorincourt at all, but was a small impostor who had sold newspapers and slept in the streets of New York before his mother imposed upon the family lawyer, who came to America to look for the Earl's heir. Then came the descriptions of the new Lord Fauntleroy and his mother. Sometimes she was a gipsy, sometimes an actress, sometimes a beautiful

Spaniard; but it was always agreed that the Earl of Dorincourt
was her deadly enemy, and would not acknowledge her son
as his heir if he could help it; and as there seemed to be some
slight flaw in the papers she had produced, it was expected
that there would be a long trial, which would be far more
interesting than anything ever carried into court before. Mr
Hobbs used to read the papers until his head was in a whirl,
and in the evening he and Dick would talk it all over. They
found out what an important personage an Earl of Dorincourt
was, and what a magnificent income he possessed, and how
many estates he owned, and how stately and beautiful was
the Castle in which he lived; and the more they learned the
more excited they became.

'Seems like somethin' orter be done,' said Mr Hobbs.
'Things like them orter be held on to – earls or no earls.'

But there really was nothing they could do but each
write a letter to Cedric, containing assurances of their friendship and sympathy. They wrote those letters as soon as they
could after receiving the news; and after having written them,
they handed them over to each other to be read.

This is what Mr Hobbs read in Dick's letter:

Dere Frend, – i got ure letter an Mr Hobbs got
his an we are sorry u are down on ure luck an we
say hold on as longs u kin and dont let no one git
ahed of u. There is a lot of ole theves wil make al
they kin of u ef u dont kepe ure i skinned. But
this is mosly to say that ive not forgot wot u did
for me an if there aint no better way cum over
here and go in pardners with me. Biznes is fine
and ile see no harm cums to u. Enny big feler
that trise to cum it over u wil hafter setle it fust
with Perfessor Dick Tipton. So no more at present
                                                    Dick

And this was what Dick read in Mr Hobbs's letter:

Dear Sir, – Yrs received and wd say things looks
bad. I believe its a put up job and them thats
done it ought to be looked after sharp. And what
I write to say is two things. I'm going to look this
thing up. Keep quiet and I'll see a lawyer and do
all I can. And if the worst happens and them
earls is too many for us theres a partnership in
the grocery business ready for you when yure old
enough and a home and a friend in

Yrs truly,
Silas Hobbs

'Well,' said Mr Hobbs, 'he's pervided for between us, if
he ain't a earl.'

'So he is,' said Dick. 'I'd ha' stood by him. Blest if I
didn't like that little feller fust rate.'

The very next morning one of Dick's customers was
rather surprised. He was a young lawyer just beginning prac-
tice; as poor as a very young lawyer can possibly be, but a
bright, energetic young fellow, with a sharp wit and a good
temper. He had a shabby office near Dick's stand, and every
morning Dick blacked his boots for him, and quite often they
were not exactly watertight, but he always had a friendly
word or a joke for Dick.

That particular morning, when he put his foot on the
rest, he had an illustrated paper in his hand – an enterprising
paper, with pictures in it of conspicuous people and things.
He had just finished looking it over, and when the last boot
was polished, he handed it to the boy.

'Here's a paper for you, Dick,' he said; 'you can look it
over when you drop in at Delmonico's for your breakfast.
Picture of an English castle in it, and an English earl's
daughter-in-law. Fine young woman too – lots of hair – though

she seems to be raising rather a row. You ought to become familiar with the nobility and gentry, Dick. Begin on the Right Honourable the Earl of Dorincourt and Lady Fauntleroy. Hallo! I say, what's the matter?'

The pictures he spoke of were on the front page, and Dick was staring at one of them with his eyes and mouth open, and his sharp face almost pale with excitement.

'What's to pay, Dick?' said the young man. 'What has paralysed you?'

Dick really did look as if something tremendous had happened. He pointed to the picture, under which was written: 'Mother of Claimant (Lady Fauntleroy).'

It was the picture of a handsome woman, with large eyes and heavy braids of black hair wound around her head.

'Her!' said Dick. 'My, I know her better'n I know you!'

The young man began to laugh.

'Where did you meet her, Dick?' he said. 'At Newport? Or when you ran over to Paris the last time?'

Dick actually forgot to grin. He began to gather his brushes and things together, as if he had something to do which would put an end to his business for the present.

'Never mind,' he said. 'I know her! An' I've struck work for this morning.'

And in less than five minutes from that time he was tearing through the streets on his way to Mr Hobbs and the corner store. Mr Hobbs could scarcely believe the evidence of his senses when he looked across the counter and saw Dick rush in with the paper in his hand. The boy was out of breath with running; so much out of breath, in fact, that he could scarcely speak as he threw the paper down on the counter.

'Hallo!' exclaimed Mr Hobbs. 'Hallo! What you got there?'

'Look at it!' panted Dick. 'Look at that woman in the picture! That's what you look at! *She* ain't no 'ristocrat, *she* ain't!' with withering scorn. 'She's no lord's wife. You may eat me, if it ain't Minna – *Minna!* I'd know her anywheres, an' so'd Ben. Jest ax him.'

Mr Hobbs dropped into his seat.

'I knowed it was a put-up job,' he said. 'I knowed it; and they done it on account o' him bein' a 'Merican!'

'Done it!' cried Dick with disgust. '*She* done it, that's who done it. She was allers up to her tricks; an' I'll tell yer wot come to me, the minnit I saw her pictur'. There was one o' them papers we saw had a letter in it that said somethin' 'bout her boy, an' it said he had a scar on his chin. Put 'em together – he 'n' that there scar! Why that there boy o' hers ain't no more a lord than I am! It's *Ben's* boy – the little chap she hit when she let fly that plate at me.'

Professor Dick Tipton had always been a sharp boy, and earning his living in the streets of a big city had made him still sharper. He had learned to keep his eyes open and his wits about him, and it must be confessed he enjoyed immensely the excitement and impatience of the moment. If little Lord Fauntleroy could only have looked into the store that morning he would certainly have been interested, even if all the discussion and plans had been intended to decide the fate of some other boy than himself.

Mr Hobbs was almost overwhelmed by his sense of responsibility, and Dick was all alive and full of energy. He began to write a letter to Ben, and he cut out the picture and enclosed it to him, and Mr Hobbs wrote a letter to Cedric and one to the Earl. They were in the midst of this letter-writing when a new idea came to Dick.

'Say,' he said, 'the feller that give me the paper, he's a lawyer. Let's ax him what we'd better do. Lawyers knows it all.'

Mr Hobbs was immensely impressed by this suggestion and Dick's business capacity.

'That's so!' he replied. 'This here calls for lawyers.'

And leaving the store in care of a substitute, he struggled

into his coat and marched down town with Dick, and the two presented themselves with their romantic story in Mr Harrison's office, much to that young man's astonishment.

If he had not been a very young lawyer, with a very enterprising mind and a great deal of spare time on his hands, he might not have been so readily interested in what they had to say, for it all certainly sounded very wild and queer; but he chanced to want something to do very much, and he chanced to know Dick, and Dick chanced to say his say in a very sharp, telling sort of way.

'And,' said Mr Hobbs, 'say what your time's worth a' hour and look into this thing thorough, and I'll pay the damage – Silas Hobbs, corner of Blank Street, Vegetables and Fancy Groceries.'

'Well,' said Mr Harrison, 'it will be a big thing if it turns out all right, and it will be almost as big a thing for me as for Lord Fauntleroy; and at any rate, no harm can be done by investigating. It appears there has been some dubiousness about the child. The woman contradicted herself in some of her statements about his age, and aroused suspicion. The first persons to be written to are Dick's brother and the Earl of Dorincourt's family lawyer.'

And actually before the sun went down, two letters had been written and sent in two different directions – one speeding out of New York harbour on a mail steamer on its way to England, and the other on a train carrying letters and passengers bound for California. And the first was addressed to 'T. Havisham Esq.', and the second to 'Benjamin Tipton'.

And after the store was closed that evening, Mr Hobbs and Dick sat in the back room and talked together until midnight.

CHAPTER 14

The Exposure

It is astonishing how short a time it takes for very wonderful things to happen. It had taken only a few minutes, apparently, to change all the fortunes of the little boy dangling his red legs from the high stool in Mr Hobbs's store, and to transform him from a small boy, living the simplest life in a quiet street, into an English nobleman, the heir to an earldom and magnificent wealth. It had taken only a few minutes, apparently, to change him from an English nobleman into a penniless little impostor, with no right to any of the splendours he had been enjoying. And surprising as it may appear, it did not take nearly so long a time as one might have expected to alter the face of everything again and to give back to him all that he had been in danger of losing.

It took the less time because, after all, the woman who had called herself Lady Fauntleroy was not nearly so clever as she was wicked; and when she had been closely pressed by Mr Havisham's questions about her marriage and her boy, she had made one or two blunders which had caused suspicion to be awakened; and then she had lost her presence of mind and her temper, and in her excitement and anger had betrayed herself still further. All the mistakes she made were about her child. There seemed no doubt that she had been married to

Bevis, Lord Fauntleroy, and had quarrelled with him and had been paid to keep away from him; but Mr Havisham found out that her story of the boy's being born in a certain part of London was false; and just when they all were in the midst of the commotion caused by this discovery, there came the letter from the young lawyer in New York, and Mr Hobbs's letters also.

What an evening it was when those letters arrived, and when Mr Havisham and the Earl sat and talked their plans over in the library!

'After my first three meetings with her,' said Mr Havisham, 'I began to suspect her strongly. It appeared to me that the child was older than she said he was, and she made a slip in speaking of the date of his birth and then tried to patch the matter up. The story these letters bring fits in with several of my suspicions. Our best plan will be to cable at once for these two Tiptons, say nothing about them to her, and suddenly confront her with them when she is not expecting it. She is only a very clumsy plotter after all. My opinion is that she will be frightened out of her wits, and will betray herself on the spot.'

And that was what actually happened. She was told nothing, and Mr Havisham kept her from suspecting anything by continuing to have interviews with her, in which he assured her he was investigating her statements; and she really began to feel so secure that her spirits rose immensely and she began to be as insolent as might have been expected.

But one fine morning, as she sat in her sitting-room at the inn called the Dorincourt Arms, making some very fine plans for herself, Mr Havisham was announced; and when he entered he was followed by no less than three persons – one was a sharp-faced boy and one was a big young man, and the third was the Earl of Dorincourt.

She sprang to her feet and actually uttered a cry of terror. It broke from her before she had time to check it. She had thought of these newcomers as being thousands of miles away, when she had ever thought of them at all, which she had scarcely done for years. She had never expected to see them again. It must be confessed that Dick grinned a little when he saw her.

'Hallo, Minna!' he said.

The big young man – who was Ben – stood still a minute and looked at her.

'Do you know her?' Mr Havisham asked, glancing from one to the other.

'Yes,' said Ben. 'I know her and she knows me.' And he turned his back on her and went and stood looking out of the window as if the sight of her was hateful to him, as indeed it was. Then the woman, seeing herself so baffled and exposed, lost all control over herself and flew into such a rage as Ben and Dick had often seen her in before. Dick grinned a trifle more as he watched her and heard the names she called them all and the violent threats she made, but Ben did not turn to look at her.

'I can swear to her in any court,' he said to Mr Havisham, 'and I can bring a dozen others who will. Her father is a respectable sort of man, though he's low down in the world. Her mother was just like herself. She's dead, but he's alive, and he's honest enough to be ashamed of her. He'll tell you who she is, and whether she married me or not.'

Then he clenched his hand suddenly and turned on her.

'Where's the child?' he demanded. 'He's going with me! He is done with you and so am I!'

And just as he finished saying the words, the door leading into the bedroom opened a little, and the boy, probably attracted by the sound of the loud voices, looked in. He was not a handsome boy, but he had rather a nice face, and he was quite like Ben, his father, as anyone could see, and there was the three-cornered scar on his chin.

Ben walked up to him and took his hand, and his own was trembling.

'Yes,' he said, 'I could swear to him too. Tom,' he said to the little fellow, 'I'm your father, I've come to take you away. Where's your hat?'

The boy pointed to where it lay on a chair. It evidently rather pleased him to hear he was going away. He had been so accustomed to queer experiences that it did not surprise him to be told by a stranger that he was his father. He objected so much to the woman who had come a few months before to the place where he had lived since his babyhood, and who had suddenly announced that she was his mother, that he was quite ready for a change. Ben took up the hat and marched to the door.

'If you want me again,' he said to Mr Havisham, 'you know where to find me.'

He walked out of the room, holding the child's hand and not looking at the woman once. She was fairly raving with fury, and the Earl was calmly gazing at her through his eye-glasses, which he had quietly placed upon his aristocratic eagle nose.

'Come, come, my young woman,' said Mr Havisham. 'This won't do at all. If you don't want to be locked up, you really must behave yourself.'

And there was something so very business-like in his tones that, probably feeling that the safest thing she could do would be to get out of the way, she gave him one savage look and dashed past him into the next room and slammed the door.

'We shall have no more trouble with her,' said Mr Havisham.

And he was right; for that very night she left the Dorincourt Arms and took the train to London, and was seen no more.

When the Earl left the room after the interview he went at once to his carriage.

'To Court Lodge,' he said to Thomas.

'To Court Lodge,' said Thomas to the coachman as he mounted the box, 'an' you may depend on it, things is taking a uniggspected turn.'

When the carriage stopped at Court Lodge, Cedric was in the drawing-room with his mother.

The Earl came in without being announced. He looked an inch or so taller and a great many years younger. His deep eyes flashed.

'Where,' he said, 'is Lord Fauntleroy?'

Mrs Errol came forward, a flush rising to her cheek. 'Is it Lord Fauntleroy?' she asked. 'Is it indeed?' The Earl put out his hand and grasped hers.

'Yes,' he answered, 'it is.'

Then he put his other hand on Cedric's shoulder.

'Fauntleroy,' he said in his unceremonious, authoritative way, 'ask your mother when she will come to us at the Castle.'

Fauntleroy flung his arms around his mother's neck.

'To live with us!' he cried. 'To live with us always!'

The Earl looked at Mrs Errol, and Mrs Errol looked at the Earl. His lordship was entirely in earnest. He had made up his mind to waste no time in arranging this matter. He had begun to think it would suit him to make friends with his heir's mother.

'Are you quite sure you want me?' said Mrs Errol with her soft, pretty smile.

'Quite sure,' he said bluntly. 'We have always wanted you, but we were not exactly aware of it. We hope you will come.'

CHAPTER 15

His Eighth Birthday

Ben took his boy and went back to his cattle ranch in California, and he returned under very comfortable circumstances. Just before his going Mr Havisham had an interview with him in which the lawyer told him that the Earl of Dorincourt wished to do something for the boy who might have turned out to be Lord Fauntleroy, and so he had decided that it would be a good plan to invest in a cattle ranch of his own, and put Ben in charge of it on terms which would make it pay him very well, and which would lay a foundation for his son's future. And so when Ben went away he went as the prospective master of a ranch which would be almost as good as his own, and might easily become his own in time, as indeed it did in the course of a few years; and Tom, the boy, grew up on it into a fine young man and was devotedly fond of his father; and they were so successful and happy that Ben used to say that Tom made up to him for all the troubles he had ever had.

But Dick and Mr Hobbs – who had actually come over with the others to see that things were properly looked after – did not return for some time. It had been decided at the outset that the Earl would provide for Dick, and would see that he received a solid education; and Mr Hobbs had decided that as he himself had left a reliable substitute in charge of his store, he could afford to wait to see the festivities which were to celebrate Lord Fauntleroy's eighth birthday. All the tenantry were invited, and there were to be feasting and dancing and games in the park, and bonfires and fireworks in the evening.

'Just like the Fourth of July!' said Lord Fauntleroy. 'It seems a pity my birthday wasn't on the Fourth, doesn't it? For then we could keep them both together.'

It must be confessed that at first the Earl and Mr Hobbs were not as intimate as it might have been hoped they would become, in the interests of the British aristocracy. The fact was that the Earl had known very few grocery-men and Mr Hobbs had not had many close acquaintances who were earls; and so in their rare interviews conversation did not flourish. It must also be owned that Mr Hobbs had been rather overwhelmed by the splendours Fauntleroy felt it his duty to show him.

The entrance gate and the stone lions and the avenue impressed Mr Hobbs somewhat at the beginning, and when he saw the Castle and the flower gardens and the hothouses and the terraces and the peacocks and the dungeon and the armour and the great staircase and the stables and the liveried servants, he really was quite bewildered. But it was the picture gallery which seemed to be the finishing stroke.

'Somethin' in the manner of a museum?' he said to Fauntleroy, when he was led into the great beautiful room.

'N-no –!' said Fauntleroy rather doubtfully. 'I don't *think* it's a museum. My grandfather says these are my ancestors.'

'Your aunt's sisters!' ejaculated Mr Hobbs. '*All* of 'em. Your great-uncle, he *must* have had a family! Did he raise 'em all?'

And he sank into a seat and looked around him with an agitated countenance, until with the greatest difficulty Lord

Fauntleroy managed to explain that the walls were not lined entirely with the portraits of the progeny of his great-uncle.

He found it necessary, in fact, to call in the assistance of Mrs Mellon, who knew all about the pictures, and could tell who painted them and when, and who added romantic stories of the lords and ladies who were the originals. When Mr Hobbs once understood, and had heard some of these stories, he was very much fascinated and liked the picture gallery almost better than anything else; and he would often walk over from the village where he stayed at the Dorincourt Arms, and would spend half an hour or so wandering about the gallery, staring at the painted ladies and gentlemen who also stared at him, and shaking his head nearly all the time.

'And they was all earls,' he would say, 'or pretty nigh it! An' *he's* goin' to be one of 'em, an' own it all!'

Privately he was not nearly so much disgusted with earls and their mode of life as he had expected to be, and it is to be doubted whether his strictly Republican principles were not shaken a little by a closer acquaintance with castles and ancestors and all the rest of it. At any rate, one day he uttered a very remarkable and unexpected sentiment.

'I wouldn't have minded bein' one of 'em myself!' he said – which was really a great concession.

What a grand day it was when little Lord Fauntleroy's birthday arrived, and how his young lordship enjoyed it! How beautiful the park looked, filled with the thronging people dressed in their gayest and best, and with the flags flying from the tents and the top of the Castle! Nobody had stayed away who could possibly come, because everybody was really glad that little Lord Fauntleroy was to be little Lord Fauntleroy still, and some day was to be the master of everything. Everyone wanted to have a look at him, and at his pretty, kind mother, who had made so many friends. And positively everyone liked the Earl rather better, and felt more amiably towards him because the little boy loved and trusted him so, and because, also, he had now made friends with and behaved respectfully to his heir's mother. It was said that he was even beginning to be fond of her too, and that between his young lordship and his young lordship's mother, the Earl might be changed in time into quite a well-behaved old nobleman, and everybody might be happier and better off.

What scores and scores of people there were under the trees, and in the tents, and on the lawns! Farmers and farmers' wives in their Sunday suits and bonnets and shawls; girls and their sweethearts; children frolicking and chasing about; and old dames in red cloaks gossiping together. At the Castle there were ladies and gentlemen who had come to see the fun, and to congratulate the Earl, and to meet Mrs Errol. Lady Lorridaile and Sir Harry were there, and Sir Thomas Asshe and his daughters, and Mr Havisham of course; and then beautiful Miss Vivian Herbert, with the loveliest white gown and lace parasol, and a circle of gentlemen to take care of her – though she evidently liked Fauntleroy better than all of them put together. And when he saw her and ran to her and put his arms around her neck, she put her arms around him too, and kissed him as warmly as if he had been her own favourite little brother, and she said:

'Dear little Lord Fauntleroy! Dear little boy! I am so glad! I am so glad!'

And afterwards she walked about the grounds with him, and let him show her everything. And when he took her to where Mr Hobbs and Dick were, and said to her, 'This is my old, old friend Mr Hobbs, Miss Herbert, and this is my other old friend Dick. I told them how pretty you were, and I told them they should see you if you came to my birthday' – she shook hands with them both, and stood and talked to them in her prettiest way, asking them about America and their voyage and their life since they had been in England; while Fauntleroy stood by, looking up at her with adoring eyes, and his cheeks quite flushed with delight because he saw that Mr Hobbs and Dick liked her so much.

'Well,' said Dick solemnly afterwards, 'she's the daisiest gal I ever saw! She's – well, she's just daisy, that's what she is, 'n' no mistake!'

Everybody looked after her as she passed, and everyone looked after little Lord Fauntleroy. And the sun shone and the flags fluttered and the games were played and the dances danced, and as the gaieties went on and the joyous afternoon passed, his little lordship was simply radiantly happy.

The whole world seemed beautiful to him.

There was someone else who was happy too – an old man, who, though he had been rich and noble all his life, had not often been very honestly happy. Perhaps indeed I shall tell you that I think it was because he was rather better than he had been that he was rather happier. He had not indeed suddenly become as good as Fauntleroy thought him; but at least he had begun to love something, and he had several times found a sort of pleasure in doing the kind things which the innocent, kind little heart of a child had suggested – and that was a beginning. And every day he had been more pleased with his son's wife. It was true, as the people said, that he was beginning to like her too. He liked to hear her sweet voice and to see her sweet face; and as he sat in his armchair, he used to watch her and listen as she talked to her boy; and he heard loving, gentle words which were new to him, and he began to see why the little fellow who had lived in a New York side street, and known grocery-men and made friends with boot-blacks, was still so well bred and manly a little fellow that he made no one ashamed of him, even when fortune changed him into the heir to an English earldom, living in an English castle.

It was really a very simple thing after all – it was only that he had lived near a kind and gentle heart, and had been taught to think kind thoughts always and to care for others.

It is a very little thing, perhaps, but it is the best thing of all. He knew nothing of earls and castles; he was quite ignorant of all grand and splendid things; but he was always lovable because he was simple and loving. To be so is like being born a king.

As the old Earl of Dorincourt looked at him that day, moving about the park among the people, talking to those he knew and making his ready little bow when anyone greeted him, entertaining his friends Dick and Mr Hobbs, or standing near his mother or Miss Herbert listening to their conversation, the old nobleman was very well satisfied with him. And he had never been better satisfied than he was when they went down to the biggest tent, where the more important tenants of the Dorincourt estate were sitting down to the grand collation of the day.

They were drinking toasts; and, after they had drunk the health of the Earl with much more enthusiasm than his name had ever been greeted with before, they proposed the health of 'Little Lord Fauntleroy'. And if there had ever been any doubt at all as to whether his lordship was popular or not, it would have been settled that instant. Such a clamour of voices and such a rattle of glasses and applause! They had begun to like him so much, those warm-hearted people, that they forgot to feel any restraint before the ladies and gentlemen from the Castle, who had come to see them. They made quite a decent uproar, and one or two motherly women looked tenderly at the little fellow where he stood, with his mother on one side and the Earl on the other, and grew quite moist about the eyes, and said to one another:

'God bless him, the pretty little dear!'

Little Lord Fauntleroy was delighted. He stood and smiled, and made bows, and flushed rosy red with pleasure up to the roots of his bright hair.

'Is it because they like me, Dearest?' he said to his mother. 'Is it, Dearest? I'm so glad!'

And then the Earl put his hand on the child's shoulder and said to him:

'Fauntleroy, say to them that you thank them for their kindness.'

Fauntleroy gave a glance up at him and then at his mother.

'Must I?' he asked just a trifle shyly, and she smiled, and so did Miss Herbert, and they both nodded. And so he made a little step forward, and everybody looked at him – such a beautiful, innocent little fellow he was, too, with his brave, trustful face! – and he spoke as loudly as he could, his childish voice ringing out quite clear and strong.

'I'm ever so much obliged to you!' he said, 'and – I hope you'll enjoy my birthday – because I've enjoyed it so much – and – I'm very glad I'm going to be an earl – I didn't think at first I should like it, but now I do – and I love this place so, and I think it is beautiful – and – and – and when I am an earl, I am going to try to be as good as my grandfather.'

And amid the shouts and clamour of applause, he stepped back with a little sigh of relief, and put his hand into the Earl's and stood close to him, smiling and leaning against his side.

And that would be the very end of my story; but I must add one curious piece of information, which is that Mr Hobbs became so fascinated with high life and was so reluctant to leave his young friend that he actually sold his corner store in New York, and settled in the English village of Erlesboro, where he opened a shop which was patronized by the Castle and consequently was a great success. And though he and the Earl never became very intimate, if you will believe me, that man Hobbs became in time more aristocratic than his lordship himself, and he read the Court news every morning, and followed all the doings of the House of Lords! And about ten years after, when Dick who had finished his education and was going to visit his brother in California, asked the good grocer if he did not wish to return to America, he shook his head seriously.

'Not to live there,' he said. 'Not to live there; I want to be near *him*, an' sort o' look after him. It's a good enough country for them that's young an' stirrin' – but there's faults in it. There's not an aunt-sister among 'em – nor a earl!'

CLASSIC LITERATURE: WORDS AND PHRASES
adapted from the *Collins English Dictionary*

Accoucheur NOUN a male midwife or doctor ❑ *I think my sister must have had some general idea that I was a young offender whom an Accoucheur Policemen had taken up (on my birthday) and delivered over to her* (*Great Expectations* by Charles Dickens)

addled ADJ confused and unable to think properly ❑ *But she counted and counted till she got that addled* (*The Adventures of Huckleberry Finn* by Mark Twain)

admiration NOUN amazement or wonder ❑ *lifting up his hands and eyes by way of admiration* (*Gulliver's Travels* by Jonathan Swift)

afeard ADJ afeard means afraid ❑ *shake it – and don't be afeard* (*The Adventures of Huckleberry Finn* by Mark Twain)

affected VERB affected means followed ❑ *Hadst thou affected sweet divinity* (*Doctor Faustus 5.2* by Christopher Marlowe)

aground ADV when a boat runs aground, it touches the ground in a shallow part of the water and gets stuck ❑ *what kep' you? – boat yet aground?* (*The Adventures of Huckleberry Finn* by Mark Twain)

ague NOUN a fever in which the patient has alternate hot and cold shivering fits ❑ *his exposure to the wet and cold had brought on fever and ague* (*Oliver Twist* by Charles Dickens)

alchemy ADJ false or worthless ❑ *all wealth alchemy* (*The Sun Rising* by John Donne)

all alike PHRASE the same all the time ❑ *Love, all alike* (*The Sun Rising* by John Donne)

alow and aloft PHRASE alow means in the lower part or bottom, and aloft means on the top, so alow and aloft means on the top and in the bottom or throughout ❑ *Someone's turned the chest out alow and aloft* (*Treasure Island* by Robert Louis Stevenson)

ambuscade NOUN ambuscade is not a proper word. Tom means an ambush, which is when a group of people attack their enemies, after hiding and waiting for them ❑ *and so we would lie in ambuscade, as he called it* (*The Adventures of Huckleberry Finn* by Mark Twain)

amiable ADJ likeable or pleasant ❑ *Such amiable qualities must speak for themselves* (*Pride and Prejudice* by Jane Austen)

amulet NOUN an amulet is a charm thought to drive away evil spirits. ❑ *uttered phrases at once occult and familiar, like the amulet worn on the heart* (*Silas Marner* by George Eliot)

amusement NOUN here amusement means a strange and disturbing puzzle ❑ *this was an amusement the other way* (*Robinson Crusoe* by Daniel Defoe)

ancient NOUN an ancient was the flag displayed on a ship to show which country it belongs to. It is also called the ensign ❑ *her ancient and pendants out* (*Robinson Crusoe* by Daniel Defoe)

antic ADJ here antic means horrible or grotesque ❑ *armed and dressed after a very antic manner* (*Gulliver's Travels* by Jonathan Swift)

antics NOUN antics is an old word meaning clowns, or people who do silly things to make other people laugh ❑ *And point like antics at his triple crown* (*Doctor Faustus 3.2* by Christopher Marlowe)

appanage NOUN an appanage is a living allowance ❑ *As if loveliness were not the special prerogative of woman*

– her legitimate appanage and heritage! (*Jane Eyre* by Charlotte Brontë)

appended VERB appended means attached or added to ❑ *and these words appended* (*Treasure Island* by Robert Louis Stevenson)

approver NOUN an approver is someone who gives evidence against someone he used to work with ❑ *Mr. Noah Claypole: receiving a free pardon from the Crown in consequence of being admitted approver against Fagin* (*Oliver Twist* by Charles Dickens)

areas NOUN the areas is the space, below street level, in front of the basement of a house ❑ *The Dodger had a vicious propensity, too, of pulling the caps from the heads of small boys and tossing them down areas* (*Oliver Twist* by Charles Dickens)

argument NOUN theme or important idea or subject which runs through a piece of writing ❑ *Thrice needful to the argument which now* (*The Prelude* by William Wordsworth).

artificially ADJ artfully or cleverly ❑ *and he with a sharp flint sharpened very artificially* (*Gulliver's Travels* by Jonathan Swift)

artist NOUN here artist means a skilled workman ❑ *This man was a most ingenious artist* (*Gulliver's Travels* by Jonathan Swift)

assizes NOUN assizes were regular court sessions which a visiting judge was in charge of ❑ *you shall hang at the next assizes* (*Treasure Island* by Robert Louis Stevenson)

attraction NOUN gravitation, or Newton's theory of gravitation ❑ *he predicted the same fate to attraction* (*Gulliver's Travels* by Jonathan Swift)

aver VERB to aver is to claim something strongly ❑ *for Jem Rodney, the mole catcher, averred that one evening as he was*

returning homeward (*Silas Marner* by George Eliot)

baby NOUN here baby means doll, which is a child's toy that looks like a small person ❑ *and skilful dressing her baby* (*Gulliver's Travels* by Jonathan Swift)

bagatelle NOUN bagatelle is a game rather like billiards and pool ❑ *Breakfast had been ordered at a pleasant little tavern, a mile or so away upon the rising ground beyond the green; and there was a bagatelle board in the room, in case we should desire to unbend our minds after the solemnity.* (*Great Expectations* by Charles Dickens)

bah EXCLAM Bah is an exclamation of frustration or anger ❑ *"Bah," said Scrooge.* (*A Christmas Carol* by Charles Dickens)

bairn NOUN a northern word for child ❑ *Who has taught you those fine words, my bairn?* (*Wuthering Heights* by Emily Brontë)

bait VERB to bait means to stop on a journey to take refreshment ❑ *So, when they stopped to bait the horse, and ate and drank and enjoyed themselves, I could touch nothing that they touched, but kept my fast unbroken.* (*David Copperfield* by Charles Dickens)

balustrade NOUN a balustrade is a row of vertical columns that form railings ❑ *but I mean to say you might have got a hearse up that staircase, and taken it broadwise, with the splinter-bar towards the wall, and the door towards the balustrades: and done it easy* (*A Christmas Carol* by Charles Dickens)

bandbox NOUN a large lightweight box for carrying bonnets or hats ❑ *I am glad I bought my bonnet, if it is only for the fun of having another bandbox* (*Pride and Prejudice* by Jane Austen)

barren NOUN a barren here is a stretch or expanse of barren land ❑ *a line of upright stones, continued the* *length of the barren* (*Wuthering Heights* by Emily Brontë)

basin NOUN a basin was a cup without a handle ❑ *who is drinking his tea out of a basin* (*Wuthering Heights* by Emily Brontë)

battalia NOUN the order of battle ❑ *till I saw part of his army in battalia* (*Gulliver's Travels* by Jonathan Swift)

battery NOUN a Battery is a fort or a place where guns are positioned ❑ *You bring the lot to me, at that old Battery over yonder* (*Great Expectations* by Charles Dickens)

battledore and shuttlecock NOUN The game battledore and shuttlecock was an early version of the game now known as badminton. The aim of the early game was simply to keep the shuttlecock from hitting the ground. ❑ *Battledore and shuttlecock's a wery good game vhen you an't the shuttlecock and two lawyers the battledores, in which case it gets too excitin' to be pleasant* (*Pickwick Papers* by Charles Dickens)

beadle NOUN a beadle was a local official who had power over the poor ❑ *But these impertinences were speedily checked by the evidence of the surgeon, and the testimony of the beadle* (*Oliver Twist* by Charles Dickens)

bearings NOUN the bearings of a place are the measurements or directions that are used to find or locate it ❑ *the bearings of the island* (*Treasure Island* by Robert Louis Stevenson)

beaufet NOUN a beaufet was a sideboard ❑ *and sweet-cake from the beaufet* (*Emma* by Jane Austen)

beck NOUN a beck is a small stream ❑ *a beck which follows the bend of the glen* (*Wuthering Heights* by Emily Brontë)

bedight VERB decorated ❑ *and bedight with Christmas holly stuck into the top.* (*A Christmas Carol* by Charles Dickens)

Bedlam NOUN Bedlam was a lunatic asylum in London which had statues carved by Caius Gabriel Cibber at its entrance ❑ *Bedlam, and those carved maniacs at the gates* (*The Prelude* by William Wordsworth)

beeves NOUN oxen or castrated bulls which are animals used for pulling vehicles or carrying things ❑ *to deliver in every morning six beeves* (*Gulliver's Travels* by Jonathan Swift)

begot VERB created or caused ❑ *Begot in thee* (*On His Mistress* by John Donne)

behoof NOUN behoof means benefit ❑ *"Yes, young man," said he, releasing the handle of the article in question, retiring a step or two from my table, and speaking for the behoof of the landlord and waiter at the door* (*Great Expectations* by Charles Dickens)

berth NOUN a berth is a bed on a boat ❑ *this is the berth for me* (*Treasure Island* by Robert Louis Stevenson)

bevers NOUN a bever was a snack, or small portion of food, eaten between main meals ❑ *that buys me thirty meals a day and ten bevers* (*Doctor Faustus 2.1* by Christopher Marlowe)

bilge water NOUN the bilge is the widest part of a ship's bottom, and the bilge water is the dirty water that collects there ❑ *no gush of bilge-water had turned it to fetid puddle* (*Jane Eyre* by Charlotte Brontë)

bills NOUN bills is an old term meaning prescription. A prescription is the piece of paper on which your doctor writes an order for medicine and which you give to a chemist to get the medicine ❑ *Are not thy bills hung up as monuments* (*Doctor Faustus 1.1* by Christopher Marlowe)

black cap NOUN a judge wore a black cap when he was about to sentence a prisoner to death ❑ *The judge* assumed the black cap, and the prisoner still stood with the same air and gesture. (*Oliver Twist* by Charles Dickens)

black gentleman NOUN this was another word for the devil ❏ *for she is as impatient as the black gentleman* (*Emma* by Jane Austen)

boot-jack NOUN a wooden device to help take boots off ❏ *The speaker appeared to throw a boot-jack, or some such article, at the person he addressed* (*Oliver Twist* by Charles Dickens)

booty NOUN booty means treasure or prizes ❏ *would be inclined to give up their booty in payment of the dead man's debts* (*Treasure Island* by Robert Louis Stevenson)

Bow Street runner PHRASE Bow Street runners were the first British police force, set up by the author Henry Fielding in the eighteenth century ❏ *as would have convinced a judge or a Bow Street runner* (*Treasure Island* by Robert Louis Stevenson)

brawn NOUN brawn is a dish of meat which is set in jelly ❏ *Heaped up upon the floor, to form a kind of throne, were turkeys, geese, game, poultry, brawn, great joints of meat, sucking-pigs* (*A Christmas Carol* by Charles Dickens)

bray VERB when a donkey brays, it makes a loud, harsh sound ❏ *and she doesn't bray like a jackass* (*The Adventures of Huckleberry Finn* by Mark Twain)

break VERB in order to train a horse you first have to break it ❏*"If a high-mettled creature like this," said he, "can't be broken by fair means, she will never be good for anything"* (*Black Beauty* by Anna Sewell)

bullyragging VERB bullyragging is an old word which means bullying. To bullyrag someone is to threaten or force someone to do something they don't want to do ❏ *and a lot of loafers bullyragging him for sport* (*The Adventures of Huckleberry Finn* by Mark Twain)

but PREP except for (this) ❏ *but this, all pleasures fancies be* (*The Good-Morrow* by John Donne)

by hand PHRASE by hand was a common expression of the time meaning that baby had been fed either using a spoon or a bottle rather than by breast-feeding ❏ *My sister, Mrs. Joe Gargery, was more than twenty years older than I, and had established a great reputation with herself . . . because she had bought me up 'by hand'* (*Great Expectations* by Charles Dickens)

bye-spots NOUN bye-spots are lonely places ❏ *and bye-spots of tales rich with indigenous produce* (*The Prelude* by William Wordsworth)

calico NOUN calico is plain white fabric made from cotton ❏ *There was two old dirty calico dresses* (*The Adventures of Huckleberry Finn* by Mark Twain)

camp-fever NOUN camp-fever was another word for the disease typhus ❏ *during a severe camp-fever* (*Emma* by Jane Austen)

cant NOUN cant is insincere or empty talk ❏ *"Man," said the Ghost, "if man you be in heart, not adamant, forbear that wicked cant until you have discovered What the surplus is, and Where it is." (A Christmas Carol* by Charles Dickens)

canty ADJ canty means lively, full of life ❏ *My mother lived til eighty, a canty dame to the last* (*Wuthering Heights* by Emily Brontë)

canvas VERB to canvas is to discuss ❏ *We think so very differently on this point Mr Knightley, that there can be no use in canvassing it* (*Emma* by Jane Austen)

capital ADJ capital means excellent or extremely good ❏ *for it's capital, so shady, light, and big* (*Little Women* by Louisa May Alcott)

capstan NOUN a capstan is a device used on a ship to lift sails and anchors ❏ *capstans going, ships going out to sea, and unintelligible sea creatures* roaring curses over the bulwarks at respondent lightermen (*Great Expectations* by Charles Dickens)

case-bottle NOUN a square bottle designed to fit with others into a case ❑ *The spirit being set before him in a huge case-bottle, which had originally come out of some ship's locker* (*The Old Curiosity Shop* by Charles Dickens)

casement NOUN casement is a word meaning window. The teacher in Nicholas Nickleby misspells window showing what a bad teacher he is ❑ *W-i-n, win, d-e-r, der, winder, a casement.'* (*Nicholas Nickleby* by Charles Dickens)

cataleptic ADJ a cataleptic fit is one in which the victim goes into a trancelike state and remains still for a long time ❑ *It was at this point in their history that Silas's cataleptic fit occurred during the prayer-meeting* (*Silas Marner* by George Eliot)

cauldron NOUN a cauldron is a large cooking pot made of metal ❑ *stirring a large cauldron which seemed to be full of soup* (*Alice's Adventures in Wonderland* by Lewis Carroll)

cephalic ADJ cephalic means to do with the head ❑ *with ink composed of a cephalic tincture* (*Gulliver's Travels* by Jonathan Swift)

chaise and four NOUN a closed four-wheel carriage pulled by four horses ❑ *he came down on Monday in a chaise and four to see the place* (*Pride and Prejudice* by Jane Austen)

chamberlain NOUN the main servant in a household ❑ *In those times a bed was always to be got there at any hour of the night, and the chamberlain, letting me in at his ready wicket, lighted the candle next in order on his shelf* (*Great Expectations* by Charles Dickens)

characters NOUN distinguishing marks ❑ *Impressed upon all forms the characters* (*The Prelude* by William Wordsworth)

chary ADJ cautious ❑ *I should have been chary of discussing my guardian too freely even with her* (*Great Expectations* by Charles Dickens)

cherishes VERB here cherishes means cheers or brightens ❑ *some philosophic song of Truth that cherishes our daily life* (*The Prelude* by William Wordsworth)

chickens' meat PHRASE chickens' meat is an old term which means chickens' feed or food ❑ *I had shook a bag of chickens' meat out in that place* (*Robinson Crusoe* by Daniel Defoe)

chimeras NOUN a chimera is an unrealistic idea or a wish which is unlikely to be fulfilled ❑ *with many other wild impossible chimeras* (*Gulliver's Travels* by Jonathan Swift)

chines NOUN chine is a cut of meat that includes part or all of the backbone of the animal ❑ *and they found hams and chines uncut* (*Silas Marner* by George Eliot)

chits NOUN chits is a slang word which means girls ❑ *I hate affected, niminy-piminy chits!* (*Little Women* by Louisa May Alcott)

chopped VERB chopped means come suddenly or accidentally ❑ *if I had chopped upon them* (*Robinson Crusoe* by Daniel Defoe)

chute NOUN a narrow channel ❑ *One morning about day-break, I found a canoe and crossed over a chute to the main shore* (*The Adventures of Huckleberry Finn* by Mark Twain)

circumspection NOUN careful observation of events and circumstances; caution ❑ *I honour your circumspection* (*Pride and Prejudice* by Jane Austen)

clambered VERB clambered means to climb somewhere with difficulty, usually using your hands and your feet ❑ *he clambered up and down stairs* (*Treasure Island* by Robert Louis Stevenson)

clime NOUN climate ❏ *no season knows nor clime* (*The Sun Rising* by John Donne)

clinched VERB clenched ❏ *the tops whereof I could but just reach with my fist clinched* (*Gulliver's Travels* by Jonathan Swift)

close chair NOUN a close chair is a sedan chair, which is an covered chair which has room for one person. The sedan chair is carried on two poles by two men, one in front and one behind ❏ *persuaded even the Empress herself to let me hold her in her close chair* (*Gulliver's Travels* by Jonathan Swift)

clown NOUN clown here means peasant or person who lives off the land ❏ *In ancient days by emperor and clown* (*Ode on a Nightingale* by John Keats)

coalheaver NOUN a coalheaver loaded coal onto ships using a spade ❏ *Good, strong, wholesome medicine, as was given with great success to two Irish labourers and a coalheaver* (*Oliver Twist* by Charles Dickens)

coal-whippers NOUN men who worked at docks using machines to load coal onto ships ❏ *here, were colliers by the score and score, with the coal-whippers plunging off stages on deck* (*Great Expectations* by Charles Dickens)

cobweb NOUN a cobweb is the net which a spider makes for catching insects ❏ *the walls and ceilings were all hung round with cobwebs* (*Gulliver's Travels* by Jonathan Swift)

coddling VERB coddling means to treat someone too kindly or protect them too much ❏ *and I've been coddling the fellow as if I'd been his grandmother* (*Little Women* by Louisa May Alcott)

coil NOUN coil means noise or fuss or disturbance ❏ *What a coil is there?* (*Doctor Faustus 4.7* by Christopher Marlowe)

collared VERB to collar something is a slang term which means to capture.

In this sentence, it means he stole it [the money] ❏ *he collared it* (*The Adventures of Huckleberry Finn* by Mark Twain)

colling VERB colling is an old word which means to embrace and kiss ❏ *and no clasping and colling at all* (*Tess of the D'Urbervilles* by Thomas Hardy)

colloquies NOUN colloquy is a formal conversation or dialogue ❏ *Such colloquies have occupied many a pair of pale-faced weavers* (*Silas Marner* by George Eliot)

comfit NOUN sugar-covered pieces of fruit or nut eaten as sweets ❏ *and pulled out a box of comfits* (*Alice's Adventures in Wonderland* by Lewis Carroll)

coming out VERB when a girl came out in society it meant she was of marriageable age. In order to 'come out' girls were expecting to attend balls and other parties during a season ❏ *The younger girls formed hopes of coming out a year or two sooner than they might otherwise have done* (*Pride and Prejudice* by Jane Austen)

commit VERB commit means arrest or stop ❏ *Commit the rascals* (*Doctor Faustus 4.7* by Christopher Marlowe)

commodious ADJ commodious means convenient ❏ *the most commodious and effectual ways* (*Gulliver's Travels* by Jonathan Swift)

commons NOUN commons is an old term meaning food shared with others ❏ *his pauper assistants ranged themselves behind him; the gruel was served out; and a long grace was said over the short commons.* (*Oliver Twist* by Charles Dickens)

complacency NOUN here complacency means a desire to please others. To-day complacency means feeling pleased with oneself without good reason. ❏ *Twas thy power that raised the first complacency in me* (*The Prelude* by William Wordsworth)

complaisance NOUN complaisance was eagerness to please ❏ *we cannot wonder at his complaisance* (*Pride and Prejudice* by Jane Austen)

complaisant ADJ complaisant means polite ❏ *extremely cheerful and complaisant to their guest* (*Gulliver's Travels* by Jonathan Swift)

conning VERB conning means learning by heart ❏ *Or conning more* (*The Prelude* by William Wordsworth)

consequent NOUN consequence ❏ *as avarice is the necessary consequent of old age* (*Gulliver's Travels* by Jonathan Swift)

consorts NOUN concerts ❏ *The King, who delighted in music, had frequent consorts at Court* (*Gulliver's Travels* by Jonathan Swift)

conversible ADJ conversible meant easy to talk to, companionable ❏ *He can be a conversible companion* (*Pride and Prejudice* by Jane Austen)

copper NOUN a copper is a large pot that can be heated directly over a fire ❏ *He gazed in stupefied astonishment on the small rebel for some seconds, and then clung for support to the copper* (*Oliver Twist* by Charles Dickens)

copper-stick NOUN a copper-stick is the long piece of wood used to stir washing in the copper (or boiler) which was usually the biggest cooking pot in the house ❏ *It was Christmas Eve, and I had to stir the pudding for next day, with a copper-stick, from seven to eight by the Dutch clock* (*Great Expectations* by Charles Dickens)

counting-house NOUN a counting house is a place where accountants work ❏ *Once upon a time – of all the good days in the year, on Christmas Eve – old Scrooge sat busy in his countinghouse* (*A Christmas Carol* by Charles Dickens)

courtier NOUN a courtier is someone who attends the king or queen – a member of the court ❏ *next the ten*

courtiers; (*Alice's Adventures in Wonderland* by Lewis Carroll)

covies NOUN covies were flocks of partridges ❏ *and will save all of the best covies for you* (*Pride and Prejudice* by Jane Austen)

cowed VERB cowed means frightened or intimidated ❏ *it cowed me more than the pain* (*Treasure Island* by Robert Louis Stevenson)

cozened VERB cozened means tricked or deceived ❏ *Do you remember, sir, how you cozened me* (*Doctor Faustus 4.7* by Christopher Marlowe)

cravats NOUN a cravat is a folded cloth that a man wears wrapped around his neck as a decorative item of clothing ❏ *we'd'a' slept in our cravats to-night* (*The Adventures of Huckleberry Finn* by Mark Twain)

crock and dirt PHRASE crock and dirt is an old expression meaning soot and dirt ❏ *and the mare catching cold at the door, and the boy grimed with crock and dirt* (*Great Expectations* by Charles Dickens)

crockery NOUN here crockery means pottery ❏ *By one of the parrots was a cat made of crockery* (*The Adventures of Huckleberry Finn* by Mark Twain)

crooked sixpence PHRASE it was considered unlucky to have a bent sixpence ❏ *You've got the beauty, you see, and I've got the luck, so you must keep me by you for your crooked sixpence* (*Silas Marner* by George Eliot)

croquet NOUN croquet is a traditional English summer game in which players try to hit wooden balls through hoops ❏ *and once she remembered trying to box her own ears for having cheated herself in a game of croquet* (*Alice's Adventures in Wonderland* by Lewis Carroll)

cross PREP across ❏ *The two great streets, which run cross and divide it into four quarters* (*Gulliver's Travels* by Jonathan Swift)

culpable ADJ if you are culpable for something it means you are to blame ❑ *deep are the sorrows that spring from false ideas for which no man is culpable.* (*Silas Marner* by George Eliot)

cultured ADJ cultivated ❑ *Nor less when spring had warmed the cultured Vale* (*The Prelude* by William Wordsworth)

cupidity NOUN cupidity is greed ❑ *These people hated me with the hatred of cupidity and disappointment.* (*Great Expectations* by Charles Dickens)

curricle NOUN an open two-wheeled carriage with one seat for the driver and space for a single passenger ❑ *and they saw a lady and a gentleman in a curricle* (*Pride and Prejudice* by Jane Austen)

cynosure NOUN a cynosure is something that strongly attracts attention or admiration ❑ *Then I thought of Eliza and Georgiana; I beheld one the cynosure of a ballroom, the other the inmate of a convent cell* (*Jane Eyre* by Charlotte Brontë)

dalliance NOUN someone's dalliance with something is a brief involvement with it ❑ *nor sporting in the dalliance of love* (*Doctor Faustus Chorus* by Christopher Marlowe)

darkling ADV darkling is an archaic way of saying in the dark ❑ *Darkling I listen* (*Ode on a Nightingale* by John Keats)

delf-case NOUN a sideboard for holding dishes and crockery ❑ *at the pewter dishes and delf-case* (*Wuthering Heights* by Emily Brontë)

determined ■ VERB here determined means ended ❑ *and be out of vogue when that was determined* (*Gulliver's Travels* by Jonathan Swift) ■ VERB determined can mean to have been learned or found especially by investigation or experience ❑ *All the sensitive feelings it wounded so cruelly, all the shame and misery it kept alive within my breast, became more poignant as I thought of this; and I determined that the life was unendurable* (*David Copperfield* by Charles Dickens)

Deuce NOUN a slang term for the Devil ❑ *Ah, I dare say I did. Deuce take me, he added suddenly, I know I did. I find I am not quite unscrewed yet.* (*Great Expectations* by Charles Dickens)

diabolical ADJ diabolical means devilish or evil ❑ *and with a thousand diabolical expressions* (*Treasure Island* by Robert Louis Stevenson)

direction NOUN here direction means address ❑ *Elizabeth was not surprised at it, as Jane had written the direction remarkably ill* (*Pride and Prejudice* by Jane Austen)

discover VERB to make known or announce ❑ *the Emperor would discover the secret while I was out of his power* (*Gulliver's Travels* by Jonathan Swift)

dissemble VERB hide or conceal ❑ *Dissemble nothing* (*On His Mistress* by John Donne)

dissolve VERB dissolve here means to release from life, to die ❑ *Fade far away, dissolve, and quite forget* (*Ode on a Nightingale* by John Keats)

distrain VERB to distrain is to seize the property of someone who is in debt in compensation for the money owed ❑ *for he's threatening to distrain for it* (*Silas Marner* by George Eliot)

Divan NOUN a Divan was originally a Turkish council of state – the name was transferred to the couches they sat on and is used to mean this in English ❑ *Mr Brass applauded this picture very much, and the bed being soft and comfortable, Mr Quilp determined to use it, both as a sleeping place by night and as a kind of Divan by day.* (*The Old Curiosity Shop* by Charles Dickens)

divorcement NOUN separation ❏ *By all pains which want and divorcement hath* (*On His Mistress* by John Donne)

dog in the manger, PHRASE this phrase describes someone who prevents you from enjoying something that they themselves have no need for ❏ *You are a dog in the manger, Cathy, and desire no one to be loved but yourself* (*Wuthering Heights* by Emily Brontë)

dolorifuge NOUN dolorifuge is a word which Thomas Hardy invented. It means pain-killer or comfort ❏ *as a species of dolorifuge* (*Tess of the D'Urbervilles* by Thomas Hardy)

dome NOUN building ❏ *that river and that mouldering dome* (*The Prelude* by William Wordsworth)

domestic PHRASE here domestic means a person's management of the house ❏ *to give some account of my domestic* (*Gulliver's Travels* by Jonathan Swift)

dunce NOUN a dunce is another word for idiot ❏ *Do you take me for a dunce? Go on?* (*Alice's Adventures in Wonderland* by Lewis Carroll)

Ecod EXCLAM a slang exclamation meaning 'oh God!' ❏ *"Ecod," replied Wemmick, shaking his head, "that's not my trade." (Great Expectations* by Charles Dickens)

egg-hot NOUN an egg-hot (see also 'flip' and 'negus') was a hot drink made from beer and eggs, sweetened with nutmeg ❏ *She fainted when she saw me return, and made a little jug of egg-hot afterwards to console us while we talked it over.* (*David Copperfield* by Charles Dickens)

encores NOUN an encore is a short extra performance at the end of a longer one, which the entertainer gives because the audience has enthusiastically asked for it ❏ *we want a little something to answer encores with, anyway* (*The Adventures of Huckleberry Finn* by Mark Twain)

equipage NOUN an elegant and impressive carriage ❏ *and besides, the equipage did not answer to any of their neighbours* (*Pride and Prejudice* by Jane Austen)

exordium NOUN an exordium is the opening part of a speech ❏ *"Now, Handel," as if it were the grave beginning of a portentous business exordium, he had suddenly given up that tone* (*Great Expectations* by Charles Dickens)

expect VERB here expect means to wait for ❏ *to expect his farther commands* (*Gulliver's Travels* by Jonathan Swift)

familiars NOUN familiars means spirits or devils who come to someone when they are called ❏ *I'll turn all the lice about thee into familiars* (*Doctor Faustus 1.4* by Christopher Marlowe)

fantods NOUN a fantod is a person who fidgets or can't stop moving nervously ❏ *It most give me the fantods* (*The Adventures of Huckleberry Finn* by Mark Twain)

farthing NOUN a farthing is an old unit of British currency which was worth a quarter of a penny ❏ *Not a farthing less. A great many back-payments are included in it, I assure you.* (*A Christmas Carol* by Charles Dickens)

farthingale NOUN a hoop worn under a skirt to extend it ❏ *A bell with an old voice – which I dare say in its time had often said to the house, Here is the green farthingale* (*Great Expectations* by Charles Dickens)

favours NOUN here favours is an old word which means ribbons ❏ *A group of humble mourners entered the gate: wearing white favours* (*Oliver Twist* by Charles Dickens)

feigned VERB pretend or pretending ❏ *not my feigned page* (*On His Mistress* by John Donne)

fence ■ NOUN a fence is someone who receives and sells stolen goods ❏

What are you up to? Ill-treating the boys, you covetous, avaricious, in-sa-ti-a-ble old fence? (Oliver Twist by Charles Dickens) ■ NOUN defence or protection ❑ *but honesty hath no fence against superior cunning* (Gulliver's Travels by Jonathan Swift)

fess ADJ fess is an old word which means pleased or proud ❑ *You'll be fess enough, my poppet* (Tess of the D'Urbervilles by Thomas Hardy)

fettered ADJ fettered means bound in chains or chained ❑ *"You are fettered," said Scrooge, trembling. "Tell me why?"* (A Christmas Carol by Charles Dickens)

fidges VERB fidges means fidgets, which is to keep moving your hands slightly because you are nervous or excited ❑ *Look, Jim, how my fingers fidges* (Treasure Island by Robert Louis Stevenson)

finger-post NOUN a finger-post is a sign-post showing the direction to different places ❑ *"The gallows," continued Fagin, "the gallows, my dear, is an ugly finger-post, which points out a very short and sharp turning that has stopped many a bold fellow's career on the broad highway."* (Oliver Twist by Charles Dickens)

fire-irons NOUN fire-irons are tools kept by the side of the fire to either cook with or look after the fire ❑ *the fire-irons came first* (Alice's Adventures in Wonderland by Lewis Carroll)

fire-plug NOUN a fire-plug is another word for a fire hydrant ❑ *The pony looked with great attention into a fire-plug, which was near him, and appeared to be quite absorbed in contemplating it* (The Old Curiosity Shop by Charles Dickens)

flank NOUN flank is the side of an animal ❑ *And all her silken flanks with garlands dressed* (Ode on a Grecian Urn by John Keats)

flip NOUN a flip is a drink made from warmed ale, sugar, spice and beaten egg ❑ *The events of the day,*

in combination with the twins, if not with the flip, had made Mrs. Micawber hysterical, and she shed tears as she replied (David Copperfield by Charles Dickens)

flit VERB flit means to move quickly ❑ *and if he had meant to flit to Thrushcross Grange* (Wuthering Heights by Emily Brontë)

floorcloth NOUN a floorcloth was a hard-wearing piece of canvas used instead of carpet ❑ *This avenging phantom was ordered to be on duty at eight on Tuesday morning in the hall (it was two feet square, as charged for floorcloth)* (Great Expectations by Charles Dickens)

fly-driver NOUN a fly-driver is a carriage drawn by a single horse ❑ *The fly-drivers, among whom I inquired next, were equally jocose and equally disrespectful* (David Copperfield by Charles Dickens)

fob NOUN a small pocket in which a watch is kept ❑ *"Certain," replied the man, drawing a gold watch from his fob* (Oliver Twist by Charles Dickens)

folly NOUN folly means foolishness or stupidity ❑ *the folly of beginning a work* (Robinson Crusoe by Daniel Defoe)

fond ADJ fond means foolish ❑ *Fond worldling* (Doctor Faustus 5.2 by Christopher Marlowe)

fondness NOUN silly or foolish affection ❑ *They have no fondness for their colts or foals* (Gulliver's Travels by Jonathan Swift)

for his fancy PHRASE for his fancy means for his liking or as he wanted ❑ *and as I did not obey quick enough for his fancy* (Treasure Island by Robert Louis Stevenson)

forlorn ADJ lost or very upset ❑ *you are from that day forlorn* (Gulliver's Travels by Jonathan Swift)

foster-sister NOUN a foster-sister was someone brought up by the same nurse or in the same household ❏ *I had been his foster-sister* (*Wuthering Heights* by Emily Brontë)

fox-fire NOUN fox-fire is a weak glow that is given off by decaying, rotten wood ❏ *what we must have was a lot of them rotten chunks that's called fox-fire* (*The Adventures of Huckleberry Finn* by Mark Twain)

frozen sea PHRASE the Arctic Ocean ❏ *into the frozen sea* (*Gulliver's Travels* by Jonathan Swift)

gainsay VERB to gainsay something is to say it isn't true or to deny it ❏ *"So she had," cried Scrooge. "You're right. I'll not gainsay it, Spirit. God forbid!"* (*A Christmas Carol* by Charles Dickens)

gaiters NOUN gaiters were leggings made of a cloth or piece of leather which covered the leg from the knee to the ankle ❏ *Mr Knightley was hard at work upon the lower buttons of his thick leather gaiters* (*Emma* by Jane Austen)

galluses NOUN galluses is an old spelling of gallows, and here means suspenders. Suspenders are straps worn over someone's shoulders and fastened to their trousers to prevent the trousers falling down ❏ *and home-knit galluses* (*The Adventures of Huckleberry Finn* by Mark Twain)

galoot NOUN a sailor but also a clumsy person ❏ *and maybe a galoot on it chopping* (*The Adventures of Huckleberry Finn* by Mark Twain)

gayest ADJ gayest means the most lively and bright or merry ❏ *Beth played her gayest march* (*Little Women* by Louisa May Alcott)

gem NOUN here gem means jewellery ❏ *the mountain shook off turf and flower, had only heath for raiment and crag for gem* (*Jane Eyre* by Charlotte Brontë)

giddy ADJ giddy means dizzy ❏ *and I wish you wouldn't keep appearing*

and vanishing so suddenly; you make one quite giddy. (*Alice's Adventures in Wonderland* by Lewis Carroll)

gig NOUN a light two-wheeled carriage ❏ *when a gig drove up to the garden gate: out of which there jumped a fat gentleman* (*Oliver Twist* by Charles Dickens)

gladsome ADJ gladsome is an old word meaning glad or happy ❏ *Nobody ever stopped him in the street to say, with gladsome looks* (*A Christmas Carol* by Charles Dickens)

glen NOUN a glen is a small valley; the word is used commonly in Scotland ❏ *a beck which follows the bend of the glen* (*Wuthering Heights* by Emily Brontë)

gravelled VERB gravelled is an old term which means to baffle or defeat someone ❏ *Gravelled the pastors of the German Church* (*Doctor Faustus 1.1* by Christopher Marlowe)

grinder NOUN a grinder was a private tutor ❏ *but that when he had had the happiness of marrying Mrs Pocket very early in his life, he had impaired his prospects and taken up the calling of a Grinder* (*Great Expectations* by Charles Dickens)

gruel NOUN gruel is a thin, watery cornmeal or oatmeal soup ❏ *and the little saucepan of gruel (Scrooge had a cold in his head) upon the hob.* (*A Christmas Carol* by Charles Dickens)

guinea, half a NOUN a half guinea was ten shillings and sixpence ❏ *but lay out half a guinea at Ford's* (*Emma* by Jane Austen)

gull VERB gull is an old term which means to fool or deceive someone ❏ *Hush, I'll gull him supernaturally* (*Doctor Faustus 3.4* by Christopher Marlowe)

gunnel NOUN the gunnel, or gunwhale, is the upper edge of a boat's side ❏ *But he put his foot on the gunnel and rocked her* (*The Adventures of Huckleberry Finn* by Mark Twain)

gunwale NOUN the side of a ship ❑ *He dipped his hand in the water over the boat's gunwale* (*Great Expectations* by Charles Dickens)

Gytrash NOUN a Gytrash is an omen of misfortune to the superstitious, usually taking the form of a hound ❑ *I remembered certain of Bessie's tales, wherein figured a North-of-England spirit, called a 'Gytrash'* (*Jane Eyre* by Charlotte Brontë)

hackney-cabriolet NOUN a two-wheeled carriage with four seats for hire and pulled by a horse ❑ *A hackney-cabriolet was in waiting; with the same vehemence which she had exhibited in addressing Oliver, the girl pulled him in with her, and drew the curtains close.* (*Oliver Twist* by Charles Dickens)

hackney-coach NOUN a four-wheeled horse-drawn vehicle for hire ❑ *The twilight was beginning to close in, when Mr. Brownlow alighted from a hackney-coach at his own door, and knocked softly.* (*Oliver Twist* by Charles Dickens)

haggler NOUN a haggler is someone who travels from place to place selling small goods and items ❑ *when I be plain Jack Durbeyfield, the haggler* (*Tess of the D'Urbervilles* by Thomas Hardy)

halter NOUN a halter is a rope or strap used to lead an animal or to tie it up ❑ *I had of course long been used to a halter and a headstall* (*Black Beauty* by Anna Sewell)

hamlet NOUN a hamlet is a small village or a group of houses in the countryside ❑ *down from the hamlet* (*Treasure Island* by Robert Louis Stevenson)

hand-barrow NOUN a hand-barrow is a device for carrying heavy objects. It is like a wheelbarrow except that it has handles, rather than wheels, for moving the barrow ❑ *his sea chest following behind him in a hand-barrow* (*Treasure Island* by Robert Louis Stevenson)

handspike NOUN a handspike was a stick which was used as a lever ❑ *a bit of stick like a handspike* (*Treasure Island* by Robert Louis Stevenson)

haply ADV haply means by chance or perhaps ❑ *And haply the Queen-Moon is on her throne* (*Ode on a Nightingale* by John Keats)

harem NOUN the harem was the part of the house where the women lived ❑ *mostly they hang round the harem* (*The Adventures of Huckleberry Finn* by Mark Twain)

hautboys NOUN hautboys are oboes ❑ *sausages and puddings resembling flutes and hautboys* (*Gulliver's Travels* by Jonathan Swift)

hawker NOUN a hawker is someone who sells goods to people as he travels rather than from a fixed place like a shop ❑ *to buy some stockings from a hawker* (*Treasure Island* by Robert Louis Stevenson)

hawser NOUN a hawser is a rope used to tie up or tow a ship or boat ❑ *Again among the tiers of shipping, in and out, avoiding rusty chain-cables, frayed hempen hawsers* (*Great Expectations* by Charles Dickens)

headstall NOUN the headstall is the part of the bridle or halter that goes around a horse's head ❑ *I had of course long been used to a halter and a headstall* (*Black Beauty* by Anna Sewell)

hearken VERB hearken means to listen ❑ *though we sometimes stopped to lay hold of each other and hearken* (*Treasure Island* by Robert Louis Stevenson)

heartless ADJ here heartless means without heart or dejected ❑ *I am not heartless* (*The Prelude* by William Wordsworth)

hebdomadal ADJ hebdomadal means weekly ❑ *It was the hebdomadal treat to which we all looked forward from Sabbath to Sabbath* (*Jane Eyre* by Charlotte Brontë)

highwaymen NOUN highwaymen were people who stopped travellers and robbed them ❏ *We are highwaymen* (*The Adventures of Huckleberry Finn* by Mark Twain)

hinds NOUN hinds means farm hands, or people who work on a farm ❏ *He called his hinds about him* (*Gulliver's Travels* by Jonathan Swift)

histrionic ADJ if you refer to someone's behaviour as histrionic, you are being critical of it because it is dramatic and exaggerated ❏ *But the histrionic muse is the darling* (*The Adventures of Huckleberry Finn* by Mark Twain)

hogs NOUN hogs is another word for pigs ❏ *Tom called the hogs 'ingots'* (*The Adventures of Huckleberry Finn* by Mark Twain)

horrors NOUN the horrors are a fit, called delirium tremens, which is caused by drinking too much alcohol ❏ *I'll have the horrors* (*Treasure Island* by Robert Louis Stevenson)

huffy ADJ huffy means to be obviously annoyed or offended about something ❏ *They will feel that more than angry speeches or huffy actions* (*Little Women* by Louisa May Alcott)

hulks NOUN hulks were prison-ships ❏ *The miserable companion of thieves and ruffians, the fallen outcast of low haunts, the associate of the scourings of the jails and hulks* (*Oliver Twist* by Charles Dickens)

humbug NOUN humbug means nonsense or rubbish ❏ *"Bah," said Scrooge. "Humbug!"* (*A Christmas Carol* by Charles Dickens)

humours NOUN it was believed that there were four fluids in the body called humours which decided the temperament of a person depending on how much of each fluid was present ❏ *other peccant humours* (*Gulliver's Travels* by Jonathan Swift)

husbandry NOUN husbandry is farming animals ❏ *bad husbandry were plentifully anointing their wheels* (*Silas Marner* by George Eliot)

huswife NOUN a huswife was a small sewing kit ❏ *but I had put my huswife on it* (*Emma* by Jane Austen)

ideal ADJ ideal in this context means imaginary ❏ *I discovered the yell was not ideal* (*Wuthering Heights* by Emily Brontë)

If our two PHRASE if both our ❏ *If our two loves be one* (*The Good-Morrow* by John Donne)

ignis-fatuus NOUN ignis-fatuus is the light given out by burning marsh gases, which lead careless travellers into danger ❏ *it is madness in all women to let a secret love kindle within them, which, if unreturned and unknown, must devour the life that feeds it; and, if discovered and responded to, must lead ignis-fatuus-like, into miry wilds whence there is no extrication.* (*Jane Eyre* by Charlotte Brontë)

imaginations NOUN here imaginations means schemes or plans ❏ *soon drove out those imaginations* (*Gulliver's Travels* by Jonathan Swift)

impressible ADJ impressible means open or impressionable ❏ *for Marner had one of those impressible, self-doubting natures* (*Silas Marner* by George Eliot)

in good intelligence PHRASE friendly with each other ❏ *that these two persons were in good intelligence with each other* (*Gulliver's Travels* by Jonathan Swift)

inanity NOUN inanity is silliness or dull stupidity ❏ *Do we not wile away moments of inanity* (*Silas Marner* by George Eliot)

incivility NOUN incivility means rudeness or impoliteness ❏ *if it's only for a piece of incivility like to-night's* (*Treasure Island* by Robert Louis Stevenson)

indigenae NOUN indigenae means natives or people from that area ❏ *an exotic that the surly indigenae will not recognise for kin* (*Wuthering Heights* by Emily Brontë)

indocible ADJ unteachable ❏ *so they were the most restive and indocible* (*Gulliver's Travels* by Jonathan Swift)

ingenuity NOUN inventiveness ❏ *entreated me to give him something as an encouragement to ingenuity* (*Gulliver's Travels* by Jonathan Swift)

ingots NOUN an ingot is a lump of a valuable metal like gold, usually shaped like a brick ❏ *Tom called the hogs 'ingots'* (*The Adventures of Huckleberry Finn* by Mark Twain)

inkstand NOUN an inkstand is a pot which was put on a desk to contain either ink or pencils and pens ❏ *throwing an inkstand at the Lizard as she spoke* (*Alice's Adventures in Wonderland* by Lewis Carroll)

inordinate ADJ without order. To-day inordinate means 'excessive'. ❏ *Though yet untutored and inordinate* (*The Prelude* by William Wordsworth)

intellectuals NOUN here intellectuals means the minds (of the workmen) ❏ *those instructions they give being too refined for the intellectuals of their workmen* (*Gulliver's Travels* by Jonathan Swift)

interview NOUN meeting ❏ *By our first strange and fatal interview* (*On His Mistress* by John Donne)

jacks NOUN jacks are rods for turning a spit over a fire ❏ *It was a small bit of pork suspended from the kettle hanger by a string passed through a large door key, in a way known to primitive housekeepers unpossessed of jacks* (*Silas Marner* by George Eliot)

jews-harp NOUN a jews-harp is a small, metal, musical instrument that is played by the mouth ❏ *A jews-harp's plenty good enough for a rat* (*The Adventures of Huckleberry Finn* by Mark Twain)

jorum NOUN a large bowl ❏ *while Miss Skiffins brewed such a jorum of tea, that the pig in the back premises became strongly excited* (*Great Expectations* by Charles Dickens)

jostled VERB jostled means bumped or pushed by someone or some people ❏ *being jostled himself into the kennel* (*Gulliver's Travels* by Jonathan Swift)

keepsake NOUN a keepsake is a gift which reminds someone of an event or of the person who gave it to them. ❏ *books and ornaments they had in their boudoirs at home: keepsakes that different relations had presented to them* (*Jane Eyre* by Charlotte Brontë)

kenned VERB kenned means knew ❏ *though little kenned the lamplighter that he had any company but Christmas!* (*A Christmas Carol* by Charles Dickens)

kennel NOUN kennel means gutter, which is the edge of a road next to the pavement, where rain water collects and flows away ❏ *being jostled himself into the kennel* (*Gulliver's Travels* by Jonathan Swift)

knock-knee ADJ knock-knee means slanted, at an angle. ❏ *LOT 1 was marked in whitewashed knock-knee letters on the brewhouse* (*Great Expectations* by Charles Dickens)

ladylike ADJ to be ladylike is to behave in a polite, dignified and graceful way ❏ *No, winking isn't ladylike* (*Little Women* by Louisa May Alcott)

lapse NOUN flow ❏ *Stealing with silent lapse to join the brook* (*The Prelude* by William Wordsworth)

larry NOUN larry is an old word which means commotion or noisy celebration ❏ *That was all a part of the larry!* (*Tess of the D'Urbervilles* by Thomas Hardy)

laths NOUN laths are strips of wood ❏ *The panels shrunk, the windows cracked; fragments of plaster fell out of the ceiling, and the naked laths were shown instead* (*A Christmas Carol* by Charles Dickens)

leer NOUN a leer is an unpleasant smile ❏ *with a kind of leer* (*Treasure Island* by Robert Louis Stevenson)

lenitives NOUN these are different kinds of drugs or medicines: lenitives and palliatives were pain relievers; aperitives were laxatives; abstersives caused vomiting; corrosives destroyed human tissue; restringents caused constipation; cephalalgics stopped headaches; icterics were used as medicine for jaundice; apophlegmatics were cough medicine, and acoustics were cures for the loss of hearing ❑ *lenitives, aperitives, abstersives, corrosives, restringents, palliatives, laxatives, cephalalgics, icterics, apophlegmatics, acoustics* (*Gulliver's Travels* by Jonathan Swift)

lest CONJ in case. If you do something lest something (usually) unpleasant happens you do it to try to prevent it happening ❑ *She went in without knocking, and hurried upstairs, in great fear lest she should meet the real Mary Ann* (*Alice's Adventures in Wonderland* by Lewis Carroll)

levee NOUN a levee is an old term for a meeting held in the morning, shortly after the person holding the meeting has got out of bed ❑ *I used to attend the King's levee once or twice a week* (*Gulliver's Travels* by Jonathan Swift)

life-preserver NOUN a club which had lead inside it to make it heavier and therefore more dangerous ❑ *and with no more suspicious articles displayed to view than two or three heavy bludgeons which stood in a corner, and a 'life-preserver' that hung over the chimney-piece.* (*Oliver Twist* by Charles Dickens)

lighterman NOUN a lighterman is another word for sailor ❑ *in and out, hammers going in ship-builders' yards, saws going at timber, clashing engines going at things unknown, pumps going in leaky ships, capstans going, ships going out to sea, and unintelligible sea creatures roaring curses over the bulwarks at respondent lightermen* (*Great Expectations* by Charles Dickens)

livery NOUN servants often wore a uniform known as a livery ❑ *suddenly a footman in livery came running out of the wood* (*Alice's Adventures in Wonderland* by Lewis Carroll)

livid ADJ livid means pale or ash coloured. Livid also means very angry ❑ *a dirty, livid white* (*Treasure Island* by Robert Louis Stevenson)

lottery-tickets NOUN a popular card game ❑ *and Mrs. Philips protested that they would have a nice comfortable noisy game of lottery tickets* (*Pride and Prejudice* by Jane Austen)

lower and upper world PHRASE the earth and the heavens are the lower and upper worlds ❑ *the changes in the lower and upper world* (*Gulliver's Travels* by Jonathan Swift)

lustres NOUN lustres are chandeliers. A chandelier is a large, decorative frame which holds light bulbs or candles and hangs from the ceiling ❑ *the lustres, lights, the carving and the guilding* (*The Prelude* by William Wordsworth)

lynched VERB killed without a criminal trial by a crowd of people ❑ *He'll never know how nigh he come to getting lynched* (*The Adventures of Huckleberry Finn* by Mark Twain)

malingering VERB if someone is malingering they are pretending to be ill to avoid working ❑ *And you stand there malingering* (*Treasure Island* by Robert Louis Stevenson)

managing PHRASE treating with consideration ❑ *to think the honour of my own kind not worth managing* (*Gulliver's Travels* by Jonathan Swift)

manhood PHRASE manhood means human nature ❑ *concerning the nature of manhood* (*Gulliver's Travels* by Jonathan Swift)

man-trap NOUN a man-trap is a set of steel jaws that snap shut when trodden on and trap a person's leg ❏ *"Don't go to him," I called out of the window, "he's an assassin! A man-trap!" (Oliver Twist* by Charles Dickens)

maps NOUN charts of the night sky ❏ *Let maps to others, worlds on worlds have shown (The Good-Morrow* by John Donne)

mark VERB look at or notice ❏ *Mark but this flea, and mark in this (The Flea* by John Donne)

maroons NOUN A maroon is someone who has been left in a place which it is difficult for them to escape from, like a small island ❏ *if schooners, islands, and maroons (Treasure Island* by Robert Louis Stevenson)

mast NOUN here mast means the fruit of forest trees ❏ *a quantity of acorns, dates, chestnuts, and other mast (Gulliver's Travels* by Jonathan Swift)

mate VERB defeat ❏ *Where Mars did mate the warlike Carthigens (Doctor Faustus Chorus* by Christopher Marlowe)

mealy ADJ Mealy when used to describe a face meant pallid, pale or colourless ❏ *I only know two sorts of boys. Mealy boys, and beef-faced boys (Oliver Twist* by Charles Dickens)

middling ADJ fairly or moderately ❏ *she worked me middling hard for about an hour (The Adventures of Huckleberry Finn* by Mark Twain)

mill NOUN a mill, or treadmill, was a device for hard labour or punishment in prison ❏ *Was you never on the mill? (Oliver Twist* by Charles Dickens)

milliner's shop NOUN a milliner's sold fabrics, clothing, lace and accessories; as time went on they specialized more and more in hats ❏ *to pay their duty to their aunt and to a milliner's shop just over the way (Pride and Prejudice* by Jane Austen)

minching un' munching PHRASE how people in the north of England used to describe the way people from the south speak ❏ *Minching un' munching! (Wuthering Heights* by Emily Brontë)

mine NOUN gold ❏ *Whether both th'Indias of spice and mine (The Sun Rising* by John Donne)

mire NOUN mud ❏ *Tis my fate to be always ground into the mire under the iron heel of oppression (The Adventures of Huckleberry Finn* by Mark Twain)

miscellany NOUN a miscellany is a collection of many different kinds of things ❏ *under that, the miscellany began (Treasure Island* by Robert Louis Stevenson)

mistarshers NOUN mistarshers means moustache, which is the hair that grows on a man's upper lip ❏ *when he put his hand up to his mistarshers (Tess of the D'Urbervilles* by Thomas Hardy)

morrow NOUN here good-morrow means tomorrow and a new and better life ❏ *And now good-morrow to our waking souls (The Good-Morrow* by John Donne)

mortification NOUN mortification is an old word for gangrene which is when part of the body decays or 'dies' because of disease ❏ *Yes, it was a mortification – that was it (The Adventures of Huckleberry Finn* by Mark Twain)

mought PARTICIPLE mought is an old spelling of might ❏ *what you mought call me? You mought call me captain (Treasure Island* by Robert Louis Stevenson)

move VERB move me not means do not make me angry ❏ *Move me not, Faustus (Doctor Faustus 2.1* by Christopher Marlowe)

muffin-cap NOUN a muffin cap is a flat cap made from wool ❏ *the old one, remained stationary in the muffin-cap and leathers (Oliver Twist* by Charles Dickens)

mulatter NOUN a mulatter was another word for mulatto, which is a person with parents who are from different races ❑ *a mulatter, most as white as a white man* (The Adventures of Huckleberry Finn by Mark Twain)

mummery NOUN mummery is an old word that meant meaningless (or pretentious) ceremony ❑ *When they were all gone, and when Trabb and his men – but not his boy: I looked for him – had crammed their mummery into bags, and were gone too, the house felt wholesomer.* (Great Expectations by Charles Dickens)

nap NOUN the nap is the woolly surface on a new item of clothing. Here the surface has been worn away so it looks bare ❑ *like an old hat with the nap rubbed off* (The Adventures of Huckleberry Finn by Mark Twain)

natural ■ NOUN a natural is a person born with learning difficulties ❑ *though he had been left to his particular care by their deceased father, who thought him almost a natural.* (David Copperfield by Charles Dickens) ■ ADJ natural meant illegitimate ❑ *Harriet Smith was the natural daughter of somebody* (Emma by Jane Austen)

navigator NOUN a navigator was originally someone employed to dig canals. It is the origin of the word 'navvy' meaning a labourer ❑ *She ascertained from me in a few words what it was all about, comforted Dora, and gradually convinced her that I was not a labourer – from my manner of stating the case I believe Dora concluded that I was a navigator, and went balancing myself up and down a plank all day with a wheelbarrow – and so brought us together in peace.* (David Copperfield by Charles Dickens)

necromancy NOUN necromancy means a kind of magic where the magician speaks to spirits or ghosts to find out what will happen in the future ❑ *He surfeits upon cursed necromancy* (Doctor Faustus chorus by Christopher Marlowe)

negus NOUN a negus is a hot drink made from sweetened wine and water ❑ *He sat placidly perusing the newspaper, with his little head on one side, and a glass of warm sherry negus at his elbow.* (David Copperfield by Charles Dickens)

nice ADJ discriminating. Able to make good judgements or choices ❑ *consequently a claim to be nice* (Emma by Jane Austen)

nigh ADV nigh means near ❑ *He'll never know how nigh he come to getting lynched* (The Adventures of Huckleberry Finn by Mark Twain)

nimbleness NOUN nimbleness means being able to move very quickly or skillfully ❑ *and with incredible accuracy and nimbleness* (Treasure Island by Robert Louis Stevenson)

noggin NOUN a noggin is a small mug or a wooden cup ❑ *you'll bring me one noggin of rum* (Treasure Island by Robert Louis Stevenson)

none ADJ neither ❑ *none can die* (The Good-Morrow by John Donne)

notices NOUN observations ❑ *Arch are his notices* (The Prelude by William Wordsworth)

occiput NOUN occiput means the back of the head ❑ *saw off the occiput of each couple* (Gulliver's Travels by Jonathan Swift)

officiously ADJ kindly ❑ *the governess who attended Glumdalclitch very officiously lifted me up* (Gulliver's Travels by Jonathan Swift)

old salt PHRASE old salt is a slang term for an experienced sailor ❑ *a 'true sea-dog', and a 'real old salt'* (Treasure Island by Robert Louis Stevenson)

or ere PHRASE before ❑ *or ere the Hall was built* (The Prelude by William Wordsworth)

ostler NOUN one who looks after horses at an inn ❑ *The bill paid, and the waiter remembered, and the ostler not forgotten, and the chambermaid taken into consideration*

197

(*Great Expectations* by Charles Dickens)

ostry NOUN an ostry is an old word for a pub or hotel ❑ *lest I send you into the ostry with a vengeance* (*Doctor Faustus 2.2* by Christopher Marlowe)

outrunning the constable PHRASE outrunning the constable meant spending more than you earn ❑ *but I shall by this means be able to check your bills and to pull you up if I find you outrunning the constable.* (*Great Expectations* by Charles Dickens)

over ADJ across ❑ *It is in length six yards, and in the thickest part at least three yards over* (*Gulliver's Travels* by Jonathan Swift)

over the broomstick PHRASE this is a phrase meaning 'getting married without a formal ceremony' ❑ *They both led tramping lives, and this woman in Gerrard-street here, had been married very young, over the broomstick (as we say), to a tramping man, and was a perfect fury in point of jealousy.* (*Great Expectations* by Charles Dickens)

own VERB own means to admit or to acknowledge ❑ *It's my old girl that advises. She has the head. But I never own to it before her. Discipline must be maintained* (*Bleak House* by Charles Dickens)

page NOUN here page means a boy employed to run errands ❑ *not my feigned page* (*On His Mistress* by John Donne)

paid pretty dear PHRASE paid pretty dear means paid a high price or suffered quite a lot ❑ *I paid pretty dear for my monthly fourpenny piece* (*Treasure Island* by Robert Louis Stevenson)

pannikins NOUN pannikins were small tin cups ❑ *of lifting light glasses and cups to his lips, as if they were clumsy pannikins* (*Great Expectations* by Charles Dickens)

pards NOUN pards are leopards ❑ *Not charioted by Bacchus and his pards*

(*Ode on a Nightingale* by John Keats)

parlour boarder NOUN a pupil who lived with the family ❑ *and somebody had lately raised her from the condition of scholar to parlour boarder* (*Emma* by Jane Austen)

particular, a London PHRASE London in Victorian times and up to the 1950s was famous for having very dense fog – which was a combination of real fog and the smog of pollution from factories ❑ *This is a London particular . . . A fog, miss'* (*Bleak House* by Charles Dickens)

patten NOUN pattens were wooden soles which were fixed to shoes by straps to protect the shoes in wet weather ❑ *carrying a basket like the Great Seal of England in plaited straw, a pair of pattens, a spare shawl, and an umbrella, though it was a fine bright day* (*Great Expectations* by Charles Dickens)

paviour NOUN a paviour was a labourer who worked on the street pavement ❑ *the paviour his pickaxe* (*Oliver Twist* by Charles Dickens)

peccant ADJ peccant means unhealthy ❑ *other peccant humours* (*Gulliver's Travels* by Jonathan Swift)

penetralium NOUN penetralium is a word used to describe the inner rooms of the house ❑ *and I had no desire to aggravate his impatience previous to inspecting the penetralium* (*Wuthering Heights* by Emily Brontë)

pensive ADV pensive means deep in thought or thinking seriously about something ❑ *and she was leaning pensive on a tomb-stone on her right elbow* (*The Adventures of Huckleberry Finn* by Mark Twain)

penury NOUN penury is the state of being extremely poor ❑ *Distress, if not penury, loomed in the distance* (*Tess of the D'Urbervilles* by Thomas Hardy)

perspective NOUN telescope ❑ *a pocket perspective* (*Gulliver's Travels* by Jonathan Swift)

phaeton NOUN a phaeton was an open carriage for four people ❑ *often condescends to drive by my humble abode in her little phaeton and ponies* (*Pride and Prejudice* by Jane Austen)

phantasm NOUN a phantasm is an illusion, something that is not real. It is sometimes used to mean ghost ❑ *Experience had bred no fancies in him that could raise the phantasm of appetite* (*Silas Marner* by George Eliot)

physic NOUN here physic means medicine ❑ *there I studied physic two years and seven months* (*Gulliver's Travels* by Jonathan Swift)

pinioned VERB to pinion is to hold both arms so that a person cannot move them ❑ *But the relentless Ghost pinioned him in both his arms, and forced him to observe what happened next.* (*A Christmas Carol* by Charles Dickens)

piquet NOUN piquet was a popular card game in the C18th ❑ *Mr Hurst and Mr Bingley were at piquet* (*Pride and Prejudice* by Jane Austen)

plaister NOUN a plaister is a piece of cloth on which an apothecary (or pharmacist) would spread ointment. The cloth is then applied to wounds or bruises to treat them ❑ *Then, she gave the knife a final smart wipe on the edge of the plaister, and then sawed a very thick round off the loaf: which she finally, before separating from the loaf, hewed into two halves, of which Joe got one, and I the other.* (*Great Expectations* by Charles Dickens)

plantations NOUN here plantations means colonies, which are countries controlled by a more powerful country ❑ *besides our plantations in America* (*Gulliver's Travels* by Jonathan Swift)

plastic ADV here plastic is an old term meaning shaping or a power that was forming ❑ *A plastic power abode with me* (*The Prelude* by William Wordsworth)

players NOUN actors ❑ *of players which upon the world's stage be* (*On His Mistress* by John Donne)

plump ADV all at once, suddenly ❑ *But it took a bit of time to get it well round, the change come so uncommon plump, didn't it?* (*Great Expectations* by Charles Dickens)

plundered VERB to plunder is to rob or steal from ❑ *These crosses stand for the names of ships or towns that they sank or plundered* (*Treasure Island* by Robert Louis Stevenson)

pommel ■ VERB to pommel someone is to hit them repeatedly with your fists ❑ *hug him round the neck, pommel his back, and kick his legs in irrepressible affection!* (*A Christmas Carol* by Charles Dickens) ■ NOUN a pommel is the part of a saddle that rises up at the front ❑ *He had his gun across his pommel* (*The Adventures of Huckleberry Finn* by Mark Twain)

poor's rates NOUN poor's rates were property taxes which were used to support the poor ❑ *"Oh!" replied the undertaker; "why, you know, Mr. Bumble, I pay a good deal towards the poor's rates."* (*Oliver Twist* by Charles Dickens)

popular ADJ popular means ruled by the people, or Republican, rather than ruled by a monarch ❑ *With those of Greece compared and popular Rome* (*The Prelude* by William Wordsworth)

porringer NOUN a porringer is a small bowl ❑ *Of this festive composition each boy had one porringer, and no more* (*Oliver Twist* by Charles Dickens)

postboy NOUN a postboy was the driver of a horse-drawn carriage ❑ *He spoke to a postboy who was dozing under the gateway* (*Oliver Twist* by Charles Dickens)

post-chaise NOUN a fast carriage for two or four passengers ❑ *Looking round, he saw that it was a* *post-chaise, driven at great speed* (*Oliver Twist* by Charles Dickens)

postern NOUN a small gate usually at the back of a building ❑ *The little servant happening to be entering the fortress with two hot rolls, I passed through the postern and crossed the drawbridge, in her company* (*Great Expectations* by Charles Dickens)

pottle NOUN a pottle was a small basket ❑ *He had a paper-bag under each arm and a pottle of strawberries in one hand . . .* (*Great Expectations* by Charles Dickens)

pounce NOUN pounce is a fine powder used to prevent ink spreading on untreated paper ❑ *in that grim atmosphere of pounce and parchment, red-tape, dusty wafers, ink-jars, brief and draft paper, law reports, writs, declarations, and bills of costs* (*David Copperfield* by Charles Dickens)

pox NOUN pox means sexually transmitted diseases like syphilis ❑ *how the pox in all its consequences and denominations* (*Gulliver's Travels* by Jonathan Swift)

prelibation NOUN prelibation means a foretaste of or an example of something to come ❑ *A prelibation to the mower's scythe* (*The Prelude* by William Wordsworth)

prentice NOUN an apprentice ❑ *and Joe, sitting on an old gun, had told me that when I was 'prentice to him regularly bound, we would have such Larks there!* (*Great Expectations* by Charles Dickens)

presently ADV immediately ❑ *I presently knew what they meant* (*Gulliver's Travels* by Jonathan Swift)

pumpion NOUN pumpkin ❑ *for it was almost as large as a small pumpion* (*Gulliver's Travels* by Jonathan Swift)

punctual ADJ kept in one place ❑ *was not a punctual presence, but a spirit* (*The Prelude* by William Wordsworth)

quadrille ■ NOUN a quadrille is a dance invented in France which is usually performed by four couples ❑ *However, Mr Swiveller had Miss Sophy's hand for the first quadrille (country-dances being low, were utterly proscribed)* (*The Old Curiosity Shop* by Charles Dickens) ■ NOUN quadrille was a card game for four people ❑ *to make up her pool of quadrille in the evening* (*Pride and Prejudice* by Jane Austen)

quality NOUN gentry or upper-class people ❑ *if you are with the quality* (*The Adventures of Huckleberry Finn* by Mark Twain)

quick parts PHRASE quick-witted ❑ *Mr Bennet was so odd a mixture of quick parts* (*Pride and Prejudice* by Jane Austen)

quid NOUN a quid is something chewed or kept in the mouth, like a piece of tobacco ❑ *rolling his quid* (*Treasure Island* by Robert Louis Stevenson)

quit VERB quit means to avenge or to make even ❑ *But Faustus's death shall quit my infamy* (*Doctor Faustus 4.3* by Christopher Marlowe)

rags NOUN divisions ❑ *Nor hours, days, months, which are the rags of time* (*The Sun Rising* by John Donne)

raiment NOUN raiment means clothing ❑ *the mountain shook off turf and flower, had only heath for raiment and crag for gem* (*Jane Eyre* by Charlotte Brontë)

rain cats and dogs PHRASE an expression meaning rain heavily. The origin of the expression is unclear ❑ *But it'll perhaps rain cats and dogs to-morrow* (*Silas Marner* by George Eliot)

raised Cain PHRASE raised Cain means caused a lot of trouble. Cain is a character in the Bible who killed his brother Abel ❑ *and every time he got drunk he raised Cain around town* (*The Adventures of Huckleberry Finn* by Mark Twain)

rambling ADJ rambling means confused and not very clear ❑ *my head began to be filled very early with rambling thoughts* (*Robinson Crusoe* by Daniel Defoe)

raree-show NOUN a raree-show is an old term for a peep-show or a fairground entertainment ❑ *A raree-show is here, with children gathered round* (*The Prelude* by William Wordsworth)

recusants NOUN people who resisted authority ❑ *hardy recusants* (*The Prelude* by William Wordsworth)

redounding VERB eddying. An eddy is a movement in water or air which goes round and round instead of flowing in one direction ❑ *mists and steam-like fogs redounding everywhere* (*The Prelude* by William Wordsworth)

redundant ADJ here redundant means overflowing but Wordsworth also uses it to mean excessively large or too big ❑ *A tempest, a redundant energy* (*The Prelude* by William Wordsworth)

reflex NOUN reflex is a shortened version of reflexion, which is an alternative spelling of reflection ❑ *To cut across the reflex of a star* (*The Prelude* by William Wordsworth)

Reformatory NOUN a prison for young offenders/criminals ❑ *Even when I was taken to have a new suit of clothes, the tailor had orders to make them like a kind of Reformatory, and on no account to let me have the free use of my limbs.* (*Great Expectations* by Charles Dickens)

remorse NOUN pity or compassion ❑ *by that remorse* (*On His Mistress* by John Donne)

render VERB in this context render means give. ❑ *and Sarah could render no reason that would be sanctioned by the feeling of the community.* (*Silas Marner* by George Eliot)

repeater NOUN a repeater was a watch that chimed the last hour when a button was pressed – as a result it was useful in the dark ❑ *And his watch is a gold repeater, and worth a hundred pound if it's worth a penny.* (*Great Expectations* by Charles Dickens)

repugnance NOUN repugnance means a strong dislike of something or someone ❑ *overcoming a strong repugnance* (*Treasure Island* by Robert Louis Stevenson)

reverence NOUN reverence means bow. When you bow to someone, you briefly bend your body towards them as a formal way of showing them respect ❑ *made my reverence* (*Gulliver's Travels* by Jonathan Swift)

reverie NOUN a reverie is a day dream ❑ *I can guess the subject of your reverie* (*Pride and Prejudice* by Jane Austen)

revival NOUN a religious meeting held in public ❑ *well I'd ben a-running' a little temperance revival thar' bout a week* (*The Adventures of Huckleberry Finn* by Mark Twain)

revolt VERB revolt means turn back or stop your present course of action and go back to what you were doing before ❑ *Revolt, or I'll in piecemeal tear thy flesh* (*Doctor Faustus 5.1* by Christopher Marlowe)

rheumatics/rheumatism NOUN rheumatics [rheumatism] is an illness that makes your joints or muscles stiff and painful ❑ *a new cure for the rheumatics* (*Treasure Island* by Robert Louis Stevenson)

riddance NOUN riddance is usually used in the form good riddance which you say when you are pleased that something has gone or been left behind ❑ *I'd better go into the house, and die and be a riddance* (*David Copperfield* by Charles Dickens)

rimy ADJ rimy is an ADJective which means covered in ice or frost ❑ *It* *was a rimy morning, and very damp* (*Great Expectations* by Charles Dickens)

riper ADJ riper means more mature or older ❏ *At riper years to Wittenberg he went* (*Doctor Faustus chorus* by Christopher Marlowe)

rubber NOUN a set of games in whist or backgammon ❏ *her father was sure of his rubber* (*Emma* by Jane Austen)

ruffian NOUN a ruffian is a person who behaves violently ❏ *and when the ruffian had told him* (*Treasure Island* by Robert Louis Stevenson)

sadness NOUN sadness is an old term meaning seriousness ❏ *But I prithee tell me, in good sadness* (*Doctor Faustus 2.2* by Christopher Marlowe)

sailed before the mast PHRASE this phrase meant someone who did not look like a sailor ❏ *he had none of the appearance of a man that sailed before the mast* (*Treasure Island* by Robert Louis Stevenson)

scabbard NOUN a scabbard is the covering for a sword or dagger ❏ *Girded round its middle was an antique scabbard; but no sword was in it, and the ancient sheath was eaten up with rust* (*A Christmas Carol* by Charles Dickens)

schooners NOUN A schooner is a fast, medium-sized sailing ship ❏ *if schooners, islands, and maroons* (*Treasure Island* by Robert Louis Stevenson)

science NOUN learning or knowledge ❏ *Even Science, too, at hand* (*The Prelude* by William Wordsworth)

scrouge VERB to scrouge means to squeeze or to crowd ❏ *to scrouge in and get a sight* (*The Adventures of Huckleberry Finn* by Mark Twain)

scrutore NOUN a scrutore, or escritoire, was a writing table ❏ *set me gently on my feet upon the scrutore* (*Gulliver's Travels* by Jonathan Swift)

scutcheon/escutcheon NOUN an escutcheon is a shield with a coat of arms, or the symbols of a family name, engraved on it ❏ *On the scutcheon we'll have a bend* (*The Adventures of Huckleberry Finn* by Mark Twain)

sea-dog PHRASE sea-dog is a slang term for an experienced sailor or pirate ❏ *a 'true sea-dog', and a 'real old salt,'* (*Treasure Island* by Robert Louis Stevenson)

see the lions PHRASE to see the lions was to go and see the sights of London. Originally the phrase referred to the menagerie in the Tower of London and later in Regent's Park ❏ *We will go and see the lions for an hour or two – it's something to have a fresh fellow like you to show them to, Copperfield* (*David Copperfield* by Charles Dickens)

self-conceit NOUN self-conceit is an old term which means having too high an opinion of oneself, or deceiving yourself ❏ *Till swollen with cunning, of a self-conceit* (*Doctor Faustus chorus* by Christopher Marlowe)

seneschal NOUN a steward ❏ *where a grey-headed seneschal sings a funny chorus with a funnier body of vassals* (*Oliver Twist* by Charles Dickens)

sensible ADJ if you were sensible of something you are aware or conscious of something ❏ *If my children are silly I must hope to be always sensible of it* (*Pride and Prejudice* by Jane Austen)

sessions NOUN court cases were heard at specific times of the year called sessions ❏ *He lay in prison very ill, during the whole interval between his committal for trial, and the coming round of the Sessions.* (*Great Expectations* by Charles Dickens)

shabby ADJ shabby places look old and in bad condition ❏ *a little bit of a shabby village named Pikesville* (*The Adventures of Huckleberry Finn* by Mark Twain)

shay-cart NOUN a shay-cart was a small cart drawn by one horse ❑ *"I were at the Bargemen t'other night, Pip;" whenever he subsided into affection, he called me Pip, and whenever he relapsed into politeness he called me Sir; "when there come up in his shay-cart Pumblechook."* (*Great Expectations* by Charles Dickens)

shilling NOUN a shilling is an old unit of currency. There were twenty shillings in every British pound ❑ *"Ten shillings too much," said the gentleman in the white waistcoat.* (*Oliver Twist* by Charles Dickens)

shines NOUN tricks or games ❑ *well, it would make a cow laugh to see the shines that old idiot cut* (*The Adventures of Huckleberry Finn* by Mark Twain)

shirking VERB shirking means not doing what you are meant to be doing, or evading your duties ❑ *some of you shirking lubbers* (*Treasure Island* by Robert Louis Stevenson)

shiver my timbers PHRASE shiver my timbers is an expression which was used by sailors and pirates to express surprise ❑ *why, shiver my timbers, if I hadn't forgotten my score!* (*Treasure Island* by Robert Louis Stevenson)

shoe-roses NOUN shoe-roses were roses made from ribbons which were stuck on to shoes as decoration ❑ *the very shoe-roses for Netherfield were got by proxy* (*Pride and Prejudice* by Jane Austen)

singular ADJ singular means very great and remarkable or strange ❑ *"Singular dream," he says* (*The Adventures of Huckleberry Finn* by Mark Twain)

sire NOUN sire is an old word which means lord or master or elder ❑ *She also defied her sire* (*Little Women* by Louisa May Alcott)

sixpence NOUN a sixpence was half of a shilling ❑ *if she had only a shilling in the world, she would be very likely to give away sixpence of it* (*Emma* by Jane Austen)

slavey NOUN the word slavey was used when there was only one servant in a house or boarding-house – so she had to perform all the duties of a larger staff ❑ *Two distinct knocks, sir, will produce the slavey at any time* (*The Old Curiosity Shop* by Charles Dickens)

slender ADJ weak ❑ *In slender accents of sweet verse* (*The Prelude* by William Wordsworth)

slop-shops NOUN slop-shops were shops where cheap ready-made clothes were sold. They mainly sold clothes to sailors ❑ *Accordingly, I took the jacket off, that I might learn to do without it; and carrying it under my arm, began a tour of inspection of the various slop-shops.* (*David Copperfield* by Charles Dickens)

sluggard NOUN a lazy person ❑ *"Stand up and repeat 'Tis the voice of the sluggard,'" said the Gryphon.* (*Alice's Adventures in Wonderland* by Lewis Carroll)

smallpox NOUN smallpox is a serious infectious disease ❑ *by telling the men we had smallpox aboard* (*The Adventures of Huckleberry Finn* by Mark Twain)

smalls NOUN smalls are short trousers ❑ *It is difficult for a large-headed, small-eyed youth, of lumbering make and heavy countenance, to look dignified under any circumstances; but it is more especially so, when superadded to these personal attractions are a red nose and yellow smalls* (*Oliver Twist* by Charles Dickens)

sneeze-box NOUN a box for snuff was called a sneeze-box because sniffing snuff makes the user sneeze ❑ *To think of Jack Dawkins – lummy Jack – the Dodger – the Artful Dodger – going abroad for a common twopenny-halfpenny sneeze-box!* (*Oliver Twist* by Charles Dickens)

snorted VERB slept ❑ *Or snorted we in the Seven Sleepers' den?* (*The Good-Morrow* by John Donne)

snuff NOUN snuff is tobacco in powder form which is taken by sniffing ❏ *as he thrust his thumb and forefinger into the proffered snuff-box of the undertaker: which was an ingenious little model of a patent coffin.* (*Oliver Twist* by Charles Dickens)

soliloquized VERB to soliloquize is when an actor in a play speaks to himself or herself rather than to another actor ❏ *"A new servitude! There is something in that," I soliloquized (mentally, be it understood; I did not talk aloud)* (*Jane Eyre* by Charlotte Brontë)

sough NOUN a sough is a drain or a ditch ❏ *as you may have noticed the sough that runs from the marshes* (*Wuthering Heights* by Emily Brontë)

spirits NOUN a spirit is the nonphysical part of a person which is believed to remain alive after their death ❏ *that I might raise up spirits when I please* (*Doctor Faustus 1.5* by Christopher Marlowe)

spleen ■ NOUN here spleen means a type of sadness or depression which was thought to only affect the wealthy ❏ *yet here I could plainly discover the true seeds of spleen* (*Gulliver's Travels* by Jonathan Swift) ■ NOUN irritability and low spirits ❏ *Adieu to disappointment and spleen* (*Pride and Prejudice* by Jane Austen)

spondulicks NOUN spondulicks is a slang word which means money ❏ *not for all his spondulicks and as much more on top of it* (*The Adventures of Huckleberry Finn* by Mark Twain)

stalled of VERB to be stalled of something is to be bored with it ❏ *I'm stalled of doing naught* (*Wuthering Heights* by Emily Brontë)

stanchion NOUN a stanchion is a pole or bar that stands upright and is used as a buidling support ❏ *and slid down a stanchion* (*The Adventures of Huckleberry Finn* by Mark Twain)

stang NOUN stang is another word for pole which was an old measurement ❏ *These fields were intermingled with woods of half a stang* (*Gulliver's Travels* by Jonathan Swift)

starlings NOUN a starling is a wall built around the pillars that support a bridge to protect the pillars ❏ *There were states of the tide when, having been down the river, I could not get back through the eddy-chafed arches and starlings of old London Bridge* (*Great Expectations* by Charles Dickens)

startings NOUN twitching or night-time movements of the body ❏ *with midnight's startings* (*On His Mistress* by John Donne)

stomacher NOUN a panel at the front of a dress ❏ *but send her aunt the pattern of a stomacher* (*Emma* by Jane Austen)

stoop VERB swoop ❏ *Once a kite hovering over the garden made a stoop at me* (*Gulliver's Travels* by Jonathan Swift)

succedaneum NOUN a succedaneum is a substitute ❏ *But as a succedaneum* (*The Prelude* by William Wordsworth)

suet NOUN a hard animal fat used in cooking ❏ *and your jaws are too weak For anything tougher than suet* (*Alice's Adventures in Wonderland* by Lewis Carroll)

sultry ADJ sultry weather is hot and damp. Here sultry means unpleasant or risky ❏ *for it was getting pretty sultry for us* (*The Adventures of Huckleberry Finn* by Mark Twain)

summerset NOUN summerset is an old spelling of somersault. If someone does a somersault, they turn over completely in the air ❏ *I have seen him do the summerset* (*Gulliver's Travels* by Jonathan Swift)

supper NOUN supper was a light meal taken late in the evening. The main meal was dinner which was eaten at four or five in the afternoon ❏ *and the supper table was all set out* (*Emma* by Jane Austen)

surfeits VERB to surfeit in something is to have far too much of it, or to overindulge in it to an unhealthy degree ❑ *He surfeits upon cursed necromancy* (*Doctor Faustus chorus* by Christopher Marlowe)

surtout NOUN a surtout is a long close-fitting overcoat ❑ *He wore a long black surtout reaching nearly to his ankles* (*The Old Curiosity Shop* by Charles Dickens)

swath NOUN swath is the width of corn cut by a scythe ❑ *while thy hook Spares the next swath* (*Ode to Autumn* by John Keats)

sylvan ADJ sylvan means belonging to the woods ❑ *Sylvan historian* (*Ode on a Grecian Urn* by John Keats)

taction NOUN taction means touch. This means that the people had to be touched on the mouth or the ears to get their attention ❑ *without being roused by some external taction upon the organs of speech and hearing* (*Gulliver's Travels* by Jonathan Swift)

Tag and Rag and Bobtail PHRASE the riff-raff, or lower classes. Used in an insulting way ❑ *"No," said he; "not till it got about that there was no protection on the premises, and it come to be considered dangerous, with convicts and Tag and Rag and Bobtail going up and down."* (*Great Expectations* by Charles Dickens)

tallow NOUN tallow is hard animal fat that is used to make candles and soap ❑ *and a lot of tallow candles* (*The Adventures of Huckleberry Finn* by Mark Twain)

tan VERB to tan means to beat or whip ❑ *and if I catch you about that school I'll tan you good* (*The Adventures of Huckleberry Finn* by Mark Twain)

tanyard NOUN the tanyard is part of a tannery, which is a place where leather is made from animal skins ❑ *hid in the old tanyard* (*The Adventures of Huckleberry Finn* by Mark Twain)

tarry ADJ tarry means the colour of tar or black ❑ *his tarry pig-tail* (*Treasure Island* by Robert Louis Stevenson)

thereof PHRASE from there ❑ *By all desires which thereof did ensue* (*On His Mistress* by John Donne)

thick with, be PHRASE if you are 'thick with someone' you are very close, sharing secrets – it is often used to describe people who are planning something secret ❑ *Hasn't he been thick with Mr Heathcliff lately?* (*Wuthering Heights* by Emily Brontë)

thimble NOUN a thimble is a small cover used to protect the finger while sewing ❑ *The paper had been sealed in several places by a thimble* (*Treasure Island* by Robert Louis Stevenson)

thirtover ADJ thirtover is an old word which means obstinate or that someone is very determined to do want they want and can not be persuaded to do something in another way ❑ *I have been living on in a thirtover, lackadaisical way* (*Tess of the D'Urbervilles* by Thomas Hardy)

timbrel NOUN timbrel is a tambourine ❑ *What pipes and timbrels?* (*Ode on a Grecian Urn* by John Keats)

tin NOUN tin is slang for money/cash ❑ *Then the plain question is, an't it a pity that this state of things should continue, and how much better would it be for the old gentleman to hand over a reasonable amount of tin, and make it all right and comfortable* (*The Old Curiosity Shop* by Charles Dickens)

tincture NOUN a tincture is a medicine made with alcohol and a small amount of a drug ❑ *with ink composed of a cephalic tincture* (*Gulliver's Travels* by Jonathan Swift)

tithe NOUN a tithe is a tax paid to the church ❑ *and held farms which, speaking from a spiritual point of view, paid highly-desirable tithes* (*Silas Marner* by George Eliot)

towardly ADJ a towardly child is dutiful or obedient ❑ *and a towardly child* (*Gulliver's Travels* by Jonathan Swift)

toys NOUN trifles are things which are considered to have little importance, value, or significance ❑ *purchase my life from them by some bracelets, glass rings, and other toys* (*Gulliver's Travels* by Jonathan Swift)

tract NOUN a tract is a religious pamphlet or leaflet ❑ *and Joe Harper got a hymn-book and a tract* (*The Adventures of Huckleberry Finn* by Mark Twain)

train-oil NOUN train-oil is oil from whale blubber ❑ *The train-oil and gunpowder were shoved out of sight in a minute* (*Wuthering Heights* by Emily Brontë)

tribulation NOUN tribulation means the suffering or difficulty you experience in a particular situation ❑ *Amy was learning this distinction through much tribulation* (*Little Women* by Louisa May Alcott)

trivet NOUN a trivet is a three-legged stand for resting a pot or kettle ❑ *a pocket-knife in his right; and a pewter pot on the trivet* (*Oliver Twist* by Charles Dickens)

trot line NOUN a trot line is a fishing line to which a row of smaller fishing lines are attached ❑ *when he got along I was hard at it taking up a trot line* (*The Adventures of Huckleberry Finn* by Mark Twain)

troth NOUN oath or pledge ❑ *I wonder, by my troth* (*The Good-Morrow* by John Donne)

truckle NOUN a truckle bedstead is a bed that is on wheels and can be slid under another bed to save space ❑ *It rose under my hand, and the door yielded. Looking in, I saw a lighted candle on a table, a bench, and a mattress on a truckle bedstead.* (*Great Expectations* by Charles Dickens)

trump NOUN a trump is a good, reliable person wo can be trusted ❑

This lad Hawkins is a trump, I perceive (*Treasure Island* by Robert Louis Stevenson)

tucker NOUN a tucker is a frilly lace collar which is worn around the neck ❑ *Whereat Scrooge's niece's sister – the plump one with the lace tucker: not the one with the roses – blushed.* (*A Christmas Carol* by Charles Dickens)

tureen NOUN a large bowl with a lid from which soup or vegetables are served ❑ *Waiting in a hot tureen!* (*Alice's Adventures in Wonderland* by Lewis Carroll)

turnkey NOUN a prison officer; jailer ❑ *As we came out of the prison through the lodge, I found that the great importance of my guardian was appreciated by the turnkeys, no less than by those whom they held in charge.* (*Great Expectations* by Charles Dickens)

turnpike NOUN the upkeep of many roads of the time was paid for by tolls (fees) collected at posts along the road. There was a gate to prevent people travelling further along the road until the toll had been paid. ❑ *Traddles, whom I have taken up by appointment at the turnpike, presents a dazzling combination of cream colour and light blue; and both he and Mr. Dick have a general effect about them of being all gloves.* (*David Copperfield* by Charles Dickens)

twas PHRASE it was ❑ *twas but a dream of thee* (*The Good-Morrow* by John Donne)

tyrannized VERB tyrannized means bullied or forced to do things against their will ❑ *for people would soon cease coming there to be tyrannized over and put down* (*Treasure Island* by Robert Louis Stevenson)

'un NOUN 'un is a slang term for one – usually used to refer to a person ❑ *She's been thinking the old 'un* (*David Copperfield* by Charles Dickens)

undistinguished ADJ undiscriminating or incapable of making a distinction between good and bad things ❏ *their undistinguished appetite to devour everything* (*Gulliver's Travels* by Jonathan Swift)

use NOUN habit ❏ *Though use make you apt to kill me* (*The Flea* by John Donne)

vacant ADJ vacant usually means empty, but here Wordsworth uses it to mean carefree ❏ *To vacant musing, unreproved neglect* (*The Prelude* by William Wordsworth)

valetudinarian NOUN one too concerned with his or her own health. ❏ *for having been a valetudinarian all his life* (*Emma* by Jane Austen)

vamp VERB vamp means to walk or tramp to somewhere ❏ *Well, vamp on to Marlott, will 'ee* (*Tess of the D'Urbervilles* by Thomas Hardy)

vapours NOUN the vapours is an old term which means unpleasant and strange thoughts, which make the person feel nervous and unhappy ❏ *and my head was full of vapours* (*Robinson Crusoe* by Daniel Defoe)

vegetables NOUN here vegetables means plants ❏ *the other vegetables are in the same proportion* (*Gulliver's Travels* by Jonathan Swift)

venturesome ADJ if you are venturesome you are willing to take risks ❏ *he must be either hopelessly stupid or a venturesome fool* (*Wuthering Heights* by Emily Brontë)

verily ADJ verily means really or truly ❏ *though I believe verily* (*Robinson Crusoe* by Daniel Defoe)

vicinage NOUN vicinage is an area or the residents of an area ❏ *and to his thought the whole vicinage was haunted by her.* (*Silas Marner* by George Eliot)

victuals NOUN victuals means food ❏ *grumble a little over the victuals* (*The Adventures of Huckleberry Finn* by Mark Twain)

vintage NOUN vintage in this context means wine ❏ *Oh, for a draught of vintage!* (*Ode on a Nightingale* by John Keats)

virtual ADJ here virtual means powerful or strong ❏ *had virtual faith* (*The Prelude* by William Wordsworth)

vittles NOUN vittles is a slang word which means food ❏ *There never was such a woman for givin' away vittles and drink* (*Little Women* by Louisa May Alcott)

voided straight PHRASE voided straight is an old expression which means emptied immediately ❏ *see the rooms be voided straight* (*Doctor Faustus 4.1* by Christopher Marlowe)

wainscot NOUN wainscot is wood panel lining in a room so wainscoted means a room lined with wooden panels ❏ *in the dark wainscoted parlor* (*Silas Marner* by George Eliot)

walking the plank PHRASE walking the plank was a punishment in which a prisoner would be made to walk along a plank on the side of the ship and fall into the sea, where they would be abandoned ❏ *about hanging, and walking the plank* (*Treasure Island* by Robert Louis Stevenson)

want VERB want means to be lacking or short of ❏ *The next thing wanted was to get the picture framed* (*Emma* by Jane Austen)

wanting ADJ wanting means lacking or missing ❏ *wanting two fingers of the left hand* (*Treasure Island* by Robert Louis Stevenson)

wanting, I was not PHRASE I was not wanting means I did not fail ❏ *I was not wanting to lay a foundation of religious knowledge in his mind* (*Robinson Crusoe* by Daniel Defoe)

ward NOUN a ward is, usually, a child who has been put under the protection of the court or a guardian for his or her protection ❏ *I call the Wards in Jarndyce. The are caged up with all the others.* (*Bleak House* by Charles Dickens)

waylay VERB to waylay someone is to lie in wait for them or to intercept them ❑ *I must go up the road and waylay him* (*The Adventures of Huckleberry Finn* by Mark Twain)

weazen NOUN weazen is a slang word for throat. It actually means shrivelled ❑ *You with a uncle too! Why, I knowed you at Gargery's when you was so small a wolf that I could have took your weazen betwixt this finger and thumb and chucked you away dead* (*Great Expectations* by Charles Dickens)

wery ■ ADV very ❑ *Be wery careful o' vidders all your life* (*Pickwick Papers* by Charles Dickens) ■ *See* wibrated

wherry NOUN wherry is a small swift rowing boat for one person ❑ *It was flood tide when Daniel Quilp sat himself down in the wherry to cross to the opposite shore.* (*The Old Curiosity Shop* by Charles Dickens)

whether PREP whether means which of the two in this example ❑ *we came in full view of a great island or continent (for we knew not whether)* (*Gulliver's Travels* by Jonathan Swift)

whetstone NOUN a whetstone is a stone used to sharpen knives and other tools ❑ *I dropped pap's whetstone there too* (*The Adventures of Huckleberry Finn* by Mark Twain)

wibrated VERB in Dickens's use of the English language 'w' often replaces 'v' when he is reporting speech. So here 'wibrated' means 'vibrated'. In Pickwick Papers a judge asks Sam Weller (who constantly confuses the two letters) 'Do you spell it with a 'v' or a 'w'?' to which Weller replies 'That depends upon the taste and fancy of the speller, my Lord' ❑ *There are strings . . . in the human heart that had better not be wibrated'* (*Barnaby Rudge* by Charles Dickens)

wicket NOUN a wicket is a little door in a larger entrance ❑ *Having rested here, for a minute or so, to collect a good burst of sobs and an imposing show of tears and terror, he knocked loudly at the wicket;* (*Oliver Twist* by Charles Dickens)

without CONJ without means unless ❑ *You don't know about me, without you have read a book by the name of The Adventures of Tom Sawyer* (*The Adventures of Huckleberry Finn* by Mark Twain)

wittles ■ NOUN vittles is a slang word which means food ❑ *I live on broken wittles – and I sleep on the coals* (*David Copperfield* by Charles Dickens) ■ *See* wibrated

woo VERB courts or forms a proper relationship with ❑ *before it woo* (*The Flea* by John Donne)

words, to have PHRASE if you have words with someone you have a disagreement or an argument ❑ *I do not want to have words with a young thing like you.* (*Black Beauty* by Anna Sewell)

workhouse NOUN workhouses were places where the homeless were given food and a place to live in return for doing very hard work ❑ *And the Union workhouses? demanded Scrooge. Are they still in operation?* (*A Christmas Carol* by Charles Dickens)

yawl NOUN a yawl is a small boat kept on a bigger boat for short trips. Yawl is also the name for a small fishing boat ❑ *She sent out her yawl, and we went aboard* (*The Adventures of Huckleberry Finn* by Mark Twain)

yeomanry NOUN the yeomanry was a collective term for the middle classes involved in agriculture ❑ *The yeomanry are precisely the order of people with whom I feel I can have nothing to do* (*Emma* by Jane Austen)

yonder ADV yonder means over there ❑ *all in the same second we seem to hear low voices in yonder!* (*The Adventures of Huckleberry Finn* by Mark Twain)